CLASSROOM GUIDE TO ACCOMPANY

POST**MODER**N

AMERICAN

POET**RY**

A Norton Anthology

CLASSROOM GUIDE TO ACCOMPANY

POSTMODERN

AMERICAN

POETRY

A Norton Anthology

by **PAUL HOOVER**

COLUMBIA COLLEGE, CHICAGO

W · W · NORTON & COMPANY

New York   London

The text of this book is composed in Caledonia with the display set in Rockwell.
Composition and manufacturing by the Haddon Craftsmen, Inc.
Book design by Jack Meserole.

ISBN 0-393-96450-7

W. W. Norton & Company, Inc., 500 Fifth Avenue, New York, N.Y. 10110
W. W. Norton & Company Ltd., 10 Coptic Street, London WC1A 1PU

2 3 4 5 6 7 8 9 0

Contents

Preface

This *Classroom Guide* is prepared to provide teaching ideas and suggestions for instructors new to the variety of poetry and poetics included in *Postmodern American Poetry: A Norton Anthology*. It may also prove useful to those more experienced with the literature. Following the same chronological order as the anthology, the *Guide* provides questions about each poem that explore not only the text and its underlying poetics, but also its literary influences and similarities to other works anthologized. Study questions are clustered under the heading "Points for Discussion and Writing," and when necessary, unfamiliar language is explicated under "Terms and References." Next to each poem title is the page number on which the poem appears in the anthology.

Postmodern American Poetry and its *Classroom Guide* can be used in a variety of poetry classes, from the undergraduate to graduate level. I have also frequently found the poems to be useful models for the creative writing classroom. In some cases, the study questions draw attention to larger concerns, such as the public and private roles of poetry, in a manner that should both stimulate discussion about the poems themselves and raise humanistic questions vital to understanding history and culture. The purpose of this anthology is to encourage a deeper understanding not only of a literature, but also of life as it is lived late in this century.

Students should be encouraged to examine issues related to field composition, indeterminacy, Projectivism, Personism, and the aleatory method—to name only a few aspects of the literature—as they relate to the larger social or historical moment. The Introduction to *Postmodern American Poetry* (pages xxv–xxxix) and the *Classroom Guide* are intended to make these and other concepts central to postmodern poetry accessible. Instructors may want to build discussions around some of the questions they raise: Is postmodern literature essentially Romantic? How does the avant-garde stand with regard to the middle class and to group identity in general? Many of the poets included are influenced by radically liberal strains of feminism and Marxism; is it possible for an avant-garde literature to be radically *conservative?* Is poetry divisible from the social or historical moment? What does "the new" represent— the introduction of new populations or new technologies? What is the process by which a poetic influence or idiom becomes dominant? What is the difference between the Personism of Frank O'Hara and the confessional poetry of Robert Lowell and Sylvia Plath? Can a personal poetry be considered objective? Why would Robert Creeley oppose poetry as a "descriptive act"? What does Clark Coolidge mean by the word "sincerity"? What might be the moral aims of obfuscation according to Bernadette Mayer? What is the importance, according to Lyn

Hejinian, of rejecting closure? All these questions resound at both the literary and cultural levels.

The "Poetics" section that completes the anthology will help students understand some of the more difficult concepts of postmodern poetry as well as its cultural contexts. Trusting in the instructor's own resources, I have chosen not to provide study questions about the essays in the "Poetics" section; I have instead taken pains to refer to issues of poetics when they are suggested by the poems themselves.

I would like to acknowledge the invaluable help of Tony Del Valle, Meredith and Peter Christensen, Art Lange, Doris Stockwell, Maxine Chernoff, Robert Kelly, Anne Waldman, George Evans, Amiri Baraka, Miguel Algarín, John Ashbery, Bob Perelman, Clark Coolidge, Jayne Cortez, Tom Mandel, Michael Davidson, Ron Silliman, Nathaniel Mackey, Barrett Watten, Diane Ward, and the reference librarians of Northwestern University, Spertus College, and Columbia College in preparing this *Classroom Guide*.

CLASSROOM GUIDE TO ACCOMPANY

POSTMODERN

AMERICAN

POETRY

A Norton Anthology

CHARLES OLSON ▪ ▪ ▪ ▪ ▪ ▪ ▪ ▪ ▪ ▪ ▪ ▪ ▪ ▪ ▪
1910–1970

In Cold Hell, in Thicket   *(p. 3)*

Points for Discussion and Writing

Olson uses the word "polytope," which means "occurring at two or more distinct places." Discuss the theme of multiple placement ("as things are constellated") in terms of Olson's overall project as a poet.

In stanza 3 of the poem's preface, "God" is put in seeming apposition to "that man." Does this placement have implications with regard to the status of God and man in Olson's metaphysics? Other elements in the same sentence come into a free-floating relationship due to the sentence's inconclusiveness. Discuss the effect of Olson's syntax on the poem in general.

Who are the "he" and "I" of the poem? Are they different characters or aspects of a single poetic self?

Hell is the poem's announced subject. Is it the Hell of Christianity? Of Dante? Or is it the personal Hell of Existentialism?

Space is feminine in the poem and "declares herself arched" in an erotic juxtaposition to her brother, who lies beneath her. What is the relationship between feminine and masculine in this work? Is the earth represented as male? Are they equal in power, or is one represented as more creative?

Examine the poem's references to clarity and richness of image versus imagelessness; also shapeliness versus wilderness, wildness, and "underbrush." Do these motifs relate to the announced impotence of the poem's "he"? Likewise, what is meant by "ya, selva oscura" at the opening of section II?

Do you feel that the "hell" of the poem is relieved or clarified at the beginning of section II, part 2?

How are men "now their own wood / and thus their own hell and paradise"? In the context of relief from Hell, what does the movement across a *field* signify? Olson writes that there is "a later wilderness" across this field; what is its significance?

I, Maximus of Gloucester, to You   *(p. 8)*

Points for Discussion and Writing

Olson lived for much of his life in Gloucester, Massachusetts, a fishing town. He was also a large man, 6 foot 9 inches in height. Is the Maximus

1

of this poem Olson himself? If so, why does he depict himself as "a metal hot from boiling water"?

In his essay, "Projective Verse," Olson writes, "For from the root out, from all over the place, the syllable comes, the figures of, the dance."[1] What is the "present dance" mentioned in the poem at hand?

With the "nest" of the poem, the kylix is a self-consciously female image, to be paired erotically with the lance and the mast. Search the rest of the poem for such images of male and female sexuality.

Discuss how the poet uses such historical references as St. Anthony of Padua to heighten his themes.

Olson writes that "love is form." Is he referring to the craft of poetry? What form does the beloved take in the poem?

Why does the bird in the poem have a "nervous beak"? In general, what does the bird represent in the poem? In what way might it serve as a figure of the artist?

Discuss what Olson means by "forwarding" at the end of section II, part 2. How might "my lady of good voyage" serve as a muse for the "forwarding" of thought in the poem?

This poem was originally addressed to Olson's wife, Connie, in the form of a letter. Is there evidence in the poem that she might represent "my lady of good voyage"?

What are the "facts" that must be played by the ear in section II, part 3? Why might Olson consider the ear a guiding principle of organization?

What role do the billboards and neon play in section II, part 3, of the poem? Do they represent the depredations of consumerism and popular culture? What about Olson's cosmology would billboards and neon unwelcome?

In section II, part 4, the theme of form returns. According to Olson, love and form come into existence when "the thing is born / born of yourself, born / of hay and cotton struts, / of street-pickings, wharves, weeds / . . . of a bell / of yourself, torn." What is "the thing" to which Olson refers? Is it poetry, or rather any creative effort? Why must it be "of yourself"? Why, especially, must it be "torn"?

In section II, part 5, what is meant by the coined word "pejorocracy," which presumably combines "pejorative" and "democracy"? How might pejorocracy "offend / a black-gold loin"?

Before devoting himself full-time to poetry, Olson was a liberal democrat employed by the Franklin Roosevelt administration. Are these politics evident in the poem at hand?

---

1. Charles Olson, "Projective Verse," in *Selected Writings*, ed. Robert Creeley, New York, 1966, p. 18.

What distinction does Olson make between "mu-sick, mu-sick, mu-sick" and "the cribbage game"? Is Olson's aim as a poet "mu-sick"? Might Olson have been influenced in this section by T. S. Eliot's *The Waste Land* in its use of popular song—for example, "O O O O that Shakespeherian Rag— / It's so elegant / So intelligent"?

Why does Olson give the advice to "kill kill kill / those / who advertise you / out)"?

Terms and References

A **kylix** is a shallow earthenware drinking cup of Ancient Greece.

St. Anthony of Padua was a Franciscan monk who lived from 1195 to 1231; he was also a patron saint of the fishing people in Gloucester.

Letter 3 ("Tansy buttons")   *(p. 11)*

Points for Discussion and Writing

What is Olson's critique of culture in this poem? What, for instance, is the relationship between what Olson calls "wondership" and "ownership"? Who are those "who use words cheap"? What effect does the cheapening of language have on the culture of Gloucester? What role does "tansy" play in this respect? Is it a restorative offered by the local gods?

Who are "the men of the Fort / who are not hired"?

The ancient city of Tyre (the Tyrian of Olson's poem) was comparable in Olson's mind to his home city of Gloucester, Massachusetts. Does Olson find "coherence" in the local culture of Gloucester?

What relation does Olson seem to draw between Gloucester and the larger culture of the United States, circa 1953?

Terms and References

Tyre was a Phoenician port and capital.

Maximus, to himself   *(p. 14)*

Points for Discussion and Writing

Does Maximus represent Olson himself? If so, do you find this part of *The Maximus Poems* more confessional or personal than the other sections selected ("I, Maximus of Gloucester, to You" and "Letter 3")? Olson is self-accusing in this poem, focusing on his "arrogances" and "distances." Compare and contrast this tone of self-loathing with the tone in "In Cold Hell, in Thicket."

The Librarian   *(p. 15)*

Points for Discussion and Writing

This poem was not included in *The Maximus Poems* but rather in *The Distances* (1960). In what ways, however, is it consistent with *The Maximus Poems?*

According to poet Tom Clarke, this poem is based in part on a dream of Olson's that he had discovered his wife, Connie, and his close friend Frank Moore making love in Olson's parents' bedroom.[2] Much of the poem, including a violent beating, is a poetic transcription of the dream's scenes. The instructor might ask the class to discuss this poem before revealing its history. Does the poem seem more, or less, personal after learning of its origin in dreaming?

JOHN CAGE ▪ ▪ ▪ ▪ ▪ ▪ ▪ ▪ ▪ ▪ ▪ ▪ ▪ ▪ ▪
1912–1992

25 Mesostics Re and Not Re Mark Tobey   *(p. 18)*

Points for Discussion and Writing

Mark Tobey is the subject and dedicatee of the poem. He also provides, by means of his name, the formal organization for the poem. To what extent does the poem appear to be a reliable report of Tobey's personal activities?

Discuss the ways in which the artifice of the mesostics form, which might have produced a randomized and therefore "unreadable" text, relates to the poem's comparatively "natural" rhetoric.

In what ways is this a narrative poem?

At what points does the poem take on the qualities of lyric? See, for example, "instead of Music: / thunder, trAffic, / biRds. . . ."

Since he is a composer, why doesn't Cage rely more heavily on a rhythmic and sonorous poetry? Is a purely musical poetry, as attempted by the British poet Algernon Swinburne and the American poet Edgar Allan Poe, possible today?

2. Tom Clark, *Charles Olson: The Allegory of a Poet's Life*, New York, 1991, p. 232.

How might the "story" of a poem heighten rather than diminish its lyricism?

What does Cage (or Tobey) mean in mesostic 14 when he comments that "up to the minute" art can be found in "thE head office / of a successful advertising companY"? Is this a critique of art as commodity or an acknowledgment of the inevitable and natural relation between the two?

While looking at the pavement at his feet, Cage comments that he "noticed no diffeRence between / looKing at art or away from it." Discuss this statement in terms of Cage's art as a whole. How might the making of art consist of creating frames (of perception) around ordinary things such as the pavement? What are the political implications of privileging ordinary objects such as the pavement?

Compare the diaristic, personal qualities of this poem with the "I do this I do that" poems of Frank O'Hara, for example, "The Day Lady Died." Does the other poem in Cage's selection, "Writing through the Cantos," have such qualities? In what other ways do the two poems differ? In what ways are they similar?

Cage uses the German word *Klangfarbenmelodie*. Does this word, defined below, characterize the poem in question? How about "Writing through the Cantos"?

Terms and References

Mesostics is a form of acrostics in which significant letters are located at the middle, rather than at the beginning, of a line.

Mark Tobey was a noted Abstract Expressionist painter and close friend of Cage.

Klangfarbenmelodie means "melody (or music) made of noise."

Writing through the Cantos   *(p. 21)*

Points for Discussion and Writing

Unlike the previous poem on Mark Tobey, this poem is difficult to read because of its gnarled and discontinuous syntax and unusual arrangement on the page. Why would Cage choose illegibility as a mode? What are the advantages and disadvantages of writing this way?

Read samples of Pound's *The Cantos*, on which Cage's work is based, to give students an idea of the difficulty of Pound's own text. How might an "opaque" text such as *The Cantos* prove more useful to Cage than the comparatively "transparent" writing of poets like William Carlos Williams?

In what sense is this a "found" poem? How radically has Pound's original text been altered?

Show or describe to the class the work of Dadaist Marcel Duchamp, especially his Readymades, or *objet trouve* (found objects). These might include "L.H.O.O.Q." (1919), a "Rectified Readymade" of a mustache and goatee drawn on an inexpensive reproduction of Da Vinci's "Mona Lisa"; "Bottlerack" (1914), a circular metal rack used in French wineries for drying recently washed bottles upside down; and "In Advance of the Broken Arm," a snow shovel Duchamp purchased in a hardware store and altered only by giving it a title. To what extent are the virtually unassisted found works of Duchamp and the cut-up poems of the greater Dada movement an influence on Cage? Are mesostics another form of the cut-up poem? (For more on Dadaist methods, see "Terms and References" below.)

To what degree is chance a factor in mesostic composition? On the other hand, how much of the work's composition is subject to a strict set of controls imposed by the author?

What does Cage's poetry have in common with that of Jackson Mac Low, who uses methods similar to mesostics? How does Cage's approach differ from Mac Low's?

Besides Cage and Mac Low, what other poets in the anthology rely on predetermined compositional methods such as acrostics and computer programs to create their work? Can work created through such methods be just as inspired as that of other poets?

Does Cage's work have any connection with the playful artifice of the French group *Oulipo,* of which American Harry Mathews, here included, is a member? (For more on *Oulipo,* see "Terms and References" below.)

How would this poem sound when read out loud? Does it communicate better or worse than when read on the page? Is communication, or accessibility to a reader or listener, necessary to poetry?

Terms and References

A **found poem** involves the use of an already established text, usually not poetry, in the creation of a poem.

The creation of a **cut-up poem** was described by Dada founder and poet Tristan Tzara (1896–1963) as follows: "Take a newspaper. Take some scissors. Choose from this paper an article of the length you want to make your poem. Cut out the article. Next carefully cut out each of the words that makes up this article and put them all in a bag. Shake gently. Next take out each cutting one after the other. Copy conscientiously in the order in which they left the bag. The poem will resemble you. And there you are—an infinitely original author of charming sensibility, even though unappreciated by the vulgar herd."[3]

3. Tristan Tzara, "Dada Manifesto on Feeble Love and Bitter Love," in *Seven Manifestoes and Lampisteries,* trans. Barbara Wright, London, 1977, p. 39.

Readymade is Marcel Duchamp's term for an art object that is found by the artist in a nonartistic context and presented in a gallery or museum as the artist's own work of art.

Dada was a literary and artistic movement founded in Zurich in 1915. Internationalist in scope and nihilist in character, it lasted until 1922, when it was supplanted in Paris by surrealism under the aggressive leadership of André Breton. According to Tristan Tzara, the movement's name "doesn't mean anything." However, he goes on to supply the following possibilities: "We read in the papers that the negroes of the Kroo race call the tail of a sacred cow: DADA. A cube, and a mother, in a certain region of Italy, are called: DADA. The word for a hobbyhorse, a children's nurse, a double affirmative in Russian and Roumanian [Tzara's native language] is also: DADA."[4] Dada's significance for the postmodern period includes the invention of the "sound poem" by Hugo Ball, an early instance of performance poetry; its redefinition of the art object, as seen in the Readymades of Marcel Duchamp which influenced the use of appropriation among artists as diverse as Andy Warhol and Sherrie Levine; and its influence on conceptual and performance art, from Eleanor Antin (whose persona Eleanora Antinova owes a debt to Marcel Duchamp's having dressed up as a woman named Rrose Selavy) to Robert Rauschenberg's "Erased de Kooning" (a drawing by the noted painter Willem de Kooning which Rauschenberg made his own work of art by erasing it).

Oulipo stands for *Ouvroir de litterature potentielle*, a group of French experimental writers that included Raymond Queneau and Georges Perec. *Oulipo* favors the use of literary games, puzzles, and unusual literary forms of the writer's invention.

JAMES LAUGHLIN ▪ ▪ ▪ ▪ ▪ ▪ ▪ ▪ ▪ ▪ ▪ ▪ ▪ ▪
b. 1914

The Inn at Kirchstetten *(p. 26)*

Points for Discussion and Writing

Do you believe that this text was actually found in an edition of Trakl's work, or is the poem entirely of Laughlin's invention? If you believe it is of Laughlin's invention, what distinguishes the poem from a work of fiction?

Identify the poem's narrator. What clues exist as to his or her identity? What "story" does he or she tell?

How much credence do you give to the "Editor's Note" that follows the poem?

4. Tristan Tzara, "Dada Manifesto 1918," in the same, p. 4.

Terms and References

Dichtungen means "poems" in German.

Georg Trakl was a leading German poet of the modern period.

Then and Now   *(p. 28)*

Points for Discussion and Writing

The Russian critic Mikhail Bahktin uses the term "dialogic" to describe the heterogenous blend of voices in works of literature. Are the two voices of this poem meant to work as dialogue or as simultaneous monologues? In this respect, compare this poem with David Trinidad's poem "Double Trouble."

What does each half of the poem communicate? Do the two halves have any relation to each other as meaning?

ROBERT DUNCAN ■ ■ ■ ■ ■ ■ ■ ■ ■ ■ ■ ■ ■ ■
1919–1988

A Poem Beginning with a Line by Pindar   *(p. 30)*

Points for Discussion and Writing

This poem makes many references to the myth of Cupid and Psyche: Psyche's sorting of the grain, the "cannibal" sheep, the help offered by ants, the monster-husband, the oil spilled on Eros' (Cupid's) shoulder, the dream at Miletus, and so on. (For more on the myth of Cupid and Psyche, see "Terms and References" below.) You may want to read a version of the myth to the class while discussing the poem. Likewise, you may want to obtain a print of Goya's painting for display in class. Is Duncan successful in relating the myth of Cupid and Psyche to his own contemporary experience?

What does the story of the mythic lovers have to do with the other elements of the poem such as the references to "factories . . . turning out commodities"?

Like some other poems from his 1960 collection *The Opening of the Field*, this poem involves Duncan's use of childhood memory, as well as a recurring dream of grass blowing in the wind. According to critic Michael Davidson, "the image of the field recurs throughout the book, derived from a childhood dream. Duncan calls it the 'Atlantis' dream, referring to its powerful evocation of a primordial flood which he associates with the death of his mother at birth."[5] Ask students to search for these dream elements. Of what importance is the recurring image of the children dancing right and left in a ring?

The poem opens and closes with references to the Latin poet Pindar. The first reference, a line from Pindar, is lyrical in character and consistent with the sumptuous tone of part I of the poem. How does this differ from Duncan's aside in part IV regarding Pindar's ode?

Discuss Duncan's use of the author as self in the poem. In what way is the announced presence of authorship at the end of the poem ("A line of Pindar / moves from the area of my lamp / toward morning.") consistent with Coleridge's poem "Kubla Khan"?

Is the prose paragraph that immediately precedes the poem's end a kind of "waking" from the dream of poetic composition? Likewise, how does this poem resemble the Keats sonnet "On First Looking into Chapman's Homer"?

Davidson makes note of Duncan's characteristically Romantic cast of mind: "the myth of an Edenic or Atlantean civilization, the cult of the child, the various permutations of Rousseau's 'noble savage,' the Hegelian dialectic of the Spirit. . . ."[6] In all of Duncan's work included, examine the above themes, as well as the common Romantic themes of despair and imagination. Is imagination a restorative power in Duncan's work? What is the role of self in his poetry?

Terms and References

The story of **Cupid and Psyche** belongs to Greek mythology. Threatened by the beauty of a king's youngest daughter named Psyche, the goddess of love, Venus, calls on her winged son, Cupid, to instill in Psyche a passionate love for a mean and contemptible being. Finding Psyche asleep, Cupid places drops from Venus' bitter fountain over her lips before accidentally wounding himself with his own arrow. Informed by the oracle that Psyche was destined to marry a monster, her parents allow her to be taken in a gloomy nuptial ceremony to a mountain top from which she is delivered by a Zephyr to the house of her mysterious husband whom she never sees and who appears in darkness only as a comforting voice. Advised by servants that her husband is a monster whom she must slay, Psyche prepares to kill him with a knife, only to discover that he is in fact the beautiful youth Cupid. As she leans over him, the oil from her lamp spills on his shoulder and causes him to awaken and flee in alarm. Psyche wanders in search of her husband and comes across a field of grain abandoned in midharvest; this is the temple of Ceres, the goddess of grain, who escorts Psyche to the temple of her enemy, Venus. Psyche is forced into a granary of mixed grains and

5. "The Book of First Things: *The Opening of the Field*," in *Robert Duncan: Scales of the Marvelous*, New York, 1979, p. 57.   6. The same, p. 56.

given the awesome task of separating all the grains from each other. As she sits in despair, a group of ants takes pity on her and sets about separating the grain. Venus discredits this work and orders Psyche to gather instead the fleece of sheep grazing on the far banks of a river. A compassionate river god instructs Psyche how to accomplish her task, and she is able to return to Venus with the fleece. Venus remains unsatisfied and requires her to perform the additional task of gathering a box full of magical cosmetics from Persephone, the goddess of the Underworld. Aided in this dangerous task by a voice, Psyche succeeds in filling the box. In her curiosity as to its contents, she opens the box only to discover that it has been filled with Stygian sleep, which causes her to fall down in a coma. Recovered from his wound, Cupid discovers Psyche asleep and awakens her with a touch of his arrow. He then implores all-powerful Jupiter to acknowledge their love. Taking pity on the young couple, Jupiter asks Psyche to drink a cup of ambrosia that makes her Cupid's equal as a god. At last united, Cupid and Psyche give birth to a daughter whose name is Pleasure.

Often I Am Permitted to Return to a Meadow (*p. 36*)

Points for Discussion and Writing

This is one of the poems based on Duncan's recurring dream of a field. Is it a simple transcription of the dream? In what ways does the poetic process resemble the act of dreaming? Who are the First Beloved, the Lady, and the Queen Under The Hill? Are they images of the poetic muse or of Duncan's mother, who died at his birth?

Discuss the similarities of this poem and "A Poem Beginning with a Line by Pindar," especially the children's game. How do the two poems differ?

Examine the lines "whose hosts are a disturbance of words within words / that is a field folded." Who are the "hosts" of the Queen Under The Hill? Why are they associated with "words within words," and, in turn, why are words associated with a "field folded"? Is the turning of the earth associated here with the poetic powers of the underworld? Compare this reference with the story of Persephone, forced to live half the year with Pluto, god of the underworld.

How is Duncan "permitted" to return to a meadow? And what does the meadow represent in Duncan's cosmology? The meadow is referred to as a "property of the mind / that certain bounds hold against chaos." Is it order? Or is it a figure of imagination, "a place of first permission"?

Poetry, a Natural Thing   (p. 37)

Points for Discussion and Writing

This poem clearly refers to the nature of poetry. How is it that "neither our vices nor our virtues / further the poem"? Is Duncan suggesting that poetry acts outside the realm of morality? What definition of poetry does Duncan seem to offer? Is poetry "a spiritual urgency" comparable to a salmon struggling for arrival and realization? Or is it the simple, awkward, but nonetheless magnificent figure of a moose? Does Duncan seem to favor one figure of poetry over the other? Which figure, salmon or moose, better represents the style of Duncan's own poetry?

The Torso   Passages 18   (p. 38)

Points for Discussion and Writing

In this poem, one of an ongoing series entitled "Passages," Duncan is open about his homosexuality. Students interested in Duncan's homosexuality will want to consult his 1944 essay, "The Homosexual in Society," reprinted in Ekbert Faas's *Young Robert Duncan: Portrait of the Poet as Homosexual in Society* (1983).

Make note of the use of upper- and lowercase in the following: "I thought a Being more than vast, His body leading / into Paradise, his eyes / quickening a fire in me. . . ." What is the relationship of "His" and "his" in these lines? In the same context, discuss the capitalization of "Self" and "Other" later in the poem.

This poem has elements of the blazon, a popular medieval form cataloguing the loved one's attributes. It might be compared to Shakespeare's Sonnet 18, a parody of the blazon form beginning "Shall I compare thee to a summer's day?" The lover's piercing look in Duncan's poem is also a convention of English Renaissance poetry. Taking into account Duncan's love of traditional usages and references, discuss the postmodern character of his writing.

Terms and References

Blazon is a literary term used to describe poetry that detailed (usually in metaphor) the various parts of a loved one's body (usually a woman's). The form is parodied by surrealist André Breton in his poem "Freedom of Love":

> My wife with the hair of a wood fire
> With the thoughts of heat lightning
> With the waist of an hourglass[7]

7. André Breton, "Freedom of Love," in *Young Cherry Trees Secured Against Hares*, trans. Edouard Roditi, Ann Arbor, 1969, n.p.

Songs of an Other   *(p. 40)*

Points for Discussion and Writing

This poem plays on the psychological concept of the double. What is the nature of the "other" in the poem? Is it the double or Duncan himself "who hides his mother / behind him mirrord in his / bride's gaze . . ."?

In the context of the double, examine the images of bride and groom in his poem. Is a marriage of two selves, male and female, suggested?

Many works of literature deal with the archetype of the double—for example, Joseph Conrad's *The Secret Sharer*. Is the double a threatening presence in Duncan's poem, or is his "strangeness" somehow comforting?

Students may be interested in comparing and contrasting this poem with D. H. Lawrence's "The Bride," included in *The Norton Anthology of Modern Poetry*.

Close   *(p. 41)*

Points for Discussion and Writing

This poem was included in the poet's final collection of poetry, *Ground Work II: In the Dark* (1987), published a year before his death. Like "Songs of an Other," it was part of a long work that was fifteen years in preparation. Students might be asked if they see any change of style or theme from Duncan's earlier to later poetry.

What is the overall subject of this poem? The images are all of fullness and completion, and so suggest knowledge of his own coming death. Is the poem therefore a self-elegy?

What is the "daimon" in "the daimon of this field"?

Duncan writes, "History / will disprove my existence." How? How do you account for the poet's reference to the "Book" containing "all the vain song I've sung"? Is the poem an expression of his defeat as a poet?

Discuss the poem's liquid images and their culmination in the falling of a tear and "the flooding into the flooding." What do the two floodings consist of?

What is meant by "the gleam of the bowl in its not holding"? Is the bowl an image of the soul, or rather the poem's ability to express the flood of emotion that is pressed into it? Moreover, does the bowl gleam all the more in *not* holding?

LAWRENCE FERLINGHETTI ▪ ▪ ▪ ▪ ▪ ▪ ▪ ▪ ▪
b. 1919

[In Goya's greatest scenes we seem to see] *(p. 43)*

Points for Discussion and Writing

Like much of Ferlinghetti's poetry, the poem is a critique of contemporary American culture. It is also sharply aware of the flux of history. What is the nature of his recognition of the human condition? Has anything changed since Goya's vision of 'suffering humanity'?

[In Golden Gate Park that day] *(p. 44)*

Points for Discussion and Writing

Are the husband and wife, the main actors of the poem, symbolic? Why, for example, does the husband carry a flute and his wife a bunch of grapes?

Why does Ferlinghetti describe the space the pair cross as "the meadow of the world" rather than an ordinary meadow?

What does it mean that the flute goes unplayed?

The poem begins on a note of celebration and ends on one of depression. Are the two figures inhabitants of some failed Eden, unable to celebrate their own lives?

[Constantly risking absurdity] *(p. 45)*

Points for Discussion and Writing

Like some of Ferlinghetti's other work, this poem comments on the existential failure of modern life ("spreadeagled on the empty air / of existence"). In this case, however, the existential acrobat is a poet. Discuss Ferlinghetti's definition of the role of the poet in relation to Beauty. Why, for instance, is the poet a "little chapleychaplin man"? Does a poet always perform "above the heads / of his audience"? Are a poet's devices simply a matter of theatrics, or do they help reveal a deeper truth?

I Am Waiting   (p. 46)

Compare and contrast this long poem with Allen Ginsberg's *Howl* and Anne Waldman's "Makeup on Empty Space." What do all these poems have in common with the psalmic tradition?

Of what advantage is the poem's use of listing and anaphora (initial repetition)? What effect would these usages have on a public reading of the poem?

Ferlinghetti suggests that America has lost its sense of wonder. What were the conditions in the United States in 1958, the date of the poem's publication, that would make a "rebirth" desirable? Have political issues in the United States changed since this poem was written?

Why would Ferlinghetti refer to Allen Tate's poem "Ode to the Confederate Dead," included in *The Norton Anthology of Modern Poetry*, as "a real farce"? Compare and contrast the poetry of Beat poets such as Ferlinghetti, Gregory Corso, and Ginsberg with that of John Crowe Ransom, Allen Tate, and Robert Penn Warren, poets of the "New Criticism." In what way does political and social difference create aesthetic and formal difference?

Monet's Lilies Shuddering   (p. 50)

Monet was one of the leading French Impressionist painters. What comment is Ferlinghetti making about the connection between Monet's paintings of lilies, clouds, and ponds and their later consumption as art?

John Cage's experimental music makes Monet's painting come to life again. Was Monet's painting also experimental in its time? How so? Discuss in this context the "outsider" status of a work of art. By what process do Monet's paintings of water lilies and haystacks become acceptable to a larger audience?

Discuss the relationship between an artist's work and an audience's later reception (or appreciation) of it? Must his or her works be received in the same spirit in which they were created?

A Dark Portrait   (p. 50)

In French, *tu* is the personal pronoun "you," to be used only among people of intimate rather than formal acquaintance. Nora Flood is a character in Djuna Barnes's modernist novel *Nightwood* (1937). "The strangest 'salon' in America was Nora's," Barnes wrote. "Her house was couched in the centre of a mass of tangled grass and weeds."[8] Barnes later describes Nora as "an early Christian" in temperament:

> Nora had the face of all people who love the people—a face that would be evil when she found out that to love without criticism is to be betrayed. Nora robbed herself for everyone; incapable of giving herself warning, she was continually turning about to find herself diminished. Wandering people the world over found her profitable in that she could be sold for a price forever, for she carried her betrayal money in her own pocket.[9]

Nora is in love with a young woman named Robin Vote but describes that love as "impossible." The "she" of this poem therefore resembles Nora Flood in her search for a lover "who would never satisfy her." Discuss the psychology of such a desire.

HILDA MORLEY ■ ■ ■ ■ ■ ■ ■ ■ ■ ■ ■ ■ ■ ■ ■
b. 1919

The Lizard   (*p. 51*)

Points for Discussion and Writing

Hilda Morley's poetry often focuses on the importance of real things in present time. She then enlarges these ordinary objects with penetrating insight by the emotion she invests in her language. Discuss the relationship between the lizard's heart and Morley's own. How is the lizard "anchored" to suspense, while "we are / anchored to nothing"? In this context, who are "we," Morley and her readers? Or is Morley referring to the general human condition?

The poem is also concerned with the human desire for mystery and meaning: "even the bicycle / on the white wall may be a glyph / and magical." A glyph is a picture or carving representing an idea. Is the poem therefore an examination of the relationship between things and their representations?

Compare this poem, and Morley's work in general, with William Carlos Williams's dictum "No ideas but in things."

It would also be useful to compare Morley's work with that of fellow Black Mountain poet Denise Levertov, as well as with the concepts implicit in Levertov's essay, "Some Notes on Organic Form." Does Morley's work suggest, for instance, that "there is a form in all things (and in our experience), which the poet can discover and reveal"?[1]

8. Djuna Barnes, *Nightwood*, New York, 1961, p. 50.   9. The same, pp. 51–52.
1. Denise Levertov, "Some Notes on Organic Form," in *The Poet in the World*, New York, 1973, p. 7.

Curve of the Water   *(p. 52)*

Points for Discussion and Writing

At the poem's end, what does Morley mean by "our slowness / itself impossible to hold"? Does she mean human mortality or the simple passing of time?

The poem begins as a portrait of a landscape. At what point does it take on a more pointed human reference?

Discuss Morley's theme of "unexpectedness." How does an object we think we know become the "not expected"? How might an "unexpectedness" of perception relate to the creation of poetry?

Made Out of Links   *(p. 53)*

Points for Discussion and Writing

This poem is probably addressed to Morley's deceased husband, composer Stefan Wolpe. It is written in present tense, yet the episode it describes happened in the past. Discuss Morley's use of memory and verb tense in the poem.

How does the "lightnesses borne down upon me" relate to her weighty knowledge of Wolpe's death? In this context, examine the poet's use of the word "nearnesses." How "near" is the person she addresses in the poem?

For Elaine de Kooning   *(p. 54)*

Points for Discussion and Writing

Elaine de Kooning was a noted Abstract Expressionist painter and wife of the painter Willem de Kooning. Compare Morley's use of color in this poem with her colorful description of the landscape in "Curve of the Water."

What does Morley mean when she refers to "the relationship between the visible & the kind of / seeing the human eye can make"? How does the eye "make" seeing?

Morley often works out of memory, in this case recalling a conversation of thirty years ago, yet she manages to do so without unwarranted nostalgia. What is it about her language that lends itself to aesthetic distance and objectivity? Likewise, compare Morley's use of memory in this poem with that in "Parents."

Parents   *(p. 55)*

Points for Discussion and Writing

Who is the "she" of this poem? Who is the "he"? How differently are they presented?

What is the relationship between strangeness and beauty in the poem? Is one to be preferred to the other?

CHARLES BUKOWSKI   ▪ ▪ ▪ ▪ ▪ ▪ ▪ ▪ ▪ ▪ ▪
1920–1994

crucifix in a deathhand   *(p. 56)*

Points for Writing and Discussion

The setting of the poem is Los Angeles, where Bukowski lived most of his life. What is his attitude toward the city? What is the logic of the metaphor, "crucifix in a deathhand," as it relates to Los Angeles?

Compare Bukowski's style in this poem with the hard-boiled detective fiction of Raymond Chandler, who also wrote about the Los Angeles area; likewise, compare Bukowski's style with the poetic minimalism of Ernest Hemingway's short stories.

startled into life like fire   *(p. 58)*

Points for Discussion and Writing

Compare this poem with the fragment from Christopher Smart's *Jubilate Agno*, ca. 1760, published in *The Norton Anthology of Poetry*. Might Bukowski have been influenced by Smart's well-known poem about his cat, Jeoffry?

What is Bukowski saying about himself (and people in general) in relation to his cat?

i am dead but i know the dead are not like this
(p. 58)

Points for Discussion and Writing

Unlike most of the poet's other work, this poem is influenced by Spanish surrealist imagery. Surrealist juxtapositions are often startling to the

point of absurdity, which is part of their strength. In this poem, surrealist detail would include the lines "a moth dies in a / freeway crash."
Does the poet mean an actual moth, or is the moth symbolic of something else?

Must poetry be rational in order to be enjoyable? Discuss the possibility
that poetry must be *irrational* in order to be enjoyable.

Compare the imagery of this poem with André Breton's definition of
surrealist beauty, quoted from the novelist Lautreamont, as "the
chance encounter on a dissecting table of a sewing machine and an
umbrella." Does the poem contain any other images in which two
things are juxtaposed for startling, dreamlike effect?

As a surrealist-influenced writing, compare this poem with Tom Clark's
"You (I)" and "You (III)," as well as elements of Gregory Corso's
"Marriage."

the mockingbird   (*p. 59*)

Points for Discussion and Writing

Compare this poem with Bukowski's "startled into life like fire," another poem about a cat.

In this poem, the cat has a ritualistic role and some of the language is
religious in nature. The bird prays to the cat, which is given certain
priest-like qualities and is described as "striding down the centuries."
What does the dynamic between the cat and bird teach Bukowski and
ourselves as readers? Why is Bukowski making use of religious imagery?

Does the poem have a moral comparable to those in Aesop's fables? If
so, what is it? Of what importance is the word "bargain" at the end of
the poem?

my old man   (*p. 60*)

Points for Discussion and Writing

This is a poem with dialogue, comparable in some ways to a short story.
How often do you encounter poetry containing dialogue? Why is dialogue comparatively infrequent in poetry?

The poem is also an example of the fictional device of the story within a
story. Of what importance is the story inside the story to the poem as a
whole?

What are Bukowski's feelings for his "old man"? Do they change during
the course of the poem?

Contrast the poems of Bukowski and Wanda Coleman, which have narrative qualities, with the prose fables of Russell Edson and Maxine Chernoff. Are the worlds of Edson and Chernoff less realistic than those of the other two poets? Or are they realistic in a different way?

Compare and contrast the work of Bukowski and Coleman with that of language poets Carla Harryman and Leslie Scalapino, who often employ fictional characters and settings, though in a much more oblique way. What differences in approach to narrative exist among the poets in question?

BARBARA GUEST ▪ ▪ ▪ ▪ ▪ ▪ ▪ ▪ ▪ ▪ ▪ ▪ ▪

b. 1920

Red Lilies   (*p. 62*)

Points for Discussion and Writing

Is the subject of this poem lilies, as the title suggests? If not, what is it? Does the poem have a central focus? Or is it a mosaic of poetic moods? How, for instance, can the snow "pour out of you"?

Examine especially the events of stanza 3, in which a scene of someone clinging to a pillow is mixed with imagery of water and branches. Is the poem the narration of a dream?

How do you account for the repeated stone imagery in the poem?

River Road Studio   (*p. 63*)

Points for Discussion and Writing

This poem resembles "Red Lilies" in compiling snatches of perception. Is it more grounded in the reality of daily experience than "Red Lilies"?

In the poem, what is the relationship between primary colors and the color black? Are these colors symbolic? What is meant, for instance, by the lines "everyone gropes toward black / where it is believed the strength lingers"?

Give special attention to the puzzle presented by the last stanza. How can quartets be bricks subject to placement by the "we" of the poem?

Prairie Houses (*p. 64*)

Points for Discussion and Writing

What kind of house on the prairie is depicted? Can you visualize it in detail, or does Guest primarily provide the essence of the house?

What does the poet mean in writing "the heavens strike hard on prairies"?

Why are the houses "hard-mouthed"? And why are they depicted as feminine, with "robust nipples"?

Wild Gardens Overlooked by Night Lights (*p. 65*)

Points for Discussion and Writing

This poem and the one to follow were published over twenty years later than the other poems in Guest's selection. Are they stylistically different from those poems? If so, in what ways? Who is the speaker of "Wild Gardens"? What are her concerns?

In what ways do the scenes outside the speaker's window and the paintings on her wall share a reality? Discuss especially Guest's presentation of "The Tale of the Genji."

How is Guest's treatment of the painting comparable to William Butler Yeats's description of a carving in his poem "Lapis Lazuli," included in *The Norton Anthology of Modern Poetry*?

An Emphasis Falls on Reality (*p. 66*)

Points for Discussion and Writing

This is yet another poem in which Guest examines the nexus between reality and its depiction in a work of visual art. What does the poet mean by "fair realism"? Why should she feel envious of it?

In the same context, how might a sunrise "revise itself"? Or is it only our perceptions of a sunrise that are revisable? Likewise, in what sense are willows "not real trees"?

Discuss the lines, "so silence is pictorial / when silence is real." Must reality be idealized in order to be understood?

What is the "emphasis" that "falls on reality"? Is it human perception or the way light falls on objects within a given scene?

Twilight Polka Dots   (*p. 67*)

Points for Discussion and Writing

The subject of this poem is a lake stocked with fish. What is "curious" about it? How might it be "edged with poetry"?

How might two figures who gaze at the lake in a "shared glance" be "admired by the lake"? Who *are* the two figures Guest introduces as lake watchers? What is their relation to what they see? For example, how might "an undercurrent of physical pleasure" cause the water to shake?

Examine the poem's fictional elements, especially the development of the torn letter. What effect does the letter have on the "twilight water"?

Barbara Guest is associated with the New York School of poets. Compare and contrast her work with that of John Ashbery, Frank O'Hara, and Kenneth Koch. Of those poets, which is most similar in approach to Guest?

JACKSON MAC LOW ▪ ▪ ▪ ▪ ▪ ▪ ▪ ▪ ▪ ▪ ▪
b. 1922

FROM *The Pronouns*   (*p. 69*)

Points for Discussion and Writing

The first three poems in Mac Low's section, published in *The Pronouns* (1964/1979), were designed for a dance performance. Discuss these works ("1st Dance—Making Things New—6 February 1964," "6th Dance—Doing Things with Pencils—17–18 February 1964," and "12th Dance—Getting Leather by Language—21 February 1964") both as instructions for dance improvisation and as poems in their own right.

How is *The Pronouns* consistent with Mac Low's later work in our selection? In what ways is it different?

How much leeway does Mac Low allow the dancers in following his instructions?

How do you explain the changing point of view, from the "he" of the "1st Dance" to the "I" of the "6th Dance"?

In performance, are the dancers called on to improvise their own language? "6th Dance," for instance, contains the line, "Again I discuss something brown." What repeated actions are required of the dancers from poem to poem?

Trope Market (*p. 71*)

Points for Discussion and Writing

Mac Low claims that this poem was created through a more deliberate, or intentional, form of composition. Is this evident in the poem?

Does the poem have any narrative elements such as character, plot, and point of view?

What are the "flashing classics" referred to in the first stanza?

A trope is a metaphor. Of what effect, then, is the title "Trope Market" on the meaning of the poem? Is Mac Low making an indirect point about poetry as commodity?

Of what importance are the words "territorialize" and "fetishistically"? What meaning do they have for poetry and language in general?

59th Light Poem: for La Monte Young and Marian Zazeela—6 November 1982 (*p. 72*)

Points for Discussion and Writing

Mac Low has indicated that this poem is, in part, an acrostic on the dedicatees' names. Compare the acrostic method of composition with John Cage's use of mesostics. What impact does the "arbitrary" nature of the acrostic form have on the poem?

How does the fact that Mac Low uses computer programs such as TRAVESTY (a randomization program based on letter count) and DIASTEX4 (a program that uses a key phrase to "read through" a given text systematically) affect your perception of him as an author? Does the use of these methods make him seem less creative than a poet who doesn't employ them? Or is the method itself part of his creativity? Do you find yourself as a reader more sympathetic to Mac Low's intuitive poems? If so, why?

What other formal elements are evident in the work? To what kinds of sentences, for example, does Mac Low limit himself?

Antic Quatrains (*p. 73*)

Points for Discussion and Writing

This poem, like "59th Light Poem," is based on the use of the dedicatee's name. Is this evident in the poem?

What other formal usages are observable? For example, count the sylla-bles in each line of the poem. What stanza form has Mac Low chosen? To what letters of the alphabet is the poem limited?

Since the poem was composed using a computer, how much of Mac Low's authorship is evident in the poem? What does the fact that we can ask such a question say about the popular concept of authorship?

Is the poem at any point lyrical or narrative? What constraints inherent in the computer method of composition makes these elements hard to achieve? Looking at Mac Low's work as a whole, is he inclined to em-ploy lyricism and narrative? If not, why not?

Is it possible to analyze the meaning of such a poem? Or does the work extend your concept of meaning in poetry?

Twenties 26 *and* Twenties 27   (*p. 74*)

Points for Discussion and Writing

Mac Low says that the poems in *Twenties* were written "intuitively, spontaneously, and directly." Such language is often associated with the Romantic tradition in poetry, which encourages a free movement of the unconscious mind in composition. Yet the poems in this sequence do not employ sentences as a means of organization; they consist instead of isolated word clusters. Do these clusters have any musical or narrative unity?

Do the poems relate to any subject matter or theme? What about "gar-ish Parkinson's twilight trim bark" in "Twenties 27"?

What are some formal constraints that Mac Low uses from poem to poem? Is there a consistency of form and word use from "Twenties 26" and "Twenties 27"?

Choose a few phrases—for example, "yield texture tenure" or "Torque normal fax center globe host"—for class discussion. Is a phrase like "yield texture tenure" devoid of meaning or does it contain potentially richer meanings than traditional poetry?

"Risible" means "of or pertaining to laughter." What is meant then by "risible stashed incomprehension"?

JACK KEROUAC ∎ ∎ ∎ ∎ ∎ ∎ ∎ ∎ ∎ ∎ ∎ ∎ ∎ ∎
1922–1969

Choruses from *Mexico City Blues*   *(p. 76)*

Points for Discussion and Writing

Kerouac believed in spontaneous composition. He also spoke against the dangers of revising one's writing. In the series of choruses in *Mexico City Blues* (1959), what evidence do you see of an improvisatory poetics?

Given the verbal energy of Kerouac's prose style, the choruses are also comparatively brief. Do you see any evidence of a predetermined formal constraint at work, for example line length or the numbers of lines per poem?

The "113th Chorus" begins with a rhyming quatrain. Is the use of rhyme in a poem implicitly nonimprovisatory? In other words, can an improvisatory poetics include so-called closed form as well as free verse?

What does Kerouac mean in "113th Chorus" by the lines "your goal / is your startingplace"? Does he believe that the universe is empty? How might it be perfect in its emptiness?

Likewise, how might a poem ("Arabies of hot / meaning") be all the more meaningful for having no starting or stopping place?

"127th Chorus" employs the rhyme of "street," "feet," and "wheedled" to unify this comparatively narrative and personal poem. It also has a very organized use of line breaks. To what extent are Kerouac's poems both improvisatory *and* formalist?

"149th Chorus" is primarily a personal poem about Kerouac's mother, to whom he was very attached. Compare and contrast it with John Wieners' poem "My Mother." What effect does the last stanza ("And I am only an Apache / smoking Hashi") have on the tone of the poem?

Compare and contrast "211th Chorus" and "228th Chorus." Both deal with the physical exigencies of life—"the wheel of the quivering meat conception" and "man . . . existing in milk." Is one poem more optimistic than the other? Discuss the religious nature of Kerouac's writing—its view of the cosmos—and compare and contrast that view with the cosmology of Allen Ginsberg's *Howl.*

The Thrashing Doves   (*p. 79*)

Points for Discussion and Writing

How is this poem comparable to "211th Chorus" and "228th Chorus"?

Neither "bibbet box" nor "otay" are defined in the dictionary. Do you need to understand their meaning in order to understand the poem? What do you imagine a "bibbet box" to be?

What is the significance of the word "Samsara" in the poem and in Kerouac's poetry as a whole? (See "Terms and References" below.) Does Maya (illusion) play a major role in his world view? Is Kerouac's cosmology one of endless suffering on the "meat wheel of conception"? To what degree may his French Catholic upbringing have influenced Kerouac's philosophy?

Of what importance are the lines "tell all the little children the little otay / story of magic, multiple madness"? Are magical stories a momentary relief against the eternal round of death and conception? Do the thrashing doves of the poem's title therefore represent the mortal fate of men and women?

Given Kerouac's freewheeling but also precise use of language, what effect does "made made" have in the poem's next to last line? Is the repetition intentional, or was the poem rushed off quickly and carelessly without concern about grammatical errors and typos?

Terms and References

Samsara is a term in Buddhism indicating the course of mundane existence, the endless cycle of birth, death, and rebirth.

In the Hindu religion, **Maya** is the mother of the world and the personified active will of the Creator; in Hindu philosophy, it is illusion, often portrayed as a young woman.

PHILIP WHALEN   ▪ ▪ ▪ ▪ ▪ ▪ ▪ ▪ ▪ ▪ ▪ ▪
b. 1923

The Slop Barrel   (*p. 81*)

Points for Discussion and Writing

According to Ezra Pound scholar Hugh Kenner, "paideuma" means "a people's whole congeries of patterned energies, from the 'ideas' down to the things they know in their bones."[2] Is Whalen's poem therefore an

2. Hugh Kenner, *The Pound Era*, Berkeley, Calif., 1971, p. 507.

attempt to capture the essence of his own people? Or is "paideuma" more broadly defined than the energies of Whalen's own cultural and ethnic background?

"The Dalles" was a location in Oregon where Whalen was born and raised. Is this also the site for the poem? Or does the poem's time and place change?

Who speaks in the poem? Is it a solitary narrator or a series of narrators?

Polydeuces in another name for Pollux of the Castor and Pollux legend, the story of the twin sons of Leda, who was raped by Zeus in the form of a swan. When Whalen writes, "You have as many scars as my brother, Polydeuces," is he announcing his identification with Castor?

Likewise, the question "Is it true your father was a swan?" probably connects to the Castor and Pollux legend. The coupling of these references from myth with scenes from Whalen's childhood may have been influenced by the poems of Ezra Pound, especially *The Cantos*, and "Leda and the Swan" by William Butler Yeats. How similar is Whalen's poem in form to the mosaic organization of *The Cantos*?

Compare and contrast "The Slop Barrel" with Ted Berrigan's "Bean Spasms."

A tonga is a light two-wheeled cart for four persons, used in India. The tonga-walla is therefore its driver. In the Hindu religion, Maya is the mother of the world and a central principle of creation. What might these references from Eastern culture have to do with Whalen's experience of childhood in The Dalles, where presumably the scene of climbing the slop barrel (section III) takes place?

To what extent are the magical injunctions of section III connected to the art of poetry?

DENISE LEVERTOV ▪ ▪ ▪ ▪ ▪ ▪ ▪ ▪ ▪ ▪ ▪ ▪

b. 1923

Overland to the Islands   (*p. 86*)

Points for Discussion and Writing

Levertov makes a comparison between the progress of a dog and that of human beings. What behavior does she advise we emulate in the dog? How might the dog's every step be an "arrival"? To what extent might the dog's haphazard movement also describe the making of a poem?

Compare Robert Frost's statement in his essay, "The Figure a Poem Makes," that a poem, like a piece of ice, "must ride on its own melting"?

Illustrious Ancestors   (*p. 87*)

Points for Discussion and Writing

Like "Overland to the Islands," this poem is partly about the writing of poetry. What kinds of poems does Levertov desire to make?

The "Rav of Northern White Russia," to which the poem refers, was Schneour Zaimon, a renowned Hasidic mystic to whom Levertov is related through her father's side of the family. Levertov's mother was descended from Angel Jones of Mold, a Welsh tailor and mystic. In what ways is Levertov's poetry consistent with the mystical tradition?

How might the writing of poetry be comparable to the act of a tailor stitching?

Why is the metaphor of pausing between stitching more effective than the act of stitching itself?

The Ache of Marriage   (*p. 87*)

Points for Discussion and Writing

This poem deals with the pain and responsibility of marriage as well as its pleasures. To what extent does this poem seem personal? Or is the poem a more general comment on the condition of marriage?

Stanza 3 begins, "We look for communion / and are turned away." Yet to some extent the "we" of the poem are safely harbored inside the leviathan of marriage. What is meant by the word "communion" in the poem? Is it communion with each other? Or with the larger world outside the marriage?

Formally, compare this and other Levertov poems with the work of Robert Creeley and Hilda Morley, two poets of the Black Mountain aesthetic. What uses does Levertov make of the poetic line? Is there a sense of cadence in its use? Might her line lengths, suggesting the rhythm of speech and its pauses, contribute to meaning in their own right? How does Levertov's poetry differ from the work of Creeley and Morley?

With regard to Levertov's metaphysics, do you find in her work "an intuition of an order, a form beyond forms, in which forms partake"?[3]

3. Denise Levertov, "Some Notes on Organic Form," in *The Poet in the World*, p. 7.

How does her inherent mysticism set her work apart from Olson's program as stated in "Projective Verse"?

Levertov's stately cadences are also similar to the work of her good friend and correspondent, Robert Duncan. What similarities and differences do you find in the work of the two poets?

How is Levertov's search for "organic form," as stated in her essay "Some Notes on Organic Form," evident in her poetry?

The Wings   (p. 88)

Points for Discussion and Writing

Like the magical realist fiction of Latin American authors such as Gabriel García Marquez, this poem has the reality and authority of a dream. How do you explain the "fictional" situation in which the narrator finds herself?

Ezra Pound wrote that in poetry "the natural object is the adequate symbol." Discuss the symbolic qualities of the wings. How might the wings symbolize Levertov's feelings about her self? Could the burden on her back, described as an embryo, represent giving birth to aspects of her own personality?

One wing is "feathered in soot"; the other is described as "blazing ciliations of ember, pale / flare-pinions." Might Levertov be referring to the flight of the Phoenix from its own ashes? Or does the sense of one white wing and one black one suggest two contrary sides of Levertov's own being? Does flying on one white wing at the poem's end suggest the need to cast off an undesireable aspect of self?

How might the metaphors of embryo and flight be seen as feminist in intention?

Stepping Westward   (p. 89)

Points for Discussion and Writing

Who is the speaker in this poem? Is it Levertov herself or a feminine character from myth—for example, Persephone? Examine the solar and lunar images of the poem, as with "I hold steady / in the black sky / and vanish by day." Could this "I" be Diana, goddess of the moon? Or is it an aspect of women in general?

It is the sun, traditionally a male figure in myth, that moves westward bearing day. The speaker of this poem, clearly feminine, describes herself as "a shadow / that grows longer as the sun / moves." Discuss the relationship between male and female figures in the poem. Does Levertov use inconstancy ("ebb and flow") to define female authority in the poem?

In discussing the role of the feminine in this work, take note of the bread image at the poem's end. Carried in a basket, the bread "hurts / my shoulders but closes me / in fragrance." This image may be intended to capture the ambivalence of a woman's life. How so?

Williams: An Essay   *(p. 90)*

Points for Discussion and Writing

Compare and contrast this work with Victor Hernandez Cruz's poem "An Essay on William Carlos Williams." Both Levertov and Cruz obviously admire the older poet. To what degree does their own poetry take its lead from Williams's work? Williams worked as a pediatrician for most of his life. Of what significance to poetry, then, are the lines "a baby's resolute fury—metaphysic / of appetite and tension"?

Like Williams, Levertov seeks a poetry of music, invention, and connection. Some commentators on language poetry believe that it takes its power from disconnectedness. Contrast Levertov's theories of organic poetry, as expressed in her essay "Some Notes on Organic Form," as well as her own mystical practice of the art, with language poetry theory.

What does Levertov mean by "Not / the bald image, but always— / undulant, elusive, beyond reach / of any dull / staring eye . . ."? How might the real poem lie "beneath the skin of image"?

Wavering   *(p. 91)*

Points for Discussion and Writing

In the midst of pastoral imagery of june bugs, curtains, fireflies, and fog, Levertov interposes the lines, "A world, the world, where *live shell* / can explode on impact." Does she mean the *words* "live shell" or the actual explosion of a shell?

Levertov writes that "The attention / sets out toward a cell, its hermit." But later this attention wavers toward the comparative mutability of the "caravan of event." Which of these seemingly opposing values of certainty and uncertainty, fixedness and mobility, does Levertov favor? Or is perception a process involving the contrary elements of identity and change?

To what extent is this a poem about poetry as an act of attention?

Where Is the Angel?   (p. 91)

Points for Discussion and Writing

Some of Levertov's other poems in this selection have made use of angel imagery. How is this poem different in its use of the figure? If the angel represents the poetic muse, what does this mean about Levertov's feelings toward herself and history? Why must one have an angel to *wrestle*, for instance? Does the angel represent an extremity of experience somehow necessary to pleasure? Of what importance are Levertov's references to inside ("It is pleasant in here") and outside ("Outside, the stark shadows / menace")?

JAMES SCHUYLER   ▪ ▪ ▪ ▪ ▪ ▪ ▪ ▪ ▪ ▪ ▪ ▪ ▪
1923–1991

A Man in Blue   (p. 93)

Points for Discussion and Writing

Who is the man in blue to whom the title refers? Is it simply a man raking leaves next to Schuyler's house? What connection does this man have to the composer Brahms, the conductor Bruno Walter, or Schuyler himself listening to their music on a sunny day?

The poem is about the occasion of listening to a symphony on a Magnavox radio "from which a forte / drops like a used Brillo pad." Discuss Schuyler's means of describing the music—for example, the reference to "beer and skittles." How is the experience of the music heightened and made more real by the ordinariness of Schuyler's references?

Compare and contrast Schuyler's use of everyday details with that of Frank O'Hara, in "The Day Lady Died." To what extent might both poets have been influenced by the poetry of William Carlos Williams in the use of "local" effects?

The Crystal Lithium   (p. 94)

Points for Discussion and Writing

Schuyler wrote some long poems of note, such as "The Crystal Lithium" (1972) and "The Morning of the Poem" (1980). In both of these works, he uses a long line. Compare and contrast his long poems with Allen Ginsberg's *Howl* and *Kaddish*, John Ashbery's *The Skaters* and *Flow Chart*, and Mei-Mei Berssenbrugge's "Alakanak Break-Up."

Although Schuyler's tone is often casual, he maintains intensity. What means does he use to achieve it? Examine, for example, the length of the poem's sentences. The entire poem consists of only three sentences, the last of which begins, "The thunder of a summer's day / rolls down the shimmering blacktop. . . ." The instructor may want to ask the class to read this last sentence out loud in order to appreciate Schuyler's highly developed ear for language.

Examine the poet's use of quotidian, or everyday, events in the poem, a practice often associated with New York School poetry. Does the use of the everyday mean that a poem's tone will become prosaic or mundane?

Lithium is a drug prescribed to level the moods of people suffering from manic-depression. Is there any evidence of these moods in the poem?

How might Schuyler, an urban dweller, be considered a nature poet?

Letter to a Friend: Who Is Nancy Daum? (*p. 98*)

Points for Discussion and Writing

The poem begins by asserting, "All things are real / no one a symbol." This view is consistent with William Carlos Williams' statement, "No idea but in things." In what ways does Schuyler's poetry concentrate on the actual rather than the symbolic?

What do you learn about Schuyler from the things on which he focuses—for example, "a compact / with a Red Sea / scene / holding little / pills (Valium / for travel strain)"? How does Schuyler's approach to the personal differ from that of confessional poets Sylvia Plath, Ann Sexton, and Robert Lowell?

To whom is the letter addressed? What does the poem reveal about their relationship?

Korean Mums (*p. 102*)

Points for Discussion and Writing

This poem, like "Letter to a Friend: Who Is Nancy Daum?", uses a very short poetic line. What effect does the shorter line have on Schuyler's language?

Compare and contrast Schuyler's use of the short line with that of Eileen Myles.

One of Schuyler's means of composition is to sit facing a landscape and absorb the actuality of the scene into language; in this respect, he is a painterly poet. How is this painterliness exhibited in "Korean Mums"?

How does the poet avoid self-consciousness when including his own presence as author in the poem?

The poem ends elegiacally. Using the figure of the Korean mums, discuss how the poet arrives at this mood.

JACK SPICER ■ ■ ■ ■ ■ ■ ■ ■ ■ ■ ■ ■ ■ ■ ■
1925–1965

FROM *Imaginary Elegies* (*p. 104*)

Points for Discussion and Writing

Spicer was an avid experimenter as a poet and readily changed his approach to composition. This sequence of poems was influenced by *The Duino Elegies* of Rainer Maria Rilke. "Morphemics" and "Phonemics" are more influenced by Ludwig Wittgenstein and the postmodern current of thought that resulted in language poetry. Discuss the difference between these two modes of expression in Spicer's poetry.

How is poetry "blind like a camera"?

Spicer writes, "The temporary tempts poetry." How?

The theme of seeing established in section I continues in section II. If seeing is power (the moon is represented as God's all-seeing yellow eye), how is it that "Lovers lose / Themselves in others" and "Do not see themselves"?

Poetry is comparable to a camera in section I; both are "blind" or objective. What is the relationship between the camera and the moon ("God's big yellow eye") in section II?

The moon perceives "What wasn't, what undoes, what will not happen." It is an *imago mundi*, or storehouse of images, of things that are never seen. Discuss the poem's images of absence and presence in this context.

Who is "Old butterface / Who always eats her lovers" in section II?

In section III, God has a second eye that is "good and gold." But "God feeds on God" in the same way that "Cat feeds on mouse." Is God a beneficient figure in the poem, a predatory figure, or both?

Of what importance is twilight in the scheme of God's two eyes (sun and moon)?

Is the figure of the "wet bat" positive or negative?

Discuss Spicer's assertion that the poet should "Be like God."

Spicer was very enthusiastic about the poetry of Federico García Lorca, a major influence on poetry of the "deep image." What elements in this poem might be considered "deep image" in influence?

Morphemics   *(p. 107)*

Points for Discussion and Writing

In part 3 of this poem, Spicer writes, "Our image shrinks to a morpheme, an -ing word. Death / Is an image of sylables [sic]." In part 4, he refers to the morpheme as "the loss of innocence." What is Spicer's attitude toward the morpheme in this poem?

How does the morpheme relate to innocence and the birth of the "Christ Child"?

What effect does Spicer's various spellings of the word "syllable" ("cantilever of sylabbles," "image of sylables") have in the poem? Are these puns on the words "able" and "babble"?

What does the morpheme—and the language as a whole—have to do with "The trees / Of some dark forest where we wander amazed at the selves of / ourselves"? Is the forest language? How might the "right woods" also be the "right words"?

Terms and References

Lew is Lew Welch, a Bay area poet who attended Reed College with Philip Whalen and Gary Snyder.

Thanatos and ***agape*** are Greek for "death" and "brotherly love."

A **morpheme** is "the smallest lexical unit of a language."

Phonemics   *(p. 109)*

Points for Discussion and Writing

A phoneme is "the smallest unit in the sound system of a language, functioning to distinguish one morpheme from another." Are phonemes comparable to "the shards of pots . . . Found but not put together"?

What is Spicer's attitude toward linguistics in this poem? Does he find it of poetic and human value?

In Keats's famous poem, "Ode to a Nightingale," the bird is a figure of transcendent imagination. What does Spicer suggest when he writes, "This is no nightingale"?

What connection exists between the "emotional disturbance" that "echoes down the canyons of the heart" and "echoes" that are "merely phonemes"?

Why are phonemes "dead before their burial"?

If in the Semitic languages consonants are male and vowels female, what implication do you see in Spicer's statement that consonants are "A pattern for imagination," whereas "The vowels / Are indistinguishable"?

KENNETH KOCH ▪ ▪ ▪ ▪ ▪ ▪ ▪ ▪ ▪ ▪ ▪ ▪ ▪
b. 1925

Permanently   (p. 112)

Points for Discussion and Writing

This poem follows, quite by coincidence, Jack Spicer's poems "Morphemics" and "Phonemics." Compare and contrast the Koch and Spicer poems on the subject of language.

Why does Koch pick an adverb for his title?

Koch's poem is narrative and personifies the parts of speech. It is also very funny. To what degree are his descriptions of nouns, verbs, and adjectives nevertheless true?

Who is the "you" the poet addresses in the poem's final stanza?

Variations on a Theme by William Carlos Williams
(p. 112)

Points for Discussion and Writing

This poem is a parody of Williams's well-known poem, "This Is Just to Say," included in *The Norton Anthology of Modern Poetry*. Read and discuss the Williams poem. Does Koch intend to make fun of the poem he is parodying?

How is the Koch poem different from "This Is Just to Say" in form?

William Carlos Williams was a pediatrician as well as a poet. Does section 4 of the poem ("I wanted you here in the wards, where I am the doctor!") refer to Williams himself?

Alive for an Instant (*p. 113*)

Points for Discussion and Writing

This poem makes use of the catalogue form; it also is influenced by surrealist collage, in which unexpected objects or events are juxtaposed—for example, "summer in my brainwater." Both forms are also used by Koch in teaching young children to write poetry. What implication does this breaking of barriers between the imaginations of adult and children have for the poem? For poetry as a whole?

While the poem is humorous and even silly at points, what traditional lyric elements does it contain?

Creative writing instructors might ask the class to imitate Koch's form of "I have a _____ in my _____" as a way of encouraging metaphor and less-rational poetic associations. This can be especially useful when students are taking relatively few risks in their uses of metaphor.

The Circus (*p. 114*)

Points for Discussion and Writing

Published in 1975, this poem refers to another Koch poem of the same title, which appeared in *Thank You and Other Poems* (1962). The instructor may want to read the earlier poem to the class. Does understanding the second poem depend on understanding the first?

Like James Schuyler in "Korean Mums," Koch announces his presence as author of the poem at hand. The reflexiveness of doing so is comparable to addressing "the fourth wall" (the audience) in theater or, in a slightly different sense, a painter doing a self-portrait. Discuss the issue of the author's self-awareness. Does it add or detract from the poem?

Does the poem have other subjects than Koch's earlier poetry? What are they?

With Janice (*p. 116*)

Points for Discussion and Writing

Like "The Circus," this poem is a meditation on events of the past. Addressed to Koch's wife Janice, it recalls the couple's visit to Greece in 1961. In what respect is it *different* from "The Circus"?

The poem contains frequent dislocations and combines sentences in a near stream of consciousness. How is this rhetorical manner consistent with the overall mood of the poem?

FRANK O'HARA ■ ■ ■ ■ ■ ■ ■ ■ ■ ■ ■ ■ ■ ■ ■

1926–1966

Poem ("The eager note on my door said 'Call me,'")
(p. 121)

Points for Discussion and Writing

This poem begins in a straightforward manner but soon makes use of eccentric details that make the reader question the narrator's reliability. What sort of person leaves for a weekend trip with nothing but tangerines in an overnight bag? Moreover, "It was autumn / by the time I got around the corner." Such detail lends a dreamlike quality to the poem that is confirmed by the horrifying and yet absurd discovery at poem's end. Discuss the overall tone of the poem. At what point do you first begin to mistrust the narrator?

Is O'Hara being ironic when he says "I did appreciate it"? What are some other examples of irony in the poem?

What effect does the "camp" language "Oh fie! / for shame!" have on the poem's tone?

Poem ("At night Chinamen jump")   (p. 122)

Points for Discussion and Writing

Examine O'Hara's use of the rhyming couplet. Because the line lengths are short and the measure is generally trimeter (three stressed syllables to the line), the rhyme comes quickly. What effect does this have on the poem?

Is O'Hara's technique flawed, or is the awkwardness of rhyme and rhythm intentional? Despite its high spirits, does the poem strive for beauty of a sort?

What sort of cultural perspective does the poem offer? Are the "Chinamen" presented as a marginalized "other," or are they regarded with sympathy?

The English metaphysical poets such as John Donne and George Herbert were fond of the concept of antipodes, places on the opposite side of the earth, that is, diametrically opposed. What similarity might this poem have with metaphysical poetry?

Meditations in an Emergency   (*p. 122*)

This is one of O'Hara's few prose poems. Of what advantage is the form? Might it have just as easily appeared in verse lines? If not, why not?

In the conservative political and artistic climate of the 1950s, how might O'Hara's "Uh huh" in paragraph 6 amount to a statement of poetics?

Discuss in general the sentiments expressed about city and country life in the same paragraph.

What does the poet mean when he asserts that "It is more important to affirm the least sincere"? What problems might sincerity present? What are the advantages of insincerity? Is O'Hara himself sincere in the poem?

Discuss O'Hara's statement in the following paragraph that he's bored but feels the duty as a poet "to be attentive." Is a poet "needed by things," as O'Hara suggests?

In a later section, what does O'Hara mean by the gnomic statement, "It is easy to be beautiful; it is difficult to appear so"?

What is the "emergency" on which this poem meditates? Is it disappointment in love?

Ode to Joy   (*p. 124*)

How is this poem different in tone from the other O'Hara work in this selection?

Each stanza consists of a single sentence. What effect does this have on the poet's tone and word choice?

An ode is an extended lyric poem on a serious theme. Is this true of O'Hara's poem?

The Day Lady Died   (*p. 125*)

The singer Billie Holiday was known as Lady Day. Mal Waldron was a pianist who accompanied her. Why does O'Hara withhold the announcement of Lady Day's death until the end of the poem?

The first stanzas of the poem are insistently casual. Do you find O'-Hara's tone inconsistent with a tone of elegy? On the other hand, how might the tone be perfectly consistent with learning the momentous news of death?

At what point does the tone of the poem change?

What affect do O'Hara's references to Verlaine, Bonnard, Hesiod, Brendan Behan, and Genet have on the poem? Some students may consider the poem's references to be comparatively "high art." What is their impression, on the other hand, of its level of rhetoric?

What is the situation with regard to "high" and "low" art today? Is it possible to make such distinctions in the poetry included here? Is John Cage's work "high" art and Charles Bukowski's "low"? Are these terms related to the perceived social class of the author? Are they justified for use in a critical discussion?

This is a poem in O'Hara's "I do this I do that" mode; it is also diaristic. What are the risks and advantages of writing in this way? What other poets in the anthology make use of the everyday?

Personal Poem   (p. 126)

Points for Discussion and Writing

This poem might be described as personal rather than confessional. How?

Is the narrator of the poem O'Hara himself? Is it possible that a persona is adopted even in writing a seemingly reliable report such as this one?

From what you know of his biography, was O'Hara's batting average as a "mover and shaker" in the art world really ".016"? How would O'-Hara's influence have compared at the time with Robert Lowell's?

The poet Wallace Stevens once wrote that poetry is "that which suffices." Was this casually written poem about a lunch date with LeRoi Jones, O'Hara's fellow poet, "sufficient" by the literary standard of 1959, which called for complexity, ambiguity, decorum, and a willingness to use traditional poetic forms?

The poem "The Day Lady Died" has levels of expression ranging from the casual to the elegiac. Is that true of this poem?

Lionel Trilling was a noted literary critic who taught at Columbia University. Don Allen is Donald Allen, editor of *The New American Poetry: 1945–1960*. Is it important that the reader know their identities? What about O'Hara's less well-known friend, Mike Kanemitsu? Discuss the use of naming, especially of his friends, in O'Hara's work. Does this naming create a democracy of detail, or do the culturally specific natures of some references make you feel excluded as a reader? In this context, discuss also James Schuyler's poem "Letter to a Friend: Who Is Nancy Daum?"

Ave Maria   *(p. 126)*

Points for Discussion and Writing

Discuss the title of this work as it relates to the content of the poem. Is O'Hara's position one of advocacy or of irony?

Is O'Hara ironic when he writes that the soul "grows in darkness, embossed by silvery images" in movie theaters?

Is a personal poetics implicit in this poem in terms of the sense of discovery and spontaneity required of composition?

What is the *moral* of this poem? Are the "darker joys" in fact important?

Steps   *(p. 127)*

Points for Discussion and Writing

In this poem, O'Hara records the events of a walk in New York City; in doing so, he adopts a method of composition employed by the French poet Guillaume Apollinaire (1880–1918), who during his walks through Paris would "combine almost at random the odd sentences and phrases that occurred to him or that he overheard."[4] Apollinaire called these works "Poemes conversations." Ask students to compare and contrast O'Hara's poems of the everyday with Apollinaire's "Monday Christine Street" and "Phantom of the Clouds," to be found in *Calligrams* and *The Selected Writings of Guillaume Apollinaire*.

A conversational idiom was also made popular in the United States by William Carlos Williams' emphasis on the vernacular. Ask students to compare and contrast the work of O'Hara and Williams—for example, "The Last Words of My English Grandmother," "The Young Housewife," and "The Catholic Bells." Which poet strikes you as employing the more poetic diction?

What is O'Hara's attitude toward the city on the day the poem is written?

What are V-days and D-days?

What evidence exists in the poem that it is truly personal rather than an objective look at "the day while the sun is still shining"?

4. Roger Shattuck, ed. and trans. *The Selected Writings of Guillaume Apollinaire*, New York, 1971, p. 21.

Poem ("Lana Turner has collapsed!") (*p. 129*)

Points for Discussion and Writing

Lana Turner was a leading film actress of the 1950s. Is the poem really about Lana Turner? That is, does it try to achieve some understanding of her character? Or is the poem about O'Hara's own casual approach to poetic composition?

Is this poem similar to or different from "The Day Lady Died," another work about a famous person?

It is part of O'Hara's legend as a poet that he wrote the poem on the Staten Island Ferry while on his way to give a reading with the more-noted poet Robert Lowell. When he arrived at the reading, O'Hara read it to the audience after announcing when and where he had written it. How does this information affect your understanding of the poem?

Why I Am Not a Painter (*p. 129*)

Points for Discussion and Writing

The painter Mike Goldberg was a friend of O'Hara's. What does this poem reveal about the creative process? Are the elements of art—for example, Goldberg's word "SARDINE"—as casually rearranged as O'-Hara suggests?

Discuss the issue of the arbitrary and the necessary when it comes to the writing of a poem. Are poems written, as some believe, out of an emotional need for expression? Does their meaning therefore preexist the words that eventually constitute the poem? Or do poems come to seem necessary after they are worked and reworked into the proper artistic shape? In this context, discuss the inclusion and alteration of the word "SARDINES" in Mike Goldberg's painting.

Compare and contrast this work, which comments on some of O'Hara's other poems, with "The Circus" by Kenneth Koch.

Discuss O'Hara's rhetorical approach in this poem. What kinds of words does he use? What kind of sentence is dominant? How important is the *pace* of the poem's narrative? What devices are used to hurry it along?

Is O'Hara sincere when he writes, "There should be / so much more, not of orange, of / words, of how terrible orange is / and life"? Discuss in general the relationship between irony and sincerity in O'Hara's work. Is it possible to be both ironic and sincere?

Discuss O'Hara's statement about his poem in progress: "It is even in / prose, I am a real poet." Under what conditions might a poem become more "real" because it is in prose (presumably free verse) rather than traditional verse?

ALLEN GINSBERG ▪ ▪ ▪ ▪ ▪ ▪ ▪ ▪ ▪ ▪ ▪ ▪ ▪
b. 1926

FROM *Howl*   (*p. 131*)

Points for Discussion and Writing

Ginsberg wrote this poem in what he calls "strophes"; that is, each indented passage in the long-lined poem acts as its own unity within the poem. According to Ginsberg's essay "Notes for *Howl and Other Poems*," the whole first section was "typed out madly in one afternoon, a huge sad comedy of wild phrasing, meaningless images for the beauty of abstract poetry of mind running along making combinations."[5] He also writes that "ideally each line of *Howl* is a single breath unit."[6] By each line, does he mean each strophe?

Ginsberg's poetry was accused by some academics of the time of being formless. In your opinion is his poetry formless? What forms does it use? Read "Notes for *Howl and Other Poems*" in the "Poetics" section of *Postmodern American Poetry* and bring it to bear on your discussion of the poem. What does he mean by "Mind is shapely, Art is shapely"? Does this suggest that anything goes in the writing of a poem? Or must one train his or her mind to the task of improvisation?

Compare Ginsberg's comments about "the elastic of a breath" with Charle's Olson's statements about breath in "Projective Verse."

Likewise, compare the poem *Howl* with the opening sections of Walt Whitman's "Song of Myself."

To what do "the sirens of Los Alamos" and "the crack of doom on the hydrogen jukebox" refer?

N.C. is Neal Cassady, a handsome young railway employee and car thief from Denver who was Ginsberg's bisexual lover for a time. In what respect is N.C. "the secret hero of these poems"?

What does Ginsberg mean by "the one eyed shrew of the heterosexual dollar"? One of the shrews "does nothing but sit on her ass and snip the intellectual golden threads of the craftsman's loom." How might this line have been influenced by the work of Ezra Pound?

Examine the implicit identities of the poem's creative figures as op-

5. Allen Ginsberg, in *The Poetics of The New American Poetry*, eds. Donald M. Allen and Warren Tallman, New York, 1973, p. 318.   6. The same, p. 319.

posed to the enemies of imagination. How might a feminist criticism apply to the poem?

What does the poet, himself gay, mean by "the nitroglycerine shrieks of the fairies of advertising"?

Several figures, including "sinister intelligent editors," are burned alive or "run down by the drunken taxicabs of Absolute Reality." Discuss Ginsberg's reference to "Absolute Reality" in the context of the relativism and indeterminacy of the language poets. Is Ginsberg's angry cosmology dependent on a God? Does language poetry depend, on the other hand, on the "death" of God?

John Cage writes, in *Themes & Variations* (1982), that "Art = imitation of nature in her manner of operation," a strongly Romantic concept. Is Cage's statement true of Ginsberg's poetry as well?

How does the Romanticism of *Howl* and Ginsberg's other poems exhibit itself?

Why does Ginsberg choose asterisks rather than words in the phrase "with mother finally °°°°°°, and the last fantastic book flung out of the tenement window"?

This poem is dedicated to Carl Solomon, whom Ginsberg met while residing in a hospital mental ward. What evidence of that experience do you find in the poem?

What surrealist images are evident in the work? How might the *politics* of surrealism have been attractive to the author of *Howl?*

The Beat poets, Ginsberg included, make many references to jazz as a compositional influence. Locate sections of the poem that are guided musically by the jazz model—for example, "and blew the suffering of America's naked mind for love into an eli eli lamma lamma sabacthani saxophone cry that shivered the cities down to the last radio."

A Supermarket in California   *(p. 135)*

Points for Discussion and Writing

How is the nineteenth-century American poet Walt Whitman a "courage teacher" to the young Allen Ginsberg? Ginsberg wonders what kind of America Whitman had at the time of his death. What kind of America does Ginsberg present in this poem? Why would both poets be lonely in America as described in the poem?

Why is it humorous that Whitman, Lorca, and Ginsberg meet in the supermarket rather than on the height of Parnassus or heaven? To what extent is the supermarket setting important to Ginsberg's political and satirical purposes?

The poem has both comedic and elegiac passages; it thus incorporates a variety of moods and dictions. Of what other poems in the anthology is this true?

Terms and References

Charon is the ferryman who transports the dead across the river Styx into Hades; he collects his fee in the form of the coins on their eyes.

With Styx and Acheron, **Lethe** is one of three rivers in Hell; crossing it causes loss of memory.

America   (*p. 136*)

Points for Discussion and Writing

Discuss the line "America after all it is you and I who are perfect not the next world." Is the America of this poem perfect? Then what does Ginsberg mean?

Ginsberg refers to his friend William Burroughs and his Uncle Max, among other personal acquaintances. Does this make the poem private or even confessional? To what extent is the poem political and public?

Who are Tom Mooney, the Spanish Loyalists, Sacco and Vanzetti, and the Scottsboro boys? Why does Ginsberg identify with them?

How would Ginsberg's announcement that he is "queer" and reads Marx have been received in the 1950s? To what extent did Ginsberg's poetry and political position alter America's reception of gays and leftists? Was W. H. Auden wrong when he wrote, "Poetry alters nothing"?

What job does Ginsberg believe he'd "better get right down to"? Is he sincere in saying that he's putting his "queer shoulder to the wheel"?

What is the purpose of Ginsberg's use of dialects late in the poem such as "Her wants to grab Chicago" and "Her make us all work sixteen hours a day"?

Terms and References

Burroughs is novelist William Burroughs, author of *Naked Lunch* and one of the central figures of the Beat movement.

Wobblies is a name for the International Workers of the World, a leftist worker's organization of the 1930s.

Scott Nearing was a radical economist and socialist.

Israel Amter and **Ella Bloor** were Communist Party leaders in the New York City area.

Nicola Sacco and Bartholomeo Vanzetti were philosophical anarchists who were convicted of murder in connection with a payroll robbery and executed in 1927.

FROM *Kaddish*   (*p. 138*)

Points for Discussion and Writing

The Kaddish is a traditional Hebrew death song, or elegy. Ginsberg "sings" it on the occasion of his mother's death. Like *Howl*, it was written in a single burst of energy. Why is the opening measure, consisting of two strong syllables followed by a trochaic emphasis in the first strophe, especially appropriate to elegy?

"Adonais" refers to Shelley's famous poem on the death of poet John Keats. To what extent is Naomi Ginsberg a figure like Adonais?

Discuss Ginsberg's presentation of his mother's life story. Is the honesty of his revelations sympathetic? What story does this elegy tell of his mother's life?

The form of this Proem to *Kaddish* is, according to Ginsberg, "completely free composition, the long line breaking up within itself into short staccato breath units. . . . Ending with a hymn in rhythm similar to the synagogue death lament."[7] Examine Ginsberg's use of the long line in this poem. Is it similar to or different from his use of the long line in *Howl*?

To Aunt Rose   (*p. 141*)

Points for Discussion and Writing

Like "A Supermarket in California," "America," and *Kaddish*, this poem begins by addressing a person or entity. It is also similar to *Kaddish* in that the poem invokes the spirit of the dead. After reading the poem out loud in class, ask a member of the class to characterize Aunt Rose in exact detail. Then do the same with Ginsberg as he presents himself in the poem.

What does Ginsberg mean in referring to himself as "an ignorant girl of family silence"? Likewise, what is the "Museum of Newark"?

Why does the poet go to such lengths to assure his Aunt Rose that Hitler is in eternity?

Ginsberg's father was Louis Ginsberg, a lyric poet of the conventional style. What do the titles of his books, *The Attic of the Past* and *Everlast-*

---

7. The same, p. 320.

ing Minute, suggest about the situation of Aunt Rose and the Ginsberg family life in general? What do they suggest about his father's poetry?

As in a letter, Ginsberg relays family news to Aunt Rose. What effect does this news have on the poem?

The final piece of information concerns the war in Spain, which "ended long ago." The poem was written in June 1958. In what year did Aunt Rose die? What invokes her memory now?

First Party at Ken Kesey's with Hell's Angels   *(p. 142)*

Points for Discussion and Writing

This and the poem to follow are among the poet's few short works. Is there anything in Ginsberg's perspective, style, or voice that lends itself especially to long poems?

Note the effectiveness of the trochaic measure (stress followed by unstressed syllables) in setting an urgent narrative pace. This "narrative" consists of a series of scenes that build into a mosaic. Examine Ginsberg's use of the catalogue, or list, to establish the scene. In what respect is the poem cinematic in approach?

Despite the "blast of loudspeakers" and the presence of the often boisterous Hell's Angels, the poem is peaceful in tone. Of what effect are the last two lines on this tone?

Novelist Ken Kesey wrote *Sometimes a Great Notion* and *One Flew Over the Cuckoo's Nest.* He was also one of the Merry Pranksters, a band of Hippies who toured the United States in a bus in the late 1960s. Of what importance is the information that it's the *first* party at Kesey's house?

Of what importance is the figure of the hanged man sculpture "dangling from a high creek branch"?

Ginsberg frequently dates his poems, in this case *December 1965.* How is this dating procedure especially appropriate to the poet's overall approach? Is the poem in any way dated or made less universal in meaning by the fact that Ginsberg has framed it in time? Or does this capturing of a moment make the poem all the stronger?

On Neal's Ashes   *(p. 143)*

Points for Discussion and Writing

Neal is Neal Cassady, Ginsberg's former lover and a folk hero of the Beat Generation. Cassady died of exposure while sleeping in a ditch during a trip with Kesey's Merry Pranksters (see Ginsberg's "First Party at Ken Kesey's with Hell's Angels"). In this small elegy, which might also serve as a prayer for the spreading of ashes, Ginsberg relies once more on a trochaic rhythm. Are trochees inherently elegiac?

Like many of Ginsberg's poems, this work is organized by means of a list. How is the catalogue or list form consistent with Romantic political philosophy, even when the poem's references are not directly political?

Given the ritual nature of this poem and the prophetic stance of some of Ginsberg's other work, discuss the role of the poet-priest in his poetry. Does the poet set himself apart from his audience through hieratic usages, or is his approach essentially democratic?

Compare and contrast Ginsberg's work with that of his older contemporary, Robert Lowell. Both have been associated with a form of "confessional" poetry. Do you find Ginsberg's work to be confessional in the same sense as Lowell's *Life Studies* or Sylvia Plath's *Ariel?* Or is Ginsberg closer in philosophy to the Personist mode of Frank O'Hara?

ROBERT CREELEY ▪ ▪ ▪ ▪ ▪ ▪ ▪ ▪ ▪ ▪ ▪ ▪
b. 1926

After Lorca   (*p. 144*)

Points for Discussion and Writing

Creeley is not generally identified as a political poet, yet this poem makes a political point. What is it? What is the meaning of the final stanza: "And the poor love it / and think it's crazy"?

Why is the poem titled "After Lorca"?

A Form of Women   (*p. 144*)

Points for Discussion and Writing

Creeley's work has the ability to be both oblique and direct; there is a painful honesty to his subjects but a cautious approach to resolution. Examine the language of the poem for these characteristics. At what points is its expression bold and direct? At what points does the syntax act to shield the poem's emotion? Why is the poem titled "A *Form* of Women"?

Creeley writes, "My face is my own, I thought. / But you have seen it / turn into a thousand years." The "I" of the poem appears to have a monstrous visage or at least a face made monstrous by some other fact. How can it be that his face, hands, and mouth are his own, but he himself is not?

The "I" of the poem initially walks out alone, in search of knowledge. But "I" encounters a "you," who cries. Who is the "you" of the poem? A form of women?

The Flower   (p. 145)

Points for Discussion and Writing

Creeley expresses a good deal of metaphysical discomfort in his poetry. In this poem especially, it is as if the form of William Carlos Williams accompanied the mystical content of William Blake or Emily Dickinson. How is this metaphysical emphasis consistent or inconsistent with a postmodern approach to composition? Is it possible to employ terms like "linearity" and "indeterminacy" in discussing such a poem?

Discuss the gestural qualities of Creeley's language at the poem's end: "like that one, / like this one."

In terms of its pained isolation, compare this poem with Creeley's poem "Bresson's Movies."

Creeley has stated his admiration for the work of William Carlos Williams. What similarity or dissimilarity do you see in the work of the two poets? How might this poem be compared with Williams' "Queen-Ann's-Lace"?

The Rain   (p. 146)

Points for Discussion and Writing

Creeley's poetry is not generally associated with the use of symbols. Does the rain invest itself with symbolism in this poem? If so, with what is it associated?

Repeatedly read out loud the poem's third sentence, typical of the complexity of Creeley's syntax. Ask the students to discuss the meaning of this sentence alone, apart from the rest of the poem. What effect does Creeley's syntax have on his meaning? Can you envision a poem constructed of syntax alone?

Creeley's poems often deal with the wounds of love and the possibility of recovery from them. To what extent is he a courtly love poet of the Petrarchan and Elizabethan traditions?

For Love   (*p. 146*)

Points for Discussion and Writing

This poem is addressed to Creeley's second wife, Bobbie Louise Hawkins. Like many of his works, it deals in the complexities of love. Does the poem have a "story" element? If the "story" is minimal or obliquely suggested, do you nevertheless gain a sense of the relationship between the two lovers?

Examine Creeley's formal usages, particularly enjambment (line breaks in midsentence). How is the short, broken line appropriate to Creeley's patterns of speech? Are the lines broken arbitrarily or by design?

Of what importance is Creeley's choice, throughout his selection, to use a regular stanza form such as the quatrain in this poem?

What effect does the break *between* stanzas have on the poem's meaning? Is the hesitation longer than that between the lines of a stanza itself? Is such an effect planned or accidental?

Look closely at the fourth and fifth stanzas of the poem. Asking several students to read the stanzas out loud, examine how the meaning of a poem can vary depending on the vocal emphasis of its reader. How important is the word "not" in these stanzas?

The poet's repetition of the word "not" at the ends of lines amounts to *rime riche,* or identical rhyme. How does the word "stopped" in stanza 5 relate to Creeley's rhyming of "not"? What about the use of "wouldn't" in stanza 4?

Ask the students what they think is being expressed in the poem as a whole. What is the face that is "gone, now" in the final stanza? Is the "company of love" elsewhere?

The Language   (*p. 148*)

Points for Discussion and Writing

In this poem the line is even more constrained than in "For Love." What effect does this have on Creeley's subject, language?

How are language and love related in the poem?

The poet writes that emptiness exists to be filled, presumably with words. But how are "words full / of holes / aching"? Likewise, what is meant by "Speech / is a mouth"?

The Window   (*p. 149*)

Points for Discussion and Writing

What is the subject of this poem? Is it the window or the way the window frames one's sight?

Why does Creeley perceive the world as "heavy" and "slow"?

Of what importance is the leaf that is "going to / fall"? How can the poem's narrator know of its impending fall? To what extent can the fall of one leaf make everything else around it drop into place?

When he was a child, Creeley lost the sight of one eye in an accident. Might this poem refer to that incident?

Compare the role of the leaf in this poem with that of the jar in Wallace Stevens' "Anecdote of the Jar," to be found in *The Norton Anthology of Modern Poetry*.

"I Keep to Myself Such Measures . . ."   (*p. 150*)

Points for Discussion and Writing

What meaning does the word "measures" have in poetry? Is that how Creeley uses it in this poem?

How can thinking make things "less tangible"? What about poetry? Does it make things more or less tangible?

In his essay "To Define," found in the "Poetics" section of *Postmodern American Poetry*, Creeley writes, "A poetry denies its end in any *descriptive* act, I mean any act which leaves the attention outside the poem."[8] In what way does this poem relate to that statement?

What is the weight that is finally held in both hands in the poem?

In the essay, "Form," also located in the "Poetics" section, Creeley writes, "Being shy as a young man, I was very formal, and still am. I make my moves fast but very self-consciously."[9] How is this statement true of this poem? Of his work in general?

Is it possible to construct a poem from nothing but language, form, and the mind's movement, that is, without substantial reference to the world at large?

8. Robert Creeley, "To Define," in *The Collected Essays of Robert Creeley*, Berkeley, 1989, p. 473.   9. Robert Creeley, "Form," in the same, p. 592.

The World   *(p. 150)*

Points for Discussion and Writing

This poem might be described as a ghost tale. How?

Is it important to know the identity of the "you" in the poem? Who does it appear to be in relation to the speaker? What comfort does the "you" need? What comfort does the apparition require?

In what respect is the narrator an "intruder"?

Examine closely the first two sentences of this poem and how they both drive the situation forward and create a wavering hesitation.

Does Creeley use any conventional devices such as rhyme? By what means does he organize the poem formally? In this respect, look closely at the value placed on the last words of each line. Is the poet rhyming silences?

Self-Portrait   *(p. 151)*

Points for Discussion and Writing

Why is the use of the third-person point of view appropriate in this poem? Are any of his other poems written in the third person?

Why would "he" *want* "to be a brutal old man"?

Is this poem consistent in tone with Creeley's earlier work?

If the poem is a self-portrait, why is there no description of Creeley's own features and specific life circumstance?

Bresson's Movies   *(p. 152)*

Points for Discussion and Writing

This poem describes two of Robert Bresson's films, the first about a young man and his girl. The second is Bresson's *Lancelot du Lac*, which concerns itself with the decline of an aging knight. Creeley notes that he identified with the young, embittered Frenchman of the first film. Does he also identify with the aging knight?

Of what importance are the figures of the horse, the castle ("itself of / no great size"), "a woods, of small trees," and the knight with his "awkward armor"? Discuss each in turn, taking into account their depiction of male consciousness, of age, and of willed self-isolation.

Creeley identifies with both a young man and an older man in Bresson's movies. What is the nature of his identity with them? Does Creeley's attitude toward himself change from the first to the second movie?

Age   (*p. 153*)

Points for Discussion and Writing

This poem is direct in its discussion of age and its personal conse-
quences. Compare and contrast its manner with Creeley's earlier work.

What is meant by the word "impedance"? To what extent has Creeley's
style as a poet always been one of hesitance, or "impedance"? How is
this word important also to the theme of aging?

What is Creeley's stance toward the *self* in the poem?

PAUL BLACKBURN   ▪ ▪ ▪ ▪ ▪ ▪ ▪ ▪ ▪ ▪ ▪ ▪
1926–1971

Brooklyn Narcissus   (*p. 155*)

Points for Discussion and Writing

Is Blackburn himself the figure of Narcissus? What physical evidence of
this exists in the poem?

How can Nemesis be "thumping down the line" in the context of a train
ride?

In what respect is this poem comparable to Robert Frost's "Stopping by
Woods on a Snowy Evening"?

What is meant by the sign "PACE O MIO DIO" (PEACE O MY GOD)?
Why is the sign repeated, followed by the word "oil"?

Examine the broken syntax of the section between the sign (PACE O
MIO DIO) and its repetition ("a bridge between / we state, one life and
the next, we state / is better so / is no / backwater"). Does this broken-
ness of expression reflect the hesitations created by the train's movement? How might this syntax compare with such usages in the poetry of
John Ashbery?

Is entering the tunnel at the poem's end symbolic?

Of what importance is the vision of Blackburn's own face?

Terms and References

Narcissus was the young man from Greek mythology who drowned
while admiring his own beauty as reflected in the water.

Nemesis was the Greek god of vengeance and retribution.

El Camino Verde   (p. 157)

Points for Discussion and Writing

Where is this poem set?

The poem opens with a choice between a "green road" (*el camino verde* in Spanish) and a "road of sand." Why does Blackburn choose the latter?

Why does Blackburn place an isolated period between "hot" and "sirocco" on two occasions? Is this a stylistic mannerism or does it correlate with other elements in the poem?

What tensions exist in the poem between the green world and the hot world of the sirocco? Are these places symbolic of Eden and Hell?

What is meant by the ending movement: "reaches of Africa / where an actual / measure / exists"? Is an "actual measure" to be found only in Africa?

Park Poem   (p. 158)

Points for Discussion and Writing

The poem begins in the third person and ends in the first person. What effect does this have on the poem's meaning?

Discuss what the "girl" of the poem is thinking. How is life "all verbs, vowels and verbs"? Compare these reference to parts of speech with those in Kenneth Koch's poem "Permanently."

How is the poem comparable to Lawrence Ferlinghetti's poem beginning "In Golden Gate Park One day"?

How might some of the poem's phrasing suggest that of Robert Creeley?

The Net of Place   (p. 160)

Points for Discussion and Writing

The poem presents two figures of a hawk, one actual and one symbolic. Distinguish them from each other.

Why is the title "The Net of Place" appropriate?

Does the poem change its setting? To what purpose?

How can Blackburn be so sure that he will never see the Rockies again?

The hawk circling over the sea is put in apposition to "My act." Discuss Blackburn's sense of personal identity in this poem, as well as his tone of self-elegy.

The last line of the poem is, "Your words are mine, at the end." How?

LARRY EIGNER ▪ ▪ ▪ ▪ ▪ ▪ ▪ ▪ ▪ ▪ ▪ ▪ ▪ ▪ ▪
b. 1927

[trees green   the quiet sun]   (*p. 162*)

Points for Discussion and Writing

Eigner rarely uses capitalization in his poems. This poem is entirely in lowercase. What effect does that have on the poem? Is the poem's appearance on the page important to its meaning? How so?

Is the "you" of the poem Eigner himself? If so, why would he choose the second-person point of view over the first?

The poem consists of pieces of perception without a connecting narrative. Discuss the relation of the poem's parts to the whole. Is each part carefully crafted to suit the adjoining part? Are the gaps or silences of the poem also crafted?

Does the poem have the rising or falling moments that occur in traditional lyrical poetry? If not, what aesthetic position might lie behind avoiding them?

Does the poem "resolve" itself or does it simply end? If you feel that resolution is achieved, how does Eigner bring it about?

[how it comes about]   (*p. 163*)

Points for Discussion and Writing

This poem has some narrative elements. What are they?

In whose "voice" might the word "ooh" be expressed? Is it, in fact, spoken? Or is it a detail of the poem as a *written* expression?

What are "the world's sharp bead / curtains"?

open air where   (p. 164)

Points for Discussion and Writing

This poem begins by casually enumerating the details of the day. Does it continue in that manner throughout?

How does this poem differ from Eigner's other poems included here?

What is meant by "the / opposite to recession"?

What is learned about the Eigner family's circumstances from the poem? Is this poem therefore personal?

How important is your knowledge of Eigner's physical handicap to your reading of his poems?

Wholes   (p. 164)

Points for Discussion and Writing

This is Eigner's only poem included here in which the title of the work does not join with the work's opening movement. Discuss Eigner's use of titles, including their typographical look on the page.

How is this poem different in approach from his other work included here?

In what way is the house a metaphor for "wholes"? Does the word "wholes" have double meaning?

What causes life to take on "a size"? What diminishes it?

[a temporary language]   (p. 165)

Points for Discussion and Writing

What is Eigner's comment on language? How is poetry the "math.. of / everyday / life"? Because it offers life a measure?

What do you make of the partial ellipsis (or two periods) following the word "math"? Do they seem necessary to the poem's meaning? Would the meaning be changed if they were absent?

What is the concern of the poem's final movement? Is Eigner addressing himself? Is Eigner concerned with his poetic career and the durability of his words?

JOHN ASHBERY ▪ ▪ ▪ ▪ ▪ ▪ ▪ ▪ ▪ ▪ ▪ ▪ ▪ ▪
b. 1927

The Picture of Little J. A. in a Prospect of Flowers
(*p. 166*)

Points for Discussion and Writing

This poem parodies, at least in its title, Andrew Marvell's "The Picture of Little T. C. in a Prospect of Flowers," ca. 1681, to be found in *The Norton Anthology of Poetry*. Read the Marvell poem in class for comparison. Are the poems similar in form or theme?

Is J. A. John Ashbery? Does Ashbery often use personal references in his poetry? If not, why not? Or does he use them in subliminal or disguised ways?

Why does Ashbery employ an antique diction? Is it for parodic purposes? Is the poem entirely an exercise in parody?

Discuss each of the three sections in turn, noting the change in tone and reference. How does the poem's diction, as well as its manner, change in section III?

How is "this comic version of myself / The true one"?

What truth exists in the statement that "change is horror"? What does this perception of change have to do with the picture of little J. A.?

"How Much Longer Will I Be Able to Inhabit the Divine Sepulcher . . ."   (*p. 168*)

Points for Discussion and Writing

Ashbery frequently changes the tone of his poems unexpectedly. How does this occur in the first stanza? What are the advantages of doing so? What disadvantages might this have for the uninitiated reader?

Discuss the sentence, "I'm / Named Tom." What does it do to your sense of the poem's voice and authorship? Is voice always variable in an Ashbery poem? Do the voices change without announcement? If so, what purpose does this serve?

Discuss the lines "which / When he'd had he would not had he of / And jests under the smarting of privet" in the fifth stanza. Why does Ashbery break with normal syntax? What comment might these lines offer about the nature of sense in a poem?

"Drink to me only with" in the seventh stanza refers to Ben Jonson's poem "Drink to Me Only with Thine Eyes." Here it appears as a fragment in passing. What do you imagine Ashbery's method of composition to be? Does he cut up found materials and rejoin them in different contexts? What other evidence exists of found materials?

Is the poem's speaker "a fool," as he asserts? Or is he even more unreliable than that? What examples of unreliable narrators can you find in works of fiction? Compare, for instance, the narrator of Vladimir Nabokov's novel *Pale Fire*.

Discuss the ways in which Ashbery acknowledges the relationship between the poem and its readers. Is the "you" of the poem always—or sometimes—the reader?

Given the poem's many burlesque moments, the class may want to discuss the issue of seriousness in poetry. Can a comic poetry be serious? Is this poem comic? Is it serious?

Leaving the Atocha Station   (*p. 170*)

Points for Discussion and Writing

This is one of the most anthologized poems of Ashbery's early career; like "How Much Longer . . ." it also appeared in his most experimental volume, *The Tennis Court Oath* (1962). Do these two poems represent a radical break with his other work? How might they be seen as a more extreme expression of Ashbery's ongoing approach to composition?

The poem's radical discontinuity is obviously intended. What means of composition might have brought it about? Why has Ashbery failed to seek more unity in the poem? Or is discontinuity itself a form of unity?

Does the poem contain hints of narrative consistent with the title? Does it have characters, settings, and points of view?

Is the ending, "next time around," a gesture toward resolution? What other signs of unity might be evident?

FROM *The Skaters*   (*p. 172*)

Points for Discussion and Writing

The poem makes frequent reference to music and other forms of sound. What does Ashbery mean by "These decibels / Are a kind of flagellation"? Does he mean the decibels (units of sound) given off by the skater's cries, the casual noise of the day (cf. John Cage), or the sounds of the poem itself?

The first stanza concludes with a sentence of philosophical grandeur. To what extent is this poem itself part of "an infinite series"? How might the skater's movements symbolize the poetic imagination?

If all the human mind can retain is "the dismal two-note theme / Of some sodden 'dump' or lament," why is Ashbery's own poem so replete and multifaceted?

Discuss the list of musical instruments, including pinball machines, electric drills, and clavicles (shoulder blades). How are these consistent with John Cage's approach to art?

Is Ashbery's value on dissonance rather than harmony? Or is dissonance ("the most dissonant night charms us") a form of harmony?

Who is the "you" of the poem?

Discuss the section beginning "So much has passed through my mind this morning / That I can give you but a dim account of it." This section suggests that the author has just returned from lunch, refreshed but confused. How common is this acknowledgement of authorship in Ashbery's poetry?

Does this poem (and poetry in general) consist of "the intensity of minor acts"?

How can there be "error / In so much precision"? Is "error," which "is plaited into desires not yet born," a necessary part of poetic composition, to be valued and employed?

Discuss the section beginning "It is time now for a general understanding of / The meaning of all this." Has that "general understanding" been the purpose all along?

Is it possible for Ashbery's poem to collapse under its load of "discarded objects"? Or is this the very point of his method? What is meant by "this leaving-out business"?

Are the poem's lines "carnivorous," capable of devouring their own nature? Discuss Ashbery's references to presence and absence in this section of the poem. Is he critical of "plain old-fashioned cause-and-effect"?

What is the difference between "the world of Schubert's lieder" and the kind of poetry Ashbery advocates? Does Ashbery reject beauty and harmony? Or is he seeking to advance our appreciation of these concepts?

Does Ashbery prefer "a 'half-man' look" even though it brings the "disgust of honest folk"? Does he intentionally present a grotesque art that is doomed to rejection by the normal reader? Who is this "normal reader"?

Farm Implements and Rutabagas in a Landscape
(p. 177)

Points for Discussion and Writing

This poem is a sestina, a thirty-nine-line form, including a three-line *envoi* at the end, in which six words repeat in a precise order at the ends of lines. Ask the class to name these words and to calculate the order of their appearance. What kinds of words has Ashbery chosen, and how easy are they to use?

Compare this poem with Dante's *Al poco giorno* . . . , beautifully translated by James Schuyler in his book *Freely Espousing*, 1969, a sestina that uses elemental repetitions such as "shadow," "stone," and "hills." What difference in tone exists between the two poems? How do the two sestinas differ in their diction, or word choice? Discuss the tension created between the poem's use of traditional form and its references to popular culture—Wimpy, Popeye, and the Sea Hag.

The One Thing That Can Save America   (p. 178)

Points for Discussion and Writing

This poem conducts a serious critique of the American condition; more than many other Ashbery poems, it can be taken at face value. Does Ashbery believe that anything is "central" in America? Do you? Is the United States a mosaic of competing interests or is there a shared ideology?

To what extent is this poem private to Ashbery alone (see stanza 3) and to what degree public?

Of what importance is the letter that belatedly arrives in the final stanza only to be unwittingly ripped in half on a plate?

The Other Tradition   (p. 180)

Points for Discussion and Writing

What does the poet mean by "the lateness / Of the hour" in the poem's first sentence? Might he refer to our cultural belatedness late in the century?

By "the other tradition," Ashbery means the experimental tradition in poetry derived from Rimbaud and Mallarme and including Dada, surrealism, the Beats, and the New York School, among others. Yet the poem itself primarily refers to culture rather than art. What evidence exists that poetry is part of the poem's reference?

What is the "event" to which the poet refers, and what is to be expected of it? Might the poem imply that all such gatherings are futile?

Discuss Ashbery's references to remembering and forgetting at the end of the poem. How might it relate to "the cool non-being of just a few minutes before"? How does forgetting as an act of rescue compare with a star that "absorbs the night"?

What is allowed to come and go "indefinitely in and out of the stockade"? Is it words spoken into a megaphone? Then why does Ashbery choose a word like "stockade" which suggests imprisonment?

Paradoxes and Oxymorons (*p. 181*)

Points for Discussion and Writing

This poem is both highly reflexive and direct. Its subject is the writing of poetry. What is Ashbery's definition of "play" as it relates to poetic composition? Would he agree with T. S. Eliot that writing poetry is a "superior amusement"?

When the poet writes, "I think you exist only / To tease me into doing it, on your level, and then you aren't there," is he referring to the reader directly?

Does the poem have the agency to set the author ("me") softly down beside the reader ("you")? Or is that agency the author's? Discuss the final statement, "The poem is you." Why is the poem not "me"?

FROM *Flow Chart* (*p. 181*)

Points for Discussion and Writing

The "published city" is probably New York, where the poet lives. Or does he refer to the state of his own authorship and career?

What is the mood of the opening section? Is there such a thing as "the central poem"? How might the central poem want the poet to feel?

What is the relationship between the river and "the painted monsters born later / out of the swift-flowing alluvial mud"?

What is "this artificial espaliered thing we have become"? What is "the book" that some advise ending? Are these disguised criticisms of Ashbery's own poetry?

What does Ashbery mean by "the world's colored paths all lead / to my mouth"? Do these lines announce the figure of poet as a generative source of enormous power? Why would this position cause him to "drop, humbled, eating from the red-clay floor"?

How might the last movement of this fragment be compared with Wordworth's *The Preludes* in its depiction of the growth of the poet's mind?

Of what significance is "the burgomaster of success" (cf. the burgomaster of *Frankenstein*, the movie) at this point in Ashbery's much-heralded career? Does Ashbery fear being consumed by his own fame? Is this long meditative poem therefore "confessional" to a degree?

HANNAH WEINER ▪ ▪ ▪ ▪ ▪ ▪ ▪ ▪ ▪ ▪ ▪ ▪ ▪
b. 1928

FROM *Clairvoyant Journal*   (*p. 185*)

Points for Discussion and Writing

Discuss Weiner's claim that she sees words on her forehead, in the air, and on other people. Is all of Weiner's work, therefore, a form of found poetry?

Does Weiner address, or report to, a reader? Or do the words of the poem address her?

To what extent is Weiner the author of her own work? Or do the clairvoyant messages simply intervene in the midst of other discourse until both discourses construct the poem at hand?

What determines the beginnings and endings—especially the endings—of such writing? Is it the moment when exhaustion or physical separation from writing materials takes place?

Is such clairvoyance willed or unwilled? If unwilled, the author is always composing. How is this different from the procedures of nonclairvoyant poets?

How might Weiner's poetry be distinguished from automatic writing?

Is Weiner's project in any way comparable to that of David Antin's talk poems? To what extent is her work *unwilled* improvisation?

The poet apparently tries to transcribe words exactly as they occur to her. Is it possible, then, for errors (typos, wrong type style and size) to be made in their presentation.

How might the typography of Weiner's poems affect their meaning when the work is read out loud?

KENWARD ELMSLIE ■ ■ ■ ■ ■ ■ ■ ■ ■ ■ ■ ■ ■
b. 1929

Feathered Dancers   (p. 190)

Points for Discussion and Writing

Elmslie's first experience as an author was as a lyricist. How is this evident in this poem?

The poem rhymes ABAB, yet the poem's details are unexpected and occasionally Surrealist. How is the inventiveness of the poem's details brought into balance by the poem's formal nature?

To what other poets in this volume might Elmslie be compared?

In the seventh stanza, third line, how is "The—" to be pronounced?

Japanese City   (p. 191)

Points for Discussion and Writing

This poem has fictional elements of a fantastic nature ("The room-clerk's pate shines up through the transparent floor") and might be compared to the work of eccentric novelists Raymond Roussel, Ronald Firbank, and Angela Carter. Joris Karl Huysmans' *Against the Grain* and T. S. Eliot's "Sweeney Among the Nightingales" also come to mind. Why is the poem titled "Japanese City"? Is there any element of literary realism in the poem—for example, the hairs in the washbasin? Or is Elmslie's procedure to give his imagination free rein?

The poem is written in five-line stanzas; this reveals the poet's formal reworking of the poem. Do you consider Elmslie a formalist?

Amazon Club   (p. 192)

Points for Discussion and Writing

This prose poem and the one to follow are part of Elmslie's abecedarium, *26 Bars*, each of which describes an unusual drinking establishment. Evident in the first paragraph is the poet's love of unusual words: "cadenzas," "imbroglios," and "yam effluvia." Discuss the effect of Elmslie's diction on his writing.

Given the ceaseless invention and rich texture of the poem, how might some of it be sung in performance, as is the poet's practice?

Big Bar   (*p. 193*)

Points for Discussion and Writing

What might a "petrocommunications system" consist of?

Describe "the Swiss Wishing Chair."

What purpose might "The Wurlitzer Suction Syphon" serve?

The bar consists of 900 feet of topiary (shaped) yucca plants, constantly attended by "snippers and shapers." How might elements of this poem compare with Tim Burton's movie *Edward Scissorhands?*

What does it mean that each section of the prose poem is paired with an ever-increasing weight? Whose weight is referred to?

What kind of rhetoric is employed in describing "Big Bar"? What kind of voice is employed in the poem? If this were a movie, who would you cast as narrator?

ED DORN ▪ ▪ ▪ ▪ ▪ ▪ ▪ ▪ ▪ ▪ ▪ ▪ ▪ ▪ ▪ ▪ ▪ ▪
b. 1929

The Rick of Green Wood   (*p. 195*)

Points for Discussion and Writing

Might this poem be easily set to music? If so, what kind?

Scan the poem for its measure and rhyme scheme. Is either set on a regular pattern?

In what year do you imagine the poem to be set? Are its situation and details comparatively timeless?

What elements does the poem have in common with the popular ballads of English literary history?

Does it break with its initial rhythm at any point, or does the poem remain song–like throughout?

Use this poem as the basis for a discussion of lyricism in poetry. What elements, such as feelings of sadness and loss, have readers come to expect from lyrical poetry?

Compare and contrast this work with the poems of Gustaf Sobin, such as "Out of the Identical." Do Sobin and Dorn have a similar approach to lyricism? In what respect does Sobin's musicality differ from Dorn's?

Geranium   (*p. 196*)

Points for Discussion and Writing

Why is the poem so titled? Is the geranium a central focus of the poem?

Like "The Rick of Green Wood," this poem has a lyrical but also courtly quality. How does the form of the poem, especially its line lengths, lend to that tone?

Is the poem in general a reflection of "the great geography of my lunacy"?

Dorn wishes he were closer to home than he is. Where *is* the poem set? Where is the home of Dorn's mind?

In what way does the poem's conception of the "handsome woman" change? What parallel exists between her and "the red Geranium of my last Washington stop"?

Dorn says that he sings "ploddingly, and out of tune as she, were she less the lapwing / as she my pale sojourner, is." What is to be made of the connection between "the lapwing" and "my pale sojourner"?

Is Dorn's "plodding" song comparable to the flight of the lapwing or the common beauty of a geranium?

In what respect is one theme of the poem "love of common object"?

Terms and References

The **lapwing** is a plover-like bird whose flight is heavy and flopping.

From Gloucester Out   (*p. 197*)

Points for Discussion and Writing

Dorn was Charles Olson's student at Black Mountain College. Gloucester, Massachusetts, was Olson's home and the setting of this poem and Olson's own *Maximus Poems*, his most noted work. The occasion of "From Gloucester Out" is remembering Dorn's visit to Olson in Gloucester at the time of a local celebration and the poets' consequent trip by car to New Jersey and New York City. Does the poem at any point reflect the influence of Olson's own style as a poet?

Dorn speaks of his own "adulterated presence." How does this relate to his complaint about his "hesitating / to know all I had now known"?

Does Dorn seem to believe that Olson lived the "Pure existence" that feels impossible for himself?

Examine the long sentence beginning "Then went / out of that city to jersey." What thematic concerns does it share with Olson's work?

What is Dorn's attitude toward Olson in this homage? Is it entirely one of admiration?

An Idle Visitation   (*p. 201*)

Points for Discussion and Writing

This poem became the opening movement of Dorn's epic of the American West, *Gunslinger*. Ask the class to characterize Gunslinger and his concerns.

What is meant by the "theater of impatience"?

Who is the "I" of the poem in relation to the poem's hero?

Does the reference to impending "Globes of fire" suggest apocalyptic prophecy on Gunslinger's part?

Of what meaning is the "grove of Gethsemane" in the context of this poem?

Explain the Gunslinger's certainty—for example, his confidence that "no *thing* is omitted." Is Gunslinger heroic in the traditional sense or is he a postmodern hero to whom all is relative?

The horse's hooves "are covered with the alkali / of the enormous space / between here and formerly." How might these lines suggest a metaphysical journey on the part of Gunslinger and his companion?

The Gunslinger's goal is to make contact with Howard Hughes, the noted millionaire of the twentieth century. Yet Gunslinger claims that the "inscrutable" Hughes has not been seen since 1832. Is this hyerbole or an attempt by Dorn to establish a parallel between the West of the past and its present-day actuality?

In the same vein, how do you account for the "genetic duels" mentioned at the poem's end? Do these genetic duels relate to "a longhorn bull half mad / half deity / who awaits an account from me / back of the sun"?

Comment on the figure of the bull as it might connect with the constellation Taurus or the Minotaur of Greek myth. Is Gunslinger a contemporary citizen, a figure from history, or a demigod in his own right?

The Sad Birds   (*p. 204*)

Points for Discussion and Writing

As a member of *Oulipo* (see "Terms and References," John Cage's "Writing Through the Cantos"), Mathews favors formal puzzles as part of his method of composition. What hidden rules of composition are observable in this poem?

Each sestet follows a certain pattern of reference in lines 5 and 6. What are they?

The poem's narrator speaks of his "ridiculous anguish." How self-conscious is the narrator in his statements? Is he, in fact, ridiculous?

In the stanza beginning, "The passive cannot laugh alone," Mathews writes, "I listen for / The bittern's crepuscular 'woomp' / From the far marshes, or 'ork,' / Passive." Is this passage good writing? Why does Mathew select such a heightened but false poetic tone? In the same context, look at the lines "Yoghurt— / My feelings are more like chiff-chaffs / Jigging, not this morose / Futility." Is the cry of the "cream-colored courser" really "Hark"? Is there, in fact, a bird called the "cream-colored courser"?

How many names of birds can you discover in the poem?

Is the cry of the "cream-colored courser" really "Hark"? Is there, in fact, a bird called the "cream-colored courser"?

Histoire   (*p. 206*)

Points for Discussion and Writing

This poem is a sestina with exceptionally long lines. Why are long lines appropriate in this case?

What other rules than those of the sestina form does Mathews set for himself?

Examine the tension created by using such comically heavy-handed end words in conjunction with the comparatively trivial story of Tina and Seth's date. How is this combination of elements comparable to John Ashbery's sestina, "Farm Implements and Rutabagas in a Landscape"?

Does this poem spoof any of the isms to which it refers? How might it be seen as a rejection of *all* of them?

GREGORY CORSO ▪ ▪ ▪ ▪ ▪ ▪ ▪ ▪ ▪ ▪ ▪ ▪
b. 1930

The Mad Yak   (p. 209)

Points for Discussion and Writing

Who or what is the speaker of this poem? What story unfolds in the process of his commentary?

Do you find this poem affecting despite the absurdity of its point of view?

Dream of a Baseball Star   (p. 209)

Points for Discussion and Writing

Why is Ted Williams weeping in Corso's dream? Is it of any significance that Williams leans against the Eiffel Tower?

Williams apparently suits Corso's ideal of the poet. How?

What is meant by "blown hands"? Is the metaphor explainable on the rational level? What would lead Corso to prefer the irrational to the rational?

What surrealist painter might have conceived the image of the "knotted and twiggy" baseball bat?

Why is it better for the poem that Williams fails to strike any of the pitches flying in from heaven? What are the metaphysical implications of Williams' being struck out by God? Are these implications intended to be highly serious?

As can be seen by "The Mad Yak" and "Dream of a Baseball Star," Corso's concepts for his poems are very unusual, even fantastic. How is he nevertheless able to arrive at some psychological truth?

I Held a Shelley Manuscript   (p. 210)

Points for Discussion and Writing

Of what value is the notation about Houghton Library following the title?

Does Corso use heightened poetic diction such as "O sovereign was my touch" in his other poems? Why is it particularly appropriate here?

What is the effect of the reference to "leopard-apples and torched-mushrooms"? Given the comedy of those lines, comment on Corso's ability to restore a tone of grandeur and dignity at the poem's end.

Is Corso sincere in his homage to the manuscript of the great English Romantic poet Percy Shelley? Is it possible, in poetry, to be silly and sincere at the same time?

Marriage   (p. 210)

Points for Discussion and Writing

This poem is a kind of epithalamion, or wedding song. Yet part of the effectiveness of "Marriage," is the indecision Corso expresses. Might the poem therefore be considered an antiepithalamion?

Examine the poem's several turns of mood with regard to the institution of marriage. Does the narrator ever come to a decision?

In stanza 1, what kind of suitor does Corso imagine he would be?

Discuss how Corso has fun at the expense of a middle-class standard of respectability. What fun does he have at his own expense?

What evidence of Surrealist behavior and expression can be found in the poem? Do these Surrealist images vary in tone and purpose within the poem?

Wilhelm Reich (1987–1957) was a noted and somewhat controversial psychologist whose therapy concentrated on orgiastic potency. Believing that psychological armor carried with it an attendant bodily armor that reflected a neurotic blockage of energy, Reich developed orgone therapy. Patients were required to sit in a metal-lined structure called an orgone accumulator which would unblock energy flow. Reich's therapy also was directed toward unblocking libidinal energy through improved orgasm. What, then, would be the behavior of "a fat Reichian wife"?

Much of this poem is humorous but still contains elements of truth. How sincere is Corso about his own feelings concerning marriage? Look especially at the poem's conclusion, starting with the lines "Because what if I'm 60 years old and not married, / all alone in a furnished room."

Who is "SHE in her lonely alien gaud" in the poem's last section?

Love Poem for Three for Kaye & Me   (*p. 213*)

Points for Discussion and Writing

Who is the "you" of the poem?

Since the poem is addressed to Corso's wife Kaye, whom he married relatively late in life, how do you explain the archaic references and diction that the poet uses?

"Wicce" is an archaic term for a female witch ("wicca" for male). How is this usage appropriate to the purpose of Corso's poem, especially in its fourth section?

What is a "thiefy wand of blood"? Likewise, what is meant by "sweet sack"?

Compare and contrast this poem on betrothal with Corso's earlier poem "Marriage."

Terms and References

Damask is a rich fabric woven in elaborate patterns.

Vair refers to furs worn by the fourteenth-century nobility.

GARY SNYDER   ▪ ▪ ▪ ▪ ▪ ▪ ▪ ▪ ▪ ▪ ▪ ▪ ▪
b. 1930

Points for General Discussion

In his essay, "The Real Work," quoted in the introduction to Snyder's section, Snyder states that he uses Buddhist meditation, or zazen, to "go into *original mind*." What does he mean by "original mind"? Does the term presume a unified human consciousness that preexists the modern condition? How is this at odds with some other postmodern views of consciousness?

How might a poem express "all of our selves," as Snyder writes, rather than the poet's personal concerns?

What is the relationship between the poet's consciousness—and consciousness in general—to the "outer world"?

In Snyder's view, why is spoken poetry to be privileged over written poetry? Is speech's privilege evident in his poems?

Riprap   *(p. 215)*

Points for Discussion and Writing

In what respect is a piece of writing like an arrangement of riprap? How does this philosophy of composition compare to the approach of Clark Coolidge? How does it differ from Coolidge?

How are the "worlds" in this poem "four-dimensional"? How do they resemble the Chinese game of *Go*?

In the poem, Snyder writes "each rock a word" and therefore a unit of meaning. How does this view compare to the Transcendentalist philosophy of Emerson and Thoreau?

Terms and References

Riprap is a loose collection of broken stones used to provide a foundation.

Go is a traditional Chinese game of war strategy.

The Bath   *(p. 216)*

Points for Discussion and Writing

Kai is Snyder's son; Masa is the poet's wife and Kai's mother. Are the family relationships clear in the poem itself?

Of what importance is the poem's varying refrain, beginning *"is this our body?"*

How might the scenes of washing and touching have religious significance?

When Snyder touches his wife's vulva, he uses the expressions "a hand of grail" and "the gates of Awe." Discuss what he means by these phrases.

How is it that a mother's milk "sends through jolts of light"?

Discuss the poem's open approach to sexuality. Do any of the students find the relationship of mother, father, and child unnatural? Is Snyder's view of the human body the essential one?

How much is our view of the human body subject to cultural conditioning? In this context, ask students from a variety of social backgrounds to comment on the poem.

Avocado   (p. 218)

Points for Discussion and Writing

How can the "Dharma" be "like an Avocado"? Why does Snyder capitalize both words?

If the seed of the avocado is "your own Original Nature," what is the significance of it slipping through the fingers rather than being planted?

Discuss Snyder's use of the avocado as a conceit (concept) through which he is able to focus on the metaphysical. Is Snyder's use of metaphor similar to or different from the practices of John Donne, George Herbert, and other Metaphysical poets of sixteenth- and seventeenth-century England?

To what extent is Snyder a moral poet? Are all poets moral in their purpose? To what degree is a moral poetry dependent on the political views of the poet in question?

Terms and References

In Hinduism and Buddhism, **dharma** is right behavior and conformity to law, thus truth and righteousness.

As for Poets   (p. 218)

Points for Discussion and Writing

Snyder presents six kinds of poets. Discuss each in turn, and attempt to identify poets of each category within this anthology. What kind of poet, for instance, is Snyder himself? Clayton Eshleman? Mei-mei Berssenbrugge? Wanda Coleman? John Ashbery? Allen Ginsberg? Of all these types, which would you rather be?

Is there one kind of poet that Snyder seems to prefer over the others?

Do poets work exclusively out of one mode? Or can one alternately be a Water Poet, Fire Poet, and Earth Poet?

How is the Mind Poet to be distinguished from the Space Poet?

Axe Handles   (p. 219)

Points for Discussion and Writing

What does this poem have in common with "The Bath"?

In this poem, Snyder honors his teachers and certain traditions with which they are associated. How then is his poetry experimental or avant-garde rather than traditional? Does avant-garde poetry *always* involve an oppositional stance with regard to earlier generations, mainstream cultural positions, and so on?

In avant-garde literature, what evidence do you see of an attempt to return literature to its roots? Are those roots always of a primitive nature? Was Lu Ji, the fourth-century AD author, primitive?

How might the word "primitive" be problematic and even racist? Give the same examination to the word "advanced" as applied to literature. Is advanced literature always produced in advanced societies such as the G-7 countries of Japan, Germany, Italy, France, Great Britain, Canada, and the United States?

What is the role of the intellectual in Snyder's poetry? Does his writing bear the imprint of years of reading and study? Why is it not considered academic? Discuss the often misused term "academic" as it is now used. Is poetry produced in university poetry workshops academic simply because of the university setting? Can poetry at once exhibit academic knowledge and fall far outside mainstream practice? Give an example of this paradox from this anthology.

Like Snyder, Ezra Pound studied Oriental poetry and philosophy. What model of behavior is taught by means of Pound's and Lu Ji's advice?

Does the axe itself bear any symbolism? What is the relationship of the axe to its handle?

What does this poem teach with regard to the human personality? Has it always been more or less the same, from culture to culture?

Terms and References

Ezra Pound (1885–1972) was the noted American modernist poet and author of *The Cantos* who was tried for treason as a result of his collaboration with the Italian Fascists in World War II.

Right in the Trail   *(p. 220)*

Points for Discussion and Writing

"Scat" refers to excrement, in this case bear droppings containing evidence of manzanita berries. What meaning does Snyder draw from its discovery?

Discuss the fable, in stanza 2, of the girl who "had some pretty children by a / Young and handsome Bear."

Why is Snyder nearly driven to tears in finding the bear droppings? What is "A shining message for all species"?

If the scats are a "Trace / of the Great One's passing," what is the significance of Snyder's use of the feminine pronoun "her" immediately following?

Compare and contrast this poem with Robert Frost's "The Bear" in *The Norton Anthology of Modern Poetry*. Do the same with Frost's "The Wood-Pile," a poem in which the figure of a wood-pile, like Snyder's scats, is discovered in a wood. To what extent do both poets write *paysages moralises*, or moralized landscapes?

JEROME ROTHENBERG ▪ ▪ ▪ ▪ ▪ ▪ ▪ ▪ ▪ ▪
b. 1931

Cokboy   (*p. 222*)

Points for Discussion and Writing

Compare and contrast this poem of the American West with Ed Dorn's "An Idle Visitation."

What are the narrator's multiple personae?

At what time and place is the poem set?

What is the importance of the repeated phrase "kabbalistic time"?

How might the Baal Shem's magical powers relate to other aspects of the poem, such as the birth of America, the references to the beaver, and so on? Likewise, how is the Baal Shem comparable to a poet or prophet?

Do Jews and Gentiles "bring the Law to Wilderness," or is this comment satirical? Why are the words "Law" and "Wilderness" capitalized?

Examine the role of the "Senator from Arizona," later referred to as "a little christian shmuck." Does any character in the poem represent a "true American"?

Discuss the meaning of the lines, "I will share / piss strained from my holy cock / will bear seed of Adonoi / & feed them [the redmen] visions / I will fill full a clamshell / will pass it around from mouth to mouth." What is Rothenberg's position in these lines with regard to his own Jewish identity? Toward the identity of the "redmen"?

Esau's twin brother was Jacob. Is the speaker in this part of the poem Jacob?

The beaver was considered sacred among the Seneca tribe of New York State; Rothenberg has made an "ethnopoetic" study of Seneca poetry. Of what importance is the beaver to PART TWO of the poem?

Discuss the mythic developments at the beginning of PART TWO of "Cokboy." What America is born to the Cacique's daughter?

Compare and contrast this poem with Gary Snyder's "The Bath," especially in connection to its representation of the human body.

The phrase, "other pure products of America," refers to the William Carlos Williams poem "To Elsie," to be found in his *Selected Poems.* Does this poem have any other connection to the work of Williams, either in style or in the nature of its cultural criticism?

What might Ishi have to do with Cokboy? Why does he look like a Jew as he waits on the crest? Who is "silent in America"?

Terms and References

In **kabbalistic** lore, time was originally a series of divine sparks or emantions that transcended the temporal. Kabbalists are Jewish mystics.

A **Baal Shem** is literally "master of the divine name," or possessor of the name of God. In the Hasidic tradition of Judaism, the Baal Shem is able to perform miracles and other forms of magic, including faith healing.

Schmuck is Yiddish for penis; it also refers to a fool.

A **shtreiml** is a broad-brimmed black hat, trimmed in velvet of fur, worn by Hasidic men from Poland and Galicia.

Adonoi and **Elohim** are Hebrew names for God.

A **cacique** is a chief among the Native American tribes of Mexico and the West Indies.

Ishi was the last member of a nearly vanished California tribe; much studied by anthropologists, he was assimilated into white society in the 1930s.

DAVID ANTIN ▪ ▪ ▪ ▪ ▪ ▪ ▪ ▪ ▪ ▪ ▪ ▪ ▪ ▪ ▪
b. 1932

a private occasion in a public place   *(p. 231)*

Points for Discussion and Writing

Antin calls his talk performances "poem-talks." In what respects are they poetic? In what respects are they stories or essays?

How dependent is the text on its performance before a public?

In the context of performance, how significant to the work's meaning is the fact that the talks are, in large part, spontaneous and unrehearsed?

If Antin were to repeat the performance of a work, would it inevitably change?

The poem-talk in question begins by comparing traditional poetry readings (from books) to "taking out a container of frozen peas." If this is so, what is the effect of your reading Antin's poem-talk in a book? Do you miss his voice even if you're not acquainted with its volume and timbre? Can you *hear* his voice in his words despite its absence?

What evidence exists that in transcribing the work Antin included everything that he said at the moment of performance?

How many narrators other than Antin exist inside the talk? What stories do they tell?

Discuss Antin's statement that "as soon as you take a position very forcefully youre immediately at the boundary of that position." How does this relate to the nexus of public and private in this talk?

When David and Eleanor laughed at their City Hall wedding, was it a private or public occasion?

Discuss the relationship of speaker and audience in the small wedding scene. For example, why does Eleanor feel it necessary to "fake crying"?

Discuss Antin's statement that artists are too "committed to making art" to be romantic. Are bourgeois people the only ones who have time for romance? Are artists by definition not bourgeois? What evidence exists to the contrary? How dependent on a middle-class audience is the literature in this anthology? Would this audience reject some of it? For what reasons?

Relate the issue of public and private to Antin's story about the voyeur and his resulting love affair with the woman being watched. How do her "performances" of fainting and singing relate to Antin's theme?

What faith does Antin place in a "private language"? Is an exclusively public language possible?

Discuss Antin's introduction of Sally Beauchamp and her four distinct personalities. In what respect does Antin, in relating the tales of his affair with Miriam and marriage to Eleanor, resemble Sally Beauchamp's neurologist?

Discuss Antin's statement, "who speaks for me when i speak?" Does any storyteller or speaker adopt a persona for the occasion? How might this persona affect the talk produced?

Can Antin's readers and audience believe him "as much as you can believe your wife   or your child   or yourself"? Is there a feeling of authenticity in what he says, or is there evidence of mythmaking and literary construction for the sake of a theme?

How much does the talk as a whole depend on a bond of authenticity, or trust, between Antin and his audience?

Examine each part of Antin's talk, especially the major narratives, for its dependence on, or relationship to, the theme of public and private.

KEITH WALDROP ▪ ▪ ▪ ▪ ▪ ▪ ▪ ▪ ▪ ▪ ▪ ▪ ▪ ▪
b. 1932

FROM *A Shipwreck in Haven*   (*p. 247*)

Points for Discussion and Writing

Might the title of this book-length poem make a pun on "heaven"? What references exist in the poem, for instance, with regard to mortality?

In section 6, "a deity enters / the world, a stranger." But to what degree is the poem set in the world?

What reference points exist as to the time, place, and intent of the poem? What passes in the street besides "pure picture"? To what degree is this poem one of "Endless beginning" (section 7)?

Section 10 has elegiac qualities such as "reflective angels," the crossing of "appointed spaces," and the sense that "something must be settled." Is the fact that "something must be settled" a requirement of life or art?

Waldrop uses four tercets per section. Each of these tercets tends to be a collection of fragments, if not what Ron Silliman calls the "New Sentence." Comment on the form of the poem. Is Waldrop influenced by language poetry theory? Or is the spirit of his work closer to Rilke and Denise Levertov?

Will to Will   (*p. 251*)

Points for Discussion and Writing

The poem begins by commenting about "the progress of a bird." Might the bird be symbolic of the progress of Waldrop's own associations as a thinker ("One's own performance can alter.")? How might a thought vanish and, later, "someone else is thinking it"?

Is Waldrop's own work a "desperate attempt to escape perplexity"? How might a focused complexity serve as an antidote to this perplexity?

To what extent does one part of the poem connect to any other part? Or does Waldrop compose by free association and the "finding" of language?

Waldrop claims that he plays deliberately on "the compositional value of inattention." Is this evident in this particular poem?

How is this poem different in tone and manner from the *A Shipwreck in Haven* excerpt?

Wandering Curves   (*p. 252*)

Points for Discussion and Writing

Though the geological reference is consistent in the poem, Waldrop's work sometimes seems to have been exploded into fragments and then reorganized into a suitable but new whole. Examine stanza 3 of the poem in this context, especially *"Despair sits brooding the putrid / eggs of hope."* What does this self-consciously poetic line have to do with the stanza's other sentences?

Who is the "me" of the poem? Who is the "she"? Do the identities of the characters really matter in such a work? Discuss how these characters might be equal to the poem's other elements as the *materials of which it is constructed.*

MICHAEL McCLURE   ▪ ▪ ▪ ▪ ▪ ▪ ▪ ▪ ▪ ▪ ▪
b. 1932

Hymn to Saint Geryon   (*p. 253*)

Points for Discussion and Writing

There was no *Saint* Geryon. Geryon was a three-headed monster of Greek mythology who was murdered by Hercules for his herd of red oxen. "Geryon" is also a mythological reference to the King of Spain. Why does McClure make him a saint?

What is McClure's strategy in beginning with strong gestural qualities, only to follow with a long quote on aesthetics from Abstract Expressionist painter Clyfford Still?

Does McClure associate his gestural approach to poetry with that of the "action" painters? He refers, for instance, to "ST. POLLOCK" and "KLINE" (the Abstract Expressionist painters Jackson Pollock and Franz Kline).

How might "politics" be distinguished from "ourselves" in the phrase, "Not politics / but ourselves"?

What is the position of ego in this poem? Does McClure place himself in the same pantheon as Shelley and Goya? When he writes, "But I love my body my face only / first and then others'," is McClure being narcissistic?

"The tygers of wrath are wiser than the horses of instruction" is quoted from William Blake's *The Marriage of Heaven and Hell*. Discuss the meaning of Blake's line. How does it relate to McClure's intent? In what way is McClure's work similar to Blake's?

The poem contains the sounds of action ("WHAP WHAP WHAP"). Is it designed to be performed with gestures? How does language relate to gesture in the poem? How are the capitalized words to be read?

Ode to Jackson Pollock   (*p. 256*)

Points for Discussion and Writing

The poem is an homage and elegy to the painter Jackson Pollock. What aspects of Pollock's own art would McClure find attractive? Do you see evidence of Pollock's influence in the present poem? Pollock worked in large gestures; is this true of McClure as well?

McClure refers to the Spanish term *duende*. Is there any attempt in McClure's work to possess the spirit of *duende*?

Who is the "beloved" who hovers in front of Pollock? Discuss her "birth" in paint and the spirit from which she is created.

Terms and References

Duende is a Spanish word denoting "depth of soul" and implies an understanding of beauty and death.

AMIRI BARAKA (LeROI JONES)   ▪ ▪ ▪ ▪ ▪ ▪ ▪
b. 1934

Political Poem   (*p. 259*)

Points for Discussion and Writing

Baraka calls this a political poem, but to what extent is all his poetry political?

The Marxist view is that all poetry is political in that it inevitably represents the beliefs and interests of one social group. Do you believe this to be true?

If political narrowness is inevitable, should all poets actively pursue a political agenda in their writing?

Is the pursuit of beauty also political?

How is luxury "a way of / being ignorant"? Does the open market depend on the ignorance of the citizen-consumer?

How is the poem "undone by my station"?

Baraka writes that "all error is forced" in the memory of "the darkness of love." Is he proposing a theory of history? Of politics?

"My dead lecturer" refers to Baraka's 1964 poetry volume *The Dead Lecturer*. Is this poem personal as well as political? Are the two inseparable in his view?

What is the political resolution of the poem? What is meant, for example, by "Undone by the logic of any specific death"?

Who are the "Old gentlemen / who still follow fires"? What do these fires represent? Righteous old causes that are forgotten by the young? Or does Baraka suggest that those fires are no longer worth following?

Three Modes of History and Culture   (*p. 260*)

Points for Discussion and Writing

Note the plosive nature of this poem's opening rhythm. Who are "we drummers"? Poets?

Why do "Maps weep"? Because of the history of slavery?

Discuss the reference to "learning / America, as speech, and a common emptiness." Why "emptiness"?

The middle part of the poem describes the migration of African-Americans from the South to the North. Which is the "Race / of madmen and giants"? "The Party of Insane Hope"?

Give special attention to the final, comparatively serene stanza. Under what conditions will Baraka "be relaxed"?

Does this poem display more optimism for social change than some of Baraka's other work?

What are the three modes of history and culture to which the poet refers?

The New World   (*p. 261*)

Points for Discussion and Writing

To whom does Baraka refer in the lines, "Our style, / and discipline, controlling the method of knowledge"?

Does Baraka identify with the Beatniks and Bohemians going "calmly out of style"? Does he set himself at a distance from them?

What is the condition of the New World as presented in this poem?

The tone of the poem is one of mild exhaustion, "wasted lyricists," and finality. Is it therefore pessimistic about the condition of the artist? How might this work be interpreted as a farewell to part of Baraka's own poetic career? To an era in American culture?

Leadbelly Gives an Autograph   (*p. 262*)

Points for Discussion and Writing

Why is the "myth of speech" described as "twisted"?

What are the implications of the lines, "We thought / it possible to enter / the way of the strongest"? What is "the way of the strongest"? Dominant white culture?

How is it "rite that the world's ills / erupt as our own"?

What role do "The possibilities of music" have in the poem? Is it from "that scripture of rhythms" in Leadbelly's music that African-American culture is to establish itself?

Who are the "savages" in the sentence, "Pay me off, savages"?

How does the "I" of the poem provide "The beasts / and myths"?

Discuss how Baraka defines history at the poem's end. Is history entirely a fable of victimization?

Terms and References

Leadbelly was another name for Huddie Ledbetter, a leading blues musician.

Nat Turner was a slave who led an uprising, for which he was executed in 1831.

Ka 'Ba (p. 263)

Points for Discussion and Writing

This uses a different syntax than some of Baraka's other poems in this selection. In what way is it different?

What "physics" do black people defy "in the stream of their will"?

The poem argues for the strength of black culture and calls for the reinstitution of "the ancient image." What is that image?

What are "the sacred words" that will initiate the "getaway" from European cultural dominance?

Ka 'Ba refers to the sacred stone at Mecca involved in Muslim ceremony. How does this information affect your reading of the poem?

Kenyatta Listening to Mozart (p. 264)

Points for Discussion and Writing

Kenyatta represents the new Africa and the composer Mozart represents the height of European culture; both are positive images. How does their conjunction affect this poem?

The poem largely consists of a simultaneity of detail which Baraka circumscribes as "A zoo of consciousness." How does Kenyatta get his access to Mozart? Through electronic mass media, received "on the back trails" while he's wearing sunglasses? What is the importance of the reference to "beings / that swim / exchanging / in- / formation"? Are these beings swimming in the great ocean of mass media?

To whom and for what reason do "Choice, and style, avail"? The words "choice" and "style" are associated with commodity capitalism. Is Baraka implicating both Kenyatta and Mozart in it?

Terms and References

Kenyatta is Jomo Kenyatta, the Kenyan nationalist leader and anthropologist. He was also for many years the president of Kenya.

Leroy (p. 264)

Points for Discussion and Writing

This is one of the most personal poems of Baraka's middle period. The title reflects his birth name, which he changed to LeRoi as a young man and later to Imamu Amiri Baraka and then Amiri Baraka. Discuss Baraka's name changes as they reflect his political focus of the moment.

What does the poem reveal about Baraka's upbringing by his mother? How was her experience of black culture in the 1920s different from his in the 1960s? Discuss especially the "black angels straining above her head, carrying life from our ancestors, / and knowledge, and the strong nigger feeling." Of what importance is the phrase "the strong nigger feeling" in this context? Does it amount to an accusation against his mother for political backwardness? Why, for instance, does the poet choose the words "Hypnotizing me"? Does this imply that some of the knowledge she passed on, especially the "white parts," is of no value?

The Nation Is Like Ourselves   (*p. 265*)

Points for Discussion and Writing

The satirical slant of this poem and its radical black nationalist politics are much stronger than in the poems of Baraka's earlier career. What is Baraka's position in the poem with regard to the "liberated nigger," by which he means the black middle class? Why *"jewish* [my emphasis] enterprise"?

The energy of the poem as speech is very high and marks a new development in Baraka's work toward performance values. What aspects of the work are designed specifically for performance?

Who is "mr mystical smasheroo . . . learning about it / from the flying dutchman"? Likewise, who is "mr ethnic meditations professor"?

What position does Baraka advocate with regard to assimilation?

Discuss Baraka's audience in this work. That is, to whom is it addressed?

Of what significance is the poem's title?

AM/TRAK   (*p. 267*)

Points for Discussion and Writing

This poem is as much meant to be performed as Coltrane's music was to be played. Ask the class to imagine—or even improvise in the classroom—what the section beginning "duh duh-duh duh-duh duh" would sound like in Baraka's own voice. Is some of this poem to be shouted and sung? What indications are there of changes in tempo?

Why is the composer Ludwig van Beethoven referred to as "Mulatto ass Beethoven"?

Discuss the difference between the music of "Street Gospel intellectual mystical survival codes" and that of "Intellectual street gospel funk modes." Do these modes also exist in Baraka's poetry?

How is the line "pink pink a cool bam groove note air breath" to be distinguished from the writing of Gertrude Stein or the language poets, especially early Clark Coolidge?

Baraka states that Don Lee is a "backward cultural nationalist / motherfucker." What is Baraka's own political position in the poem?

"I lay in solitary confinement, July 67" refers to Baraka's "imprisonment on charges of unlawfully carrying weapons and resisting arrest during the Newark riots."[1] Of what importance was Coltrane's music to Baraka at the time? What was its message to him "last night"?

Terms and References

Trane is John Coltrane, the tenor saxophonist.

Other jazz references in the poem are alto saxophonist Johnny Hodges (**Rabbit**), alto saxophonist Eddie "**Cleanhead**" Vinson, trumpeter and band leader Dizzy Gillespie (**Diz**), and **Big Maybelle**, a rhythm and blues singer of the 1950s and 1960s.

Miles is trumpeter Miles Davis.

Monk is pianist Thelonious Monk.

The 5 Spot was a New York City jazz club.

Duke is composer and band leader Duke Ellington.

"**Captain Marvel Elvin / on drums**" refers to Elvin Jones.

Lyric Wilbur is probably Wilbur de Paris.

Don Lee is Don L. Lee, the African-American poet.

DIANE DI PRIMA ▪ ▪ ▪ ▪ ▪ ▪ ▪ ▪ ▪ ▪ ▪ ▪
b. 1934

The Practice of Magical Evocation   (p. 273)

Points for Discussion and Writing

"Ductile" means easily led, tractable, or pliant. Does di Prima believe this is true of women, or is her poem wholly satirical of Snyder's position on women?

1. *The LeRoi Jones/Amiri Baraka Reader*, ed. William J. Harris, New York, 1991, p. xxii.

Discuss the feminist viewpoint of the poem, for example, the assertion that women are "built for masochistic / calm." Of what importance is the statement that "men children only" are brought forth at birth?

With whom is "Will" identified in the poem?

In what way is woman "twice torn" in relationship with man?

Describe the tone of the poem. Is it bitter, angry, or wisely observant?

Why is the poem titled "The Practice of Magical Evocation"?

On Sitting Down to Write, I Decide Instead to Go to Fred Herko's Concert   (*p. 273*)

Points for Discussion and Writing

Fred Herko was a dancer, choreographer, and friend of di Prima. Does the poem refer to Herko, or does it deal primarily with di Prima's own experience?

Who is the "you" of the poem who has "scurried already / hurried already / uptown / on a Third Avenue Bus"?

What is suggested by "crabs I'll never get / and you all perfumed too / as if they'd notice"? Likewise, who are "they"?

The second movement of the poem, beginning "O the dark caves of obligation" carries a different sense of address. What is di Prima's mood on leaving her apartment? On arriving at the concert? Why does she perceive everything so blankly?

Obviously, di Prima did eventually sit down to write. When do you imagine the poem to be written? The same evening? Is it likely to have been much later in time?

Given the poem's title, discuss the ending, "Hello / I came here / after all."

For H.D.   (*p. 274*)

Points for Discussion and Writing

The mood of the poem is pained throughout. Why do you think it is addressed to H.D.? As a fellow woman poet from whom she might take comfort? As another woman who has "lived passionately"?

What do the poem's diamonds, quartz, and ice represent?

In section 3, di Prima writes, " 'I am a woman of pleasure' & give back / salt for salt." What is meant by giving "salt for salt"? How is the metaphor of salt employed in the rest of this section?

Is the desert symbolic of love's cruelty? The desert theme and the praying for flood is reminscent of Eliot's *The Waste Land*. Does the poem resemble Eliot's poem in any other respect?

Are the hyenas, vultures, and other carrion eaters symbolic of the men di Prima has known?

What is the tone of section 5? Is it in any way different from the first four sections?

How is song related to salt in the poem's final lines?

What is the "power of incantation stirring to life / what shd sleep, like stone"?

Terms and References

H.D. refers to the poet Hilda Doolittle, who attended the University of Pennsylvania at the same time as Ezra Pound and William Carlos Williams, and whose poetry "founded" the Imagist movement in poetry. Lasting from roughly 1910 to 1920 but profoundly influencing the poetry to follow, Imagism called for a physical, rather than rhetorical, poetry in which, according to Pound, there would be "Direct treatment of the 'thing,' whether subjective or objective." Other guidelines set by Pound were "to use absolutely no word that does not contribute to the presentation" and "to compose in the sequence of the musical phrase, not in sequence of a metronome."

Dis is the Underworld in Roman mythology; also a god of that place.

In Egyptian myth, **Anubis** is the jackal-headed guide of the dead to the place of judgment.

Backyard   (*p. 276*)

Points for Discussion and Writing

How is the form of this poem different from di Prima's other poems included here?

The poet's use of initial repetition is called "anaphora." What other poets in the anthology make use of it? What are the advantages of the form? The shortcomings?

What is learned of di Prima's upbringing in Brooklyn? How might the poet's use of personal detail compare with that of Allen Ginsberg in his poem "To Aunt Rose"?

The Loba Addresses the Goddess / or The Poet as Priestess Addresses the Loba-Goddess   *(p. 277)*

Points for Discussion and Writing

In his poem "Wichita Vortex Sutra" Allen Ginsberg wrote, "Poet is priest!" What is the relationship between poet as priestess and the Loba-Goddess? Between the Loba and the Goddess?

Read di Prima's account of her dream encounter with the "huge white wolf," or wolf-goddess, in the introduction to her section. What might the wolf represent? Ask the class for dream interpretations of this experience. Might the appearance of the wolf have been influenced by di Prima's living in Wyoming at the time? Of what importance is the fact that European wolf-goddesses existed long before di Prima's dream of them, although she was apparently not aware of this fact?

The poem opens with a description to the goddess of the exhausting services women offer to children and "the niggardly / dying fathers / healing each other w / water & bitter herbs." Are the "dying fathers" the husbands of these women and father to the children? If so, do they offer healing only to each other?

Discuss the ritual qualities of section II. Who are the "we" who stand naked in a circle of lamps? A society of women? What bearing does the goddess Nut have on the poem? On di Prima's selection as a whole?

Terms and References

Nut is the Egyptian goddess of the sky from whose back the sun god Ra raised himself.

TED BERRIGAN ▪ ▪ ▪ ▪ ▪ ▪ ▪ ▪ ▪ ▪ ▪ ▪ ▪ ▪ ▪
1934–1983

Sonnet II ("Dear Margie, hello. It is 5:15 a.m.")
(p. 279)

See p. 6 for Tristan Tzara's instructions on how to unite a Dada poem. The Beat novelist William Burroughs has also used the cut-up method in writing his works of fiction. How might Berrigan have employed a similar method in writing his sonnets? Does he follow it systematically? What lines repeat from poem to poem?

When Berrigan writes, "It is 5:15 a.m.," is he reporting the actual time? Only a few lines later, the time is reported as 8:30 p.m. Has time passed or is Berrigan purposely undermining the reader's sense of temporal (and therefore authorial) reliability? What effect does the second reference to "5:15 a.m." have, especially as followed by "fucked til 7 now she's late to work"?

The line "How Much Longer Shall I Be Able To Inhabit The Divine" refers to a poem by John Ashbery, included here. Do you see any other evidence of Ashbery's influence?

Berrigan was himself much older than 18 when this poem was written, yet he writes "and I'm / 18 so why are my hands shaking." Does the poem contain a shifting persona?

Despite its fragmentation and intentional undercutting of consecutive sense, is this poem's lyricism nevertheless effective?

Sonnet XXXVI ("It's 8:54 a.m. in Brooklyn, it's the 28th of July and") (*p. 279*)

Points for Discussion and Writing

To what extent is the opening movement a parody or imitation of Frank O'Hara's "The Day Lady Died"?

When an author reports events in present time, is he or she transcribing them as they actually happen? Or are such reports only illusions of real time? Is it possible to transcribe experience as it happens into a poem? With this in mind, compare Diane di Prima's "On Sitting Down to Write I Decide Instead to Go to Fred Herko's Concert."

Like other New York School poets, Berrigan offers the names of his friends such as Carol and Dick. Is it necessary to know who these people are? Does the poem itself reveal what is necessary to know about them?

Berrigan himself lived in the more rundown section of Manhattan's East Village. What role does "Perry street," located in the more prosperous district of the West Village, have in the poem?

The expression "badly loved" is taken from the poem "La Chanson du Mal-Aimé" by Guillaume Apollinaire. Are there any other literary references in the poem?

To what extent might the words "feminine marvelous and tough" describe a poetic ideal for Berrigan?

Sonnet LXXXVIII: A Final Sonnet (*p. 280*)

Points for Discussion and Writing

This was, in fact, the final sonnet in Berrigan's *The Sonnets*. Discuss the line "A man / Signs a shovel and so he digs" in terms of Berrigan's "signing off" at the book's end.

The lines from "But this rough magic" to "And deeper than did ever plummet sound / I'll drown my book" are taken from Prospero's final speech at the end of *The Tempest*, Shakespeare's final play. Most readers of the play believe that Shakespeare was himself speaking through the voice of Prospero. Comment on Berrigan's use of Shakespeare's lines.

Of what significance is the book's final line immediately following the quote from Shakespeare?

Words for Love   (*p. 280*)

Points for Discussion and Writing

Out of amusement and a love of language, Berrigan delighted in making use of a heightened poetic diction. Examine his word choices ("smites," "Oubliette," "parrot fever") and levels of rhetoric (from the hieratic [refined] to the demotic [everyday]). How might it be that Berrigan's love of poetry "smites" him?

Discuss the use of tone in the sentence, "I watch / my psyche, smile, dream wet dreams, and sigh." Is Berrigan parodying the high seriousness of some poetry, or does he employ it ultimately to a serious purpose? Regarding the reliability of Berrigan's tone, look especially at the final sections, beginning "Only this."

Robert Creeley's books include *Words* (1967) and *For Love* (1962). Might they have influenced the title of this poem?

Bean Spasms   (*p. 281*)

Points for Discussion and Writing

This poem was originally published in a collaborative book (with Ron Padgett) of the same title. At that time, none of the poems was assigned authorship. Compare and contrast this project with the collaborative venture *The Lyrical Ballads* by William Wordsworth and Samuel Taylor Coleridge.

The poem was later republished in Berrigan's own volume *Many Happy Returns* (1969). Discuss the issues of ownership and authorship raised by collaboration. Does collaboration compromise a poet's aura of originality or genius? To what extent is the work of other poets always an influence on a poet's work?

Is there any evidence of the cut-up method in the poem "Bean Spasms"? One of Berrigan's methods in writing his long poems was to compose at the typewriter over a period of days and allow new events and references at hand to enter the poem. He would also encourage friends who were visiting his New York City apartment to contribute lines to the ongoing work. Do you find evidence of this compositional mode in the poem?

What is Berrigan's attitude in the poem toward Henry James? To what extent might the lines "minute by minute GENEROSITY!" describe the poetic impulse of the work at hand?

To what does "I'm the Wonderer" refer? The Del Shannon song?

Why is the poem divided into parts? Is there any dramatic or logical necessity to doing so? Or does each part equal a day's writing?

What does Berrigan mean by "Praising, that's it!" Is praising an activity of poetry?

What is meant by "You have it seems a workshop nature"?

Discuss Fairfield Porter's statement, "Art is art & Life / is home" in connection to Berrigan's blend of art and life. Given his open, collaborative nature and love of "found" detail, can Berrigan's life be separated from his art? Are some poet's lives more separate from their art than others? Who, for example?

Why would Berrigan describe the surrealist poet André Breton as "a shit"?

How are the double columns at the poem's end to be read out loud? Can the elements be read in a different order and still make sense?

Throughout the poem, there is a noticeable lack of closure and summation that would gather the poem into a unity; instead, the poem simply continues. Is Berrigan's closure in this poem designed as such or is it an incidental part of the ongoing process? Might the poem have just as successfully ended elsewhere?

Terms and References

"Those long skinny *Rivers* [my emphasis] / So well hung, in New York City" is a wicked reference to Larry Rivers, a painter closely associated to Frank O'Hara and other poets of the New York School.

Fairfield Porter was also a painter associated with the poets of the New York School.

Mr. Macadams is Lewis MacAdams, a poet and contemporary of Berrigan.

ANSELM HOLLO ▪ ▪ ▪ ▪ ▪ ▪ ▪ ▪ ▪ ▪ ▪ ▪ ▪
b. 1934

Journey, 1966   (p. 287)

Points for Discussion and Writing

The title refers to a journey. In the poem, does it prove to be a physical or psychological journey? What details of the external landscape are given?

There is a reference to "the blueing desert / encased in time." Is this detail symbolic or actual?

What is "that constant spear" which "watched us"?

The lighting and staging of the poem could be described as heroic. How consistent or inconsistent is this with Hollo's other work?

To whom might the poem be addressed?

Shed the Fear   (p. 288)

Points for Discussion and Writing

How is this poem consistent with "Journey, 1966"?

Compare and contrast Hollo's use of the line and stanza with that of Robert Creeley. What use is made, for instance, of enjambment (line breaks)?

Discuss the meaning of the poem's first sentence. In what way is the world "not / to be borne"?

What is the poem's subject? What does Hollo wish to shed the fear of?

The Dream of Instant Total Representation   (p. 288)

Points for Discussion and Writing

What is "postnomadic time"? How does it relate to "Instant Total Representation"?

When was the turnip "the new technology"?

What condition of communication does the poet find desirable? Is the existing system desireable?

In the last stanza, what is the explicitly stated philosophy with regard to communication?

Godlike   (p. 289)

Points for Discussion and Writing

This poem is a single sentence fragment in which the text serves to define "godlike." Is it "godlike" to resist talking about what an idiot you once were?

What is the importance of the fact that "you" are sitting at the *head* of the table?

Italics   (p. 290)

Points for Discussion and Writing

Why does this poem bear the title "Italics"? Is Hollo referring primarily to his own use of italics such as *yearned, thought, are,* and *think*?

How might the title relate to the lines, "make sure you're reading / what you think you're reading"? Is it possible for the use of italics to lend a false authority to words?

What are the larger political implications of the poem? Do some authority figures in fact deserve awe?

Does Hollo himself use italics appropriately? Are some of his uses more striking than others?

Wild West Workshop Poem   (p. 290)

Points for Discussion and Writing

Of what importance is the word "workshop" in the poem's title? What might Hollo be saying about the value of poetry workshops? Since the rise of the academic creative writing workshop system, which began at the University of Iowa, there has been controversy about the role of these workshops and the kind of poetry they promulgate. Is Hollo advocating a poetry that pops "'em in the back" whenever it gets a chance, that is, a spontaneous and untutored poetry?

Is a spontaneous poetry necessarily anti-intellectual? Which "tradition," the academic or the innovative, tends to be more intellectual in its concerns? Do these allegiances change with the times?

JOSEPH CERAVOLO ■ ■ ■ ■ ■ ■ ■ ■ ■ ■ ■ ■
1934–1988

Ho Ho Ho Caribou   (p. 291)

Points for Discussion and Writing

Discuss the realism of this poem. Despite its fantastic detail (such as kangaroos leaping on fruit trees), how might the poem be considered realistic?

Do the detail and tone vary? If so, characterize these differences.

In what way does the narrator characterize himself?

What is the "plot situation" of the poem?

Examine the syntax of the following two sentences: "Tell us where to / stop and eat. And / drink which comes to use out / in the sand is / at a star." Although Ceravolo uses discontinuity inventively, what separates his work from that of the language poets?

The poem is set in unusual places, such as a desert, the edge of a cliff, and a "firm lake." The poem also places diners next to herds of caribou. Discuss this melange of detail. What unifying force fuses such disparate detail?

How does the last section (X) affect all that went before?

How might Freudian or Jungian approaches to literature be applied to this poem?

Pregnant, I Come   (p. 294)

Points for Discussion and Writing

The narrator is clearly male, bearing semen and babies. Discuss the title, especially the word "pregnant," in terms of this maleness. Does "I come" have a double meaning?

How does the "you" "go up / in your consciousness"?

Geological Hymn   (p. 295)

Points for Discussion and Writing

Ceravolo has the ability to simultaneously perceive events in the present and in the far past in a very compressed form. In what way is this poem consistent with Clayton Eshleman's poetry? How is it vastly different from Eshleman's work?

What might be an example of "non-visual reality"? Are any examples offered by the poem itself?

The center of the poem contains a view of the "cambrian worm." What does the cambrian worm represent?

To what degree was Ceravolo's imagination Paleozoic rather than postmodern? Or is it both?

Discuss Ceravolo's careful distinction that the desert, an ocean, or a tundra in the cambrian worm "lies before me" but "not from me or in me / but from some foreign night / falling and falling in snow." Why the care to distance these things from his own imaginative agency?

Ceravolo writes, "But I still come around / while the wind itself is gone." To what place does he come?

Discuss the poem's images of arrival and departure, presence and absence. For instance, the "falling in snow" seems very present as imagery, yet it occurs "from some foreign night."

Terms and References

The **Cambrian** period in geological history was the first period of the Paleozoic era, characterized by warm seas and desert land areas.

New Realism   (p. 295)

Points for Discussion and Writing

What is "a stab / of preservation" to which Ceravolo refers? Is it a dream or the procreative act ("a mouth between ourselves").

What is a "preserver of heaven between our legs"?

Ceravolo seems to be teetering imaginatively between the worlds of life and death, summer and fall. Examine the poem's images of death and generation, such as "seeding the whirlpool / of earth's magnified fall." Why would a coyote's song be "wet with death"?

Why does he call his poem "New Realism"? Has the old realism changed or needed to be replaced? Or is this "New Realism" in fact a fresh realization of the cycle of existence?

JOHN WIENERS ■ ■ ■ ■ ■ ■ ■ ■ ■ ■ ■ ■ ■ ■ ■
b. 1934

A poem for the insane   (p. 296)

Points for Discussion and Writing

How much of the artist Edvard Munch's work is evident in this poem? Why would Wieners be drawn to Munch's work? Is all of the poem set in the nightmarish world of Munch? In what ways does Wieners conjoin Munch's world with his own contemporary experience?

On at least three occasions, Wieners was hospitalized for mental disorder. At what points in the poem does he seem to refer to his own emotional turmoil?

Terms and References

Munch refers to the paintings of Scandanavian artist Edvard Munch, best known for his disturbing work, "The Scream."

The Waning of the Harvest Moon   (p. 298)

Points for Discussion and Writing

What evidence exists that Persephone, who resides with the king of Hades half the year, might be "my daughter" in the poem?

Why is my soul referred to as "daughter"? Is the speaker Ceres, the mother of Persephone? If so, is Persephone's absence the cause of "famine and empty / altars"?

What is the "descent" for which one dresses in blue, the one into Hell? Do the dogs at the gate represent Cerberus, the three-headed dog of Greek myth?

If the setting is mythic, how do you explain the line, "I want to go out and rob a grocery store"? Has the narrator changed from the first stanza? Whose perspective are we in at the poem's conclusion when words are "gone from my mouth"?

Do you see any connection in style and tone between Wieners's poems and those of Joseph Ceravolo?

A Poem for Trapped Things   (*p. 298*)

Points for Discussion and Writing

Wieners expresses an intense concern for the butterfly that becomes trapped in his room. To what does he compare the butterfly? To what extent do his perceptions about the butterfly amount to self-examination?

Why might "we" vanish from sight?

If Wieners feels such sympathy with the butterfly, why doesn't he free it? Instead he sits all morning long, "amid debris," with his hand over his mouth. Does Wieners also feel like a "trapped thing"?

Examine the poem's color scheme: the "blue flame," "yellow being," "black border," "red robe amid debris," and "blue diamonds on your back."

My Mother   (*p. 299*)

Points for Discussion and Writing

Is Wieners's observation of his mother voyeuristic? How might it be compared to his fascination with the butterfly in the previous poem?

Of what importance is the word "underground" in the poem? The reference to "the wire grates of a cage"?

If Wieners loves his mother as he says, why does he hide in a booth when she enters the subway?

Two Years Later   (*p. 300*)

Points for Discussion and Writing

This poem probably deals with the poet's experience of shock therapy as a mental patient. Discuss the curiously effective imagery of the poem's last two lines. What is Wieners expressing about his condition two years later? Is he saying that the beauty of men becomes as indelible an image as the blue car in the stars, no matter what woe befalls them? Or that the beauty of men becomes a distant event lost in the stars, irretrievable after such woeful events?

How might this be considered an Imagist poem? Compare and contrast the Ezra Pound poem, "In a Station of the Metro."

The Loneliness   (*p. 300*)

Points for Discussion and Writing

Wieners's poetry often reflects on moments of isolation, pain, and fail-ure. In this sexually explicit poem about Wieners's homosexuality, what is meant by "How can a man have pride / without a wife"? Does he desire a wife and feel ashamed of his homosexual acts? Or does the poet mean, "How can a man have pride *in this homophobic society* without a wife?"

Why has the encounter with the other man been so unsatisfactory?

What do you make of the poet's final statement, "Feeling like a girl / stinking beneath my clothes"?

Are any other poets in the anthology so honest in the depiction of their affairs and sorrows?

ROBERT KELLY ▪ ▪ ▪ ▪ ▪ ▪ ▪ ▪ ▪ ▪ ▪ ▪ ▪ ▪
b. 1935

Coming   (*p. 301*)

Points for Discussion and Writing

Discuss the unifying images of blue in the poem. What connection ap-pears between "the blue mouth of the shark," "a great blue harp," "Hevajra," and "the blue silk hung canopy at Versailles"? What does Kelly mean by the title, "Coming," in this context?

Terms and References

Yama is the Sanskrit word for the god of the dead.

Hevajra is the "laughing vajra" or "tantric yidam" on whom meditation focuses. He is also the blue figure depicted as holding the "mandala," or wheel of life, in his hands.

Lama, or "high one," refers to one's spiritual director or guru.

The **Scythians** were great horsepeople of ancient Greece; the setting here, however, is a central Asian plain.

The Rainmakers   (*p. 302*)

Points for Discussion and Writing

Who are the rainmakers to whom the poem refers?

How do we "daily anthologize" the work of the Demiurge?

The reference at first is cosmic and mythic; it then turns to the subject of semiotics. Who are these contemporary "rainmakers" who "sell us the sexy / isotherms of semiotics"? How might contemporary literary critics, guided by the fashion of deconstruction and semiotics, be compared to rainmakers?

In section 2, the subject advances into the realm of poetry. Here, Kelly quotes the poet Robert Duncan in support of his own position. What *is* the position Kelly holds? Naturalness of expression? Must naturalness be "charmed" in order to appear natural?

Is it a "world we speak," language alone, or both? What would Kelly's position appear to be concerning language poetry?

What does the poet mean in section 3 by "the numbers are not governors, / the numbers are white, every one is one"?

Is Kelly's model of poetry "one thing listening always to another, / an old woman visiting her bees"?

Terms and References

The **Demiurge** was the name used by Plato to designate the deity who fashions the material world; it is also the Gnostic creator of the material world.

[Bittersweet growing up the red wall]   (*p. 303*)

Points for Discussion and Writing

How does the information in the "Terms and References" section clarify your understanding of Kelly's poem?

The setting is Providence, Rhode Island. Does Kelly see "the continuity / of actual effort" in the "wharves and bait shacks" of the city?

How are the shacks that "stand in their difference" to be valued? Is there a force in our culture working against this difference?

How might this poem be compared with the work of Charles Olson in style and theme?

Terms and References

Bittersweet is a North American fruity vine with fleshy scarlet fruit both bitter and sweet to the taste; in Europe bittersweet is called nightshade and its fruit is poisonous.

Tantra refers to Buddhist and Hindu mystical writings on the subject of magic; literally, it means "loom," and metaphorically, it suggests the continuity of all experience.

Chlamyses are short mantles fastened at the shoulder and worn by men in Greece; here they are worn by women.

Menhaden are abundant inedible fish used primarily for fertilizer (*menhaden* means "old wife" in Algonquin).

Tansy, a yellow buttonlike flower that is also the subject of Charles Olson's "Letter 3" in *The Maximus Poems,* takes its name from *atanasia,* the Greek word for immortality.

A Woman with Flaxen Hair in Norfolk Heard
(*p. 304*)

Points for Discussion and Writing

Basil Bunting was a poet from Durham, England, closely allied to the Pound tradition. Besides the dedication, what evidence exists in the poem that it is an homage or elegy to Bunting?

Who is the speaker of the first section? A woman with flaxen hair? Is her speech overheard? Of what importance is her reference to being "a mouth / in the middle of things"?

Each section of the poem is fairly distinct in manner. Is section 2 entirely dreamed, and therefore apocryphal as fact?

The word *'ud* originally meant "oriental religious instrument"; it has since become our word "lute." Of what significance is it that this information appears to the author in a dream? What is the importance of the figure of the lute for poetry? Is a feminist poetics implied in the "womb" metaphor?

Who speaks in the second section? Kelly himself or someone overheard?

Kelly says that the third section is based on a conversation between a British working-class man and wife about a house they planned to purchase in the small town of Trunch, England. Is the language of this section in their voices or the voice of another narrator?

In what respect are "we" to be considered "saints of a sort, gaudy / in our private way"? Are "we" the joiner and his wife? How might these citizens be "doomed / in a fresco on a wall"?

CLAYTON ESHLEMAN ■ ■ ■ ■ ■ ■ ■ ■ ■ ■ ■ ■

b. 1935

The Lich Gate   (*p. 307*)

Points for Discussion and Writing

Eshleman's mother's name was Gladys; his father's was Wallace. This would indicate that Eshleman himself is the narrator. Whose burial is he attending? His own? What evidence exists in the poem that we are experiencing a dream?

Why is memory "not a friend"?

Discuss the metaphor of the clapper and bell. Of what importance is the fact that the "I" of the poem is the clapper? Are Gladys and Wallace the bell rope? Who is being instructed to pull on this rope?

Who are "the you-hordes / leaning over my sleep with / needle-shaped / fingers"?

When the poet writes, "I have come here / to bleed this gate, to make my language fray," does he refer to the act of writing? Why is fraying the language a positive value for Eshleman? Of what connection is this fraying to the line, "or to let my dying pass into the poem"?

Of what importance is the scene at the "The Mayan Ballcourt of the Dead"? Is the description of "struggling intently" a suggestion of his impending loss at the game?

Terms and References

A **lich gate** is a roofed gateway to a churchyard originally used as a resting place for the bier before burial. *Lich* in Middle English means "body" or "corpse."

A **hominid** is a member of the family *hominidae* of the primate order, now represented by only one living species, *Homo sapiens*.

"The Mayan Ballcourt of the Dead" refers to the practice of sacrificing the game's losing players.

Notes on a Visit to Le Tuc d'Audoubert   (*p. 308*)

Points for Discussion and Writing

This poem concerns itself with Eshleman's revelatory early visits to the caves of the Dordogne region of France. Compare Gary Snyder's search for "Original Mind" with Eshleman's desire to understand Paleolithic imagination.

How is the descent into the cave symbolic of rebirth?

Eshleman writes, "grotesque = movement." Discuss the poet's privileging of the grotesque in this poem and in his work in general. Is life seen "at full vent" inherently grotesque?

Discuss the prose section beginning with the word "useful." How might this be seen as a statement of Eshleman's poetics? Is "Any plan a coincidence" in his approach? Or is his work an insistent struggle for an "image" of history?

The juxtaposition of " 'naturalistic' ibex" over the figure of an " 'abstract' vulva already gouged there" are for Eshleman "the rudiments of poetry." How so? Did the same elements of poetry exist in 30,000 BC as today? Is poetry in the images themselves: the juxtaposition of *two* images, the palimpsest or overwriting of figures, or the relation of naturalistic and abstract? Is one figure more "abstract" than the other because it is more faded or because it is less detailed? With this in mind, what *are* the essential elements of poetry?

Eshleman writes that to be alive as a poet is to be *"in conversation with one's eyes."* Is the visual element of his poetry (its phanopoeia) dominant over its music (melopoeia)?

Much of the poem is written in an essayistic prose. To what extent is the poem an argument with history? With Eshleman's own psyche?

ROSMARIE WALDROP ▪ ▪ ▪ ▪ ▪ ▪ ▪ ▪ ▪ ▪ ▪
b. 1935

FROM *Inserting the Mirror*   (p. 314)

Points for Discussion and Writing

Part 1 of the poem establishes important tensions between the world of rain (material reality) and language, presence and absence, the human body (pubic hair) and mind (arid speculation). Do these dualities continue throughout the selection?

In part 2, how might the body go on an errand while "I stay in bed"? Is the true "I" other than the body?

In part 4, is one's image in the mirror a presence or absence? How about one's name or the concept of "me"? What might the statement "all resonance grows from consent to emptiness" have to do with poetry? Examine the concept of identity as presented in this section.

Waldrop also writes fiction. How does her skill at narrative, especially in part 5, influence its poetic character?

Discuss Waldrop's sentence in part 6, "I closed my eyes, afraid to resemble." What does closing one's eyes resemble?

In part 8, Waldrop writes, "I know, but cannot say, what a violin sounds like." How is such a statement consistent with the writings of philosopher Wittgenstein, whose views concerned the linguistic construction of thought?

Discuss the feminist themes of part 9, for example, "The whole idea of depth smells fishy." Is woman "deep"? Is depth admirable to Waldrop, or, like the language poets, does she prefer a poetics of surface?

Many of the poem's sections include the figure of rain or a reference to wetness ("Wet laundry flapped in the wind"). Are these the poem's means to unity?

Compare and contrast this series of prose poems with the Lyn Hejinian sequence, *My Life*.

GUSTAF SOBIN ▪ ▪ ▪ ▪ ▪ ▪ ▪ ▪ ▪ ▪ ▪ ▪ ▪ ▪
b. 1935

Out of the Identical   (*p. 318*)

Points for Discussion and Writing

What is Sobin's poem about? A hand is "writing / the rocks." Is the hand, rather than the rocks, the subject of the poem?

What does "weeks, / now, without" mean? Weeks without writing?

What is "the identical" to which the title refers?

Is the world (nature, the rocks, "flowing light") indistinguishable and without difference until a hand (human imagination) traces its features? Why are these features associated with "smoke" and "its shimmers"?

Of what importance to the poem is the expression "verb-driven"? To what extent is Sobin's own poem "verb-driven"?

To what extent are formal qualities such as alliteration and assonance the dominant features of this poem?

Discuss in detail the *form* of the following:

> its

> tissues, that
> tissue, that

> smoke, with its
> vaporous,
> verb-

> driven shimmers.

In the passage, what value is placed on the short "i" sound? The "s" sound?

What the Music Wants   (*p. 319*)

Points for Discussion and Writing

Sobin's claims to have been influenced by the "focused intensity" of the work of Objectivist poet George Oppen. Read sections of Oppen's "Of Being Numerous," to be found in *Collected Poems* (1975). Oppen writes about the city, Sobin about rural France. Nevertheless, what similarities do you find in the work of the two poets?

In what respect is the music of poetry comparable to the volute shape of a gastropod shell (such as a snail's) into which "ourselves" are inserted?

How does the metaphor of the volute relate to the search for a place to stand? How might one stand "with-in / sound alone"? Do Sobin's poems do this?

To what do the "pod and tentacle" of the poem's opening refer?

What inspires the poem's ecstatic tone?

Terms and References

A **volute** is a twisted or spiral formation, such as the whorls of a gastropod shell or the capital of an Ionic column.

Eleven Rock Poems   (*p. 320*)

Points for Discussion and Writing

Sobin begins midsentence: "sent myself the   length / of my own metaphors (boxwood, then cistus. . . ." In what respect does he send himself the length of his metaphors? What is the advantage of beginning *in medias res*, or "in the middle of things"?

Where is this poem set? How important is the setting to the poem? How does its starkness and altitude lend the poem ceremonial qualities?

Give the "plot" of the poem insofar as it exists. What is the nature of events in the poem? Is the landscape or the climber/narrator the poem's chief actor?

What does Sobin mean by " 'the harmonies' as they shattered"?

An interval refers to a measure of time or music. What might "fixed intervals / moving" refer to?

What are the "opaque vocables" to which the poet refers? The sound of the wind in the grotto?

How might this poem be compared to Clayton Eshleman's "Notes on a Visit to Le Tuc d'Audoubert"? How does Sobin's work differ from Eshleman's?

Compare the packed syntax of Sobin's poetry ("that the / emptiness be edged, wedged, that   pierced, it / spread / open)" with that of Gerard Manley Hopkins. Like Hopkins, does Sobin owe a debt to the Anglo-Saxon origins of English? As with Hopkins's devotional poetry, does Sobin's poetry bear any relation to the transcendent?

Formally, what is the basic unit of organization in Sobin's poetry: the syllable, the word, or the sentence?

The poem's title is "Eleven Rock Poems." Does each section work independently of the rest?

Terms and References

A **cirque** is a steep hollow, often containing a lake, to be found at the upper end of some mountain valleys.

Ilex is a kind of holly; in the Mediterranean region it is known as "holm oak."

Cade is also a Mediterranean shrub.

RUSSELL EDSON ▪ ▪ ▪ ▪ ▪ ▪ ▪ ▪ ▪ ▪ ▪ ▪ ▪ ▪
b. 1935

Conjugal   (p. 323)

Points for Discussion and Writing

What does Edson's poetry have in common with fables?

One of Edson's shorter prose poems was once published as a "novel" in an anthology of experimental fiction. Why is "Conjugal" a poem and not a work of fiction?

Ezra Pound divided poetry into three aspects: phanopoeia (its visual qualities), melopoeia (its music), and logopoeia (its diction or word choices). Which of these elements is dominant in Edson's work?

Is the *sound* of his words of any concern to Edson? Is the rhythm of his sentences that of poetry or prose? Can you conceive of these words being set in lines of verse?

How might an elemental diction serve his overall purpose better than an elaborate diction?

What is the difference between the use of stanza breaks in a work of verse and Edson's use of the paragraph? Is the paragraph used to separate his material thematically? Or is it primarily used as a timing device?

Discuss the fact that the third section of the poem contains two joined paragraphs.

Discuss the sexual politics of the poem. Who has the more active agency in the conjugal act? Why does the *male* figure do all the teaching?

How can the narrator be "bending her around something that / she has bent herself around"?

Ape   (*p. 323*)

Points for Discussion and Writing

This poem contains a lot of dialogue. Might it be staged as a play?

This poem is consistent with many of Edson's other works in that it makes use of a family romance or melodrama. How are the politics of family relations expressed by means of its outrageous narrative? Or is this work simply a grotesque comedy, without moral purpose?

Is Edson interested in beauty? If so, how might he define it?

Edson writes that the prose poem is "a personal form disciplined not by other literature but by unhappiness; thus a way to be happy."[2] Is there any evidence in his work that he is exorcizing his personal fears by means of his poetry? Is it possible to be confessional by means of fable?

A Performance at Hog Theater   (*p. 324*)

Points for Discussion and Writing

Might this work have begun, "Once upon a time"?

Despite the childish nature of Edson's fabulism, this poem expresses serious concerns about the nature of art. Discuss the issue of seriousness as it relates to the writing of poetry. Does Edson's work fail Matthew Arnold's test of "high seriousness"?

Distinguish between the kinds of plays advocated by the two hogs. The first is very conscious of art; the second calls for simply acting as hogs, a

2. Russell Edson, "Portrait of the Writer as a Fat Man," *Field*, No. 13, Fall 1975, p. 25.

view that wins the day. What might Edson be saying about the nature of art? About the audience for art? Do poets hold such opposing views as well? With which hog would Edson himself identify?

The Toy-Maker   (p. 324)

Points for Discussion and Writing

Is the function of Edson's work to shock the reader? What moral agency might this shock serve?

As a reader, do you find yourself being lulled by Edson's lyricism ("He made a getting-old toy, and he made a dying toy"), only to be subverted by the reference to "toy shit"? Do you feel tricked or pleased?

Is it possible for Edson to anger his audience through these subversions? Or does he play to an audience's expectation of having the rug pulled out from under it? How might this subversion compare to the sudden changes of tone in the work of John Ashbery, a poet much different in approach and kinds of expression?

In subverting the reader's expectation, what point is Edson making about the social contract between author and reader?

The Optical Prodigal   (p. 324)

Points for Discussion and Writing

This poem begins with a conceit based on optical perspective. How might such a use place Edson in the Metaphysical tradition of John Donne, George Herbert, and Emily Dickinson?

To what extent is Edson influenced by surrealism? What characteristics do surrealism and metaphysical poetry share? How might they lend themselves to Edson's fabulistic approach?

The son in the poem goes into the distance and finds that his parents are still small. Is this distance symbolic or a practical part of the poem's conceit?

What does the poem express about relations between parents and child?

What do you imagine relations between Edson and his own parents to be? Is it fair to assume that what is expressed in a work of art has anything to do with the author's own life?

JOHN GIORNO ■ ■ ■ ■ ■ ■ ■ ■ ■ ■ ■ ■ ■ ■ ■

b. 1936

Life Is a Killer   (p. 326)

Points for Discussion and Writing

Giorno's work characteristically uses repetition of key phrases. How is this useful in performance? How might it be compared to the refrain of a popular song?

Is it possible to appreciate Giorno's poetry as poetry when read on the page? Or does it require the attentions of his own voice?

Play a CD or videotape of Giorno in performance (for example, Ron Mann's video, *Poetry in Motion*). How does Giorno's volume and register affect the poem's meaning?

To what extent is Giorno a moral poet intent on communicating wisdom?

Do the various movements or sections of the poem relate to each other by theme?

To what extent is Giorno personal in the poem?

As declaratory poetry, does Giorno's work have anything in common with that of Allen Ginsberg, Jerome Rothenberg, or Anne Waldman?

Scum & Slime   (p. 330)

Points for Discussion and Writing

Does Giorno personally want to be "filthy and anonymous" or clean and successful? In other words, is he making use of a persona?

Discuss the gender politics of Giorno's reference to Adam and Eve, especially his explanation of "why the ocean smells of fish."

When Giorno writes, "We don't take / drugs no more, / we sit around / praying for money," is he satirizing those of the 1960s generation who joined the upwardly mobile "Me Generation" of the 1980s?

Discuss the straightforward, declaratory nature of Giorno's poetry. Much declaimed poetry is written on political themes. Is Giorno's?

Is Giorno's work personal to him or does he use an anonymous mosaic of voices and personae?

On the surface, Giorno's work appears simple, open, and direct. Is it really? Does it have intellectual content?

JAYNE CORTEZ ■ ■ ■ ■ ■ ■ ■ ■ ■ ■ ■ ■ ■ ■ ■ ■
b. 1936

For the Poets (Christopher Okigbo & Henry Dumas)
(*p. 333*)

Points for Discussion and Writing

This poem is both an homage and an elegy. Does it deal exclusively with the situations of Christopher Okigbo and Henry Dumas, or are they two of many black heros? What is Cortez's scope in the poem, and how does it relate to her political purpose?

For what purpose does Cortez need "kai kai" and "akpetesie"? Why would these be drawn from the "torn arm of Bessie Smith," the noted blues singer who died after being refused care in a white hospital in the South?

This poem is designed to be performed and has certain elements of chant and song; the "ah," for instance, is in the form of a choral response. The poem is also written as a ritual invocation of helpful spirits. How are the objects invoked (kai kai, canefields, ashes, snakes) to be used?

Cortez's work has been published in the contemporary surrealist journal *Arsenal*. What evidence of surrealism do you find in her writing?

How does Cortez's use of the list or catalogue form compare with Anne Waldman's in "Makeup on Empty Space"?

In what ways are the performance values of the poem announced even as it appears on the page?

Terms and References

Born in 1932, **Christopher Okigbo** is an important Nigerian poet who was killed in 1967 during a civil war in that country.

Henry Dumas was a young African-American poet of great promise who was shot to death by a police officer in a Harlem subway station in a case of mistaken identity. His poems are collected in *Knees of a Natural Man* (1989).

Kai kai is a homemade gin in Nigeria.

Akpetesie is a homemade gin in Ghana.

Lucumi is a religious cult in Cuba.

Abakwa is a secret society cult in Cuba.

Damballah is the god of fertility in Haiti.

A **durbar** is a reception hall, also a state reception given formerly by an Indian prince by a British governor in India.

Lobito is a city in Angola.

"Sahelian zone" refers to an area of devastating drought in the 1970s consisting of Senegal, Mauritania, Mali, Upper Volta, Niger, and Chad, known collectively as the Sahel.

Basuto is a group of people in Lesotho, South Africa.

Ju ju is a West African term referring to traditional religious practices.

B. J. Vorster was Prime Minister of the apartheid regime of South Africa in the 1960s and 1970s.

I See Chano Pozo   (*p. 335*)

Points for Discussion and Writing

Chano Pozo is described as "connector of two worlds." What are the two worlds to which Cortez refers?

How might Cortez as a poet be compared to Chano Pozo as a drummer? Does her work also have a chanting and percussive quality?

Discuss Cortez's work in terms of its priestly and oracular functions. Is her poetry therefore traditional? Discuss in general the role of religion and politics in Cortez's writing.

Is it possible to appreciate the power and mystery of Cortez's work without understanding all its references?

Cortez's performance of this poem, accompanied by her band, can be found on Ron Mann's video, *Poetry in Motion.* Ask the class to discuss the poem before viewing the video; then discuss it further *after* hearing Cortez's voice. What difference does the poet's voice and presence make with regard to the poem's meaning? Does it become a different poem?

When you read a poem like this to yourself, whose voice do you hear before you hear the "real" one?

Terms and References

Chano Pozo is a famous Afro-Cuban drummer.

Atamo, Mpebi, Donno, Obonu, Atumpan, Mpintintoa, Ilya Ilu, Ntenga, Siky Akkua, Bata, and **Fontomfrom** are the names of various African drums.

Antonio Maceo is the most important Cuban general in the nineteenth-century war for Cuban independence.

"Nago tongue" refers to the language group of the Yorubas of Da-
homey, West Africa.

Encuentro means "encounter" in Spanish.

Rape   (p. 337)

Points for Discussion and Writing

Discuss the politics of the poem. Do you feel that the two raped women
are justified in their actions?

The explicitness of the poem is one of its notable features. How does
this openness aid the poem's argument for revenge?

Discuss Cortez's unexpected use of humor—for example, "hee haw like
a California burro."

What are the sexual politics of a *woman* writing in this way? Are your
expectations different for a woman than for a man when it comes to
transgressive reference?

How do the conjunction and sound of the words "swat freak motherfucker" create a different entity than "fat . . . racist policeman"? Does
the explosiveness of the words replicate the act of stabbing him?

CLARENCE MAJOR ▪ ▪ ▪ ▪ ▪ ▪ ▪ ▪ ▪ ▪ ▪ ▪
b. 1936

Swallow the Lake   (p. 339)

Points for Discussion and Writing

Who or what are "blank monkeys of the hierarchy"? Major's inexpressi-
ble feelings? Of what importance, especially, is the word "hierarchy"?

The middle passage refers to the midocean part of the voyage of slave
ships. Is Major experiencing "middle passage" in personal terms as
well? What effect does his "corroding hate" have on Major personally?

How does social injustice such as racism make one "come up abstract"?

Who "gave me things I / could not use"? What things in turn could
Major "not give back"?

What are the "ideas I could not break nor form"?

Isolate   *(p. 340)*

Points for Discussion and Writing

This poem is about the breakup of a love affair. Is the woman about whom Major writes of another culture? What difference does she feel from Americans?

Discuss the lines, "Sees difficulty more in her 'church' blood / than in her cycle." What is "church" blood?

What is meant by "the crude / Cramming of Nothing"?

The effectiveness of the woman's bold statement at the poem's end may have to do with the comparative obliqueness of some earlier lines—for example, "This pilgrimage she bled into her principles. / Higher, deeper than my closed eye." Discuss the poem's rhetorical style. What is meant by "These violet people in gentle expenditures!"?

Inside Diameter   *(p. 340)*

Points for Discussion and Writing

What is "the position" to which Major refers? Inside a diameter of meaning? The known? One's cultural position seen from a different culture, in this case France? Or does Major refer to an aesthetic position ("People praise the wrong works")?

A central figure in this poem is the horse's eye fluttering "just above the buckle on the strap." What is the eye's meaning?

In section 3, what is "The original position" that is already known?

In what respect is this poem concerned with locating "the cathedral / of the imagination"?

When "battles are won and lost . . . prophets have their day." Is Major critical of these prophets? In this context, discuss the two images of nuns in section 4.

What is the impact of the second reference to the horse's eye?

DIANE WAKOSKI ▪▪▪▪▪▪▪▪▪▪▪▪▪
b. 1937

Blue Monday *(p. 343)*

Points for Discussion and Writing

This poem is a catalogue of blue images. Why is blue an effective color for making such a list? Is it inherently poetic?

What other colors appear in the poem? At the end of the poem, when the "blue jugular" spouts, what color comes out?

What is the position of Wakoski (or the "I") with regard to the world?

Is the final movement suicidal ("my blood / . . . tumbling into the ocean") or celebratory, depicting woman as volcanic force?

Wakoski's early style, of which this poem is an example, has been associated with the deep image. Give some examples of the deep image in "Blue Monday." How close are they to surrealist images?

Is the change of point of view from third person to first of any significance? The universality of the "I" in the poem may suggest the work of Walt Whitman. Is "Blue Monday" in any way comparable to sections of "Song of Myself"?

To what extent is Wakoski satirical in the stanzas referring to "Mr. Love," a businessman in a fedora?

Hummingbird Light *and* For Craig Who Leapt Off a Cliff in to Hummingbird Light *(p. 345)*

Points for Discussion and Writing

Compare and contrast "Hummingbird Light" with Jackson Mac Low's "59th Light Poem." Does Wakoski use the same formal organization?

Does she adopt something like it in the connected poem, "For Craig"?

Is the group named, mostly poets, *in* the hummingbird house? Or is it a house near the presence of hummingbirds?

The setting is magical, filled with "jewel engines." Does the comparison of Wakoski to an owl and Jerome Rothenberg to a "Jack-O-Lantern" make sense from what you know of their work? Does Wakoski's writing emanate wisdom and watchfulness and Rothenberg warm light through a scary grin?

Merlin and Lancelot are figures from Arthurian legend. Is the act of naming that the poets perform in "For Craig" comparable to the magical powers of Merlin? Is naming transformative?

Might "For Craig" have been composed as a collaboration by the poets and dinner guests?

How might the occasional nature of the paired poems, as well as Wakoski's listing of friend's names, compare to the poetry of Ted Berrigan?

"For Craig" also refers to the act of leaping off a cliff in "To Hummingbird Light," yet there is no report of such an event in the first poem. How do you explain this?

Compare and contrast "For Craig" with Anne Waldman's list poem "Makeup on Empty Space."

SUSAN HOWE ▪ ▪ ▪ ▪ ▪ ▪ ▪ ▪ ▪ ▪ ▪ ▪ ▪ ▪ ▪
b. 1937

FROM *Speeches at the Barriers*   (*p. 347*)

Points for Discussion and Writing

Speeches at the barriers of what? Of meaning?

How is "a ballad / wrapped in a ballad" comparable to "we are language   Lost / in language"? How can "we" consist of language?

How does the presence of Iseult of Ireland affect the poem?

Is "an old woman prowling / Genial telling her story" a figure for the author? Examine the meaning of the word "Genial" (capital "G") in the context of authorship.

Discuss the line "Sleet whips the page." How does it pair with "Earth of ancient ballad" and "earth as thought of the sea"?

What is the "reality" of images provoked in the mind by reading? Are they as immediate as the page? More so?

In part 2, words are "wind or web." What is the difference? Is Howe's work guided more by the wind or the web metaphor?

How are schoolboys "stemmed" in sleep?

Who or what is the "you" the narrator will "draw"?

Part 3 continues the reference to historical England. Are the houses of vision those of "tatterdemalion" revel or those of "Quiet remembered precepts"? Might they be the same?

In part 4, why is the heart "misgiving" in its charity of "all / Verisimilitude"? Is a complete "verisimilitude" possible in poetry? In what ways does language poetry, with which Howe's work is sometimes associated, attempt such a verisimilitude?

Terms and References

In Arthurian legend, **Iseult** (Isolde) was an Irish princess who married the king of Cornwall and had a love affair with his knight Tristan (Tristram).

A **wassail** is a toast or drinking festivity.

A **tatterdemalion** is a person in ragged clothing.

White Foolscap: Book of Cordelia   (*p. 351*)

Points for Discussion and Writing

Trace the references to the story of Lear (Lir) in this poem. Does the urgency of the language in parts of the poem suggest Lear's voice or consciousness?

Examine the word "Whowe" in the poem. What words are contained in it besides the name of the author?

In what way is Lear himself a "recreant"? Is poetry also recreant?

How might Lear be "nuclear (hooded)"?

Who is the "I" who will go quietly to his or her desk?

What do you make of the repeating section, beginning "I can re / trac / my steps / Iwho / crawl / between thwarts"? Why, for instance, is the "e" missing from "trace" in this passage?

Before she was a poet, Howe was an artist. Take a look at the visual design of Howe's words on the page. Does it dramatically affect her meaning?

KATHLEEN FRASER ■ ■ ■ ■ ■ ■ ■ ■ ■ ■ ■ ■ ■
b. 1937

re:searches (fragments, after Anakreon,
for Emily Dickinson)   (p. 356)

Points for Discussion and Writing

Why is the language "jittery" and "burned"? Because, like the fragments of Sappho, time has burned it to a nervous disjunction?

Discuss the stanza, "latent content / extant context" in detail. Examine the puns in the stanza, "equalibrium / (cut her name / out of every / scribble) / hymn   himnal now, equal- / lateral."

In light of the "jittery" nature of some preceding stanzas, discuss the manner of the final stanza.

Is "lyric forever error"? How can something be "embarrassingly clear" in terms of language?

TONY TOWLE ■ ■ ■ ■ ■ ■ ■ ■ ■ ■ ■ ■ ■ ■ ■ ■
b. 1939

North   (p. 360)

Points for Discussion and Writing

Is this poem directed toward a focused or specific meaning, or like John Ashbery's work, does it employ a periphrastic or roundabout rhetoric?

Does Towel put credence in "miracles of divine reaches and words spinning from infancy"?

The poetic rhetoric of the poem swirls beautifully, but around what center?

Discuss stanza 3 in some detail. What is its leading focus? In what way might that focus provide a key to the rest?

Painting the Eaves   (*p. 360*)

Points for Discussion and Writing

What do you make of the passage of time in this poem?

The poem begins with a reference to an event of light "some months ago" and ends in night and a return to "visionary gloom." To what extent is the concern of this poem not a subject matter but rather the sustenance of poetic rhetoric?

What are "wafers of solemn translation"?

How is the speaker "the author of all I see," that is, of "all the wavering lines I can think of in English"?

Random (Re-arrangeable) Study for *Views*   (*p. 361*)

Points for Discussion and Writing

How does this poem differ from the first two in Towle's selection?

The poem is dedicated to the artist Robert Rauschenberg, who made inventive use of collage, often three dimensional, in his paintings. How is the column to the right, in italics, consistent with this dedication?

Describe the colors "deep whale," "policy orange," and "literary chrome."

The title indicates random selection. Does each color to the right necessarily match with the line to the left? Is the connection altogether arbitrary? Is the column to the left also re-arrangeable?

BILL BERKSON   ▪ ▪ ▪ ▪ ▪ ▪ ▪ ▪ ▪ ▪ ▪ ▪ ▪
b. 1939

Russian New Year   (*p. 363*)

Points for Discussion and Writing

Berkson's poetry, like Towle's, is associated with the New York School. What evidence of this allegiance exists in the poems themselves?

Language poetry is noted for its attention to the fragment or part and is often discontinuous. Is that true of this work? In this context, discuss the line "The pricks incorporate all jolly in the lurch." Can such a work be discussed in terms of its "whole"?

Is the poem realistic? Or is it a colliding series of inventions? What about the realism of "when it is snowing heat remains / In the cupboard"?

How might this poem be compared to John Ashbery's "How Much Longer Will I Be Able to Inhabit the Divine Sepulcher"?

Rebecca Cutlet   (*p. 364*)

Points for Discussion and Writing

What do you make of the large number of literary references such as "language," "text," "revisionism," and "the first hundred-or-so pages"? Is Rebecca Cutlet a character in a novel?

Discuss the lines, "the tricks fade / away into indestructible charm, the least / common denominator of what you took this dive for in the first place." Is the poem's "you" its reader? How might reading be compared to taking a dive?

Is the woman hopping up and down at the end of the poem a figure of "capable imagination," as Harold Bloom writes of the Romantic poets? Or is she a parody of such a figure and such expectations? Is this same woman the mysterious Rebecca Cutlet?

Melting Milk   (*p. 365*)

Points for Discussion and Writing

To some degree, this poem has a different look and tone than the two earlier Berkson works. In what way? Is the author more in pursuit of a theme?

In what ways are the last two lines, "Ash is crystal. / Ecstasy is near," related in syntax and sound? Are ash and ecstasy comparable? In what way?

ED SANDERS ■ ■ ■ ■ ■ ■ ■ ■ ■ ■ ■ ■ ■ ■ ■ ■

b. 1939

The Cutting Prow   (*p. 366*)

Points for Discussion and Writing

Is there an "investigative" element to this work?

Sanders frequently performs the poem using homemade electronic instruments, a pair of scissors, and his own singing voice. What parts do you imagine to be sung? What parts are spoken?

Compare the text with Sanders's performance of the poem on Ron Mann's video, *Poetry in Motion*. Is the "swawk" to be spoken by Sanders or produced by instruments?

What symbolism exists in the "flashing scissors"? In the "scepter"? In the "cutting prow"? How might the cutting of scissors be compared to the prow of a boat?

What is the meaning, for an artist, to be pushed over "next to Plato's door"?

CLARK COOLIDGE ■ ■ ■ ■ ■ ■ ■ ■ ■ ■ ■ ■

b. 1939

Brill   (*p. 370*)

Points for Discussion and Writing

What means might have been used to create this work? Might it have been created intuitively, as Jackson Mac Low says of his own "intentional" poems? Or did Coolidge make use of an already existing text, which he then trimmed down to his own use?

Ask the students to choose a preexisting text unrelated to poetry and then to cross out words until only a poem remains. Does the resulting text have a lot of continuity, color, and meaning in the conventional sense? If so, ask them to do it again, isolating the pieces of the resulting mosaic with a firmer hand.

Is there any evidence that parts of Coolidge's poem were "found" elsewhere? To what extent is all poetry influenced by found materials?

Is there any evidence of lyricism in "Brill"? What about the lines "dim after him" and "his the / like darkness   past is root"?

Ask a student to read this poem out loud at a brisk pace, as if it had expressive meaning so that connections may be made as the reader improvises with the text. How does the meaning change as the poem moves to monosyllables? Does the pace of the reading increase?

As a reader, do you find yourself wanting to alter the sense of the poem's ending to a more conventional sense such as "air   when nod   no"? Has Coolidge anticipated this possibility and used the more unexpected "air   wen   hod   no" to focus attention more on the individual words?

How important is "you / get   here" as a narrative "staging device" just before the ending?

Styro   *(p. 370)*

Points for Discussion and Writing

Is this a better poem than "Brill"? What standard is to be used in comparing the two works?

Discuss in detail the opening movement: "quite is high / quatic." Why is "quatic" better than "aquatic," for instance? Do the same with "trees palling steins   ing." In this line, Coolidge uses the morpheme "ing" instead of a full word. Does it seem correct in the context?

What meaning might be expressed in the closing lines, "whom whine / it, state"? Is Coolidge interested primarily in the alliteration of "whom   whine" or is he placing emphasis on the word "whine"? If there is an emphasis, what might it be? Is it possible that "elicit of haunt," "and ever attack," and "whom   whine / it, state" comprise a comment on the nature of writing?

On Induction of the Hand   *(p. 371)*

Points for Discussion and Writing

How does this poem differ from the two preceding Coolidge works? Are any elements similar?

Ask a student to read the sentence beginning "There is a wrench that a certain staring." Now ask to hear it again. After discussing the sentence for its sound qualities, like a jazz riff, ask what thematic concerns it contains. Are words "humours"? What is the role of "edgy fondness bound useless in calm of lucidity"? Is lucidity possible in poetry? Is this poem lucid?

What is the relation between language and the world in this poem? How might the world be seen as "an evening of syntax"?

What does Coolidge mean by "A poet used the word / 'lozenge,' he didn't write it"? Isn't using the same as writing?

Discuss at length the sentence, "Writing *is* a prayer for / always it starts at the portal lockless to me at last leads / to the mystery of everything that has always been written." Did you expect Coolidge to seek the mystery of lived experience instead? In what way is writing "a prayer"?

To what extent do all poets, even narrative poets, live in the world of *text*?

What does Coolidge mean by the line, "I / would rather confess, but there's no mouth to pour toward at / the poem"?

Piero is probably Piero della Francesca, an Italian painter of the fifteenth century. What is the significance of Piero's blue being "Christless"? Who or what is the "demon" addressed in the poem?

Discuss the poem's title. Why induction of the *hand*? Does Coolidge refer to the hand in the act of writing?

The Hand Further (*p. 372*)

Points for Discussion and Writing

This poem is contained in the same collection, *Solution Passage: Poems 1978–1981* (1986), as "On Induction of the Hand," "Noon Point," and "The Crack." It is a sequel to "On Induction of the Hand"? To what degree does it share that poem's concerns?

Why does Coolidge feel that he must "stop wishing / the outer other things nearly me"? How is this concern comparable to Charles Olson's statement regarding "the getting rid of the lyrical interference of the individual as ego"?[3]

Is lyricism (music, feeling in language) possible without egoism? Or does it make egoism impossible?

What confusion between subject and object, self and nature, tends to exist in the mainstream practice of lyricism? Can you provide an example of this confusion?

Why would Coolidge state that he must "stop / washing this window out"? Is a dirty window better for the poem because it helps us realize the presence of the window?

At the poem's conclusion, what do you make of the mysterious figure of the dress "of a white all tongues are on"?

3. Charles Olson, "Projective Verse," in *Selected Writings*, p. 24.

Noon Point (*p. 372*)

Points for Discussion and Writing

Is there an apostrophe missing in the phrase "trees shake"?

How could he not know whether he wrote a poem "today"?

Why should everyone rise? To acknowledge that everything lies? Wouldn't this very agreement be a socially constructed truth?

Why is the poem called "Noon Point"?

The Crack (*p. 372*)

Points for Discussion and Writing

What is the "story" of the poem?

What distinct images occur to you as a reader? What is the process by which words become images? Would Coolidge consider his work as Imagist?

To use Coolidge's essay, "Words," found in the "Poetics" section of *Postmodern American Poetry,* do words as well as things "light and sculpt their own particular spaces"? How does one "think *around* things"?

An "ort" is a useless or discarded item, as of food. What then is an "ort bath"?

How does Coolidge's own poetry relate to his line "the lining rhyme of a lagging tongue run"?

What are "my organ selves"?

Why is the poem titled "The Crack"?

Discuss the role of sex in the poem. Is the poem confessional in this respect?

FROM *At Egypt* (*p. 373*)

Points for Discussion and Writing

This excerpt is from Coolidge's long poem included in his 1988 book of the same title. How does the length of the poem affect its organization and manner?

Why is there an extra "you" in the fourth line?

How might history be considered "a coming which was done"?

Who is the "copier" in stanza II, and what are his "styles"?

In what respect is time a "failure"?

Of what effect does the use of the third person in the occasional in-dented stanzas ("As he has said it / That it needs to") have on the poem? Is this a gloss on coolidge's authorial "I"?

The poem is based on the experience of visiting Egypt. To what extent is Egypt "painted" in language? Is there an image of that country to be found in "black bottle taxi to fire totter doorway"?

Discuss the *form* of the line, "Those gentlemen roentgens routing the rhythms."

What is meant by "I write clear to window with my elbow follow-through"?

Discuss the line "as the things sign this paper." Is "this face" the face of things, the face of the place, or Coolidge's own features "no longer man's"?

STEPHEN RODEFER ▪ ▪ ▪ ▪ ▪ ▪ ▪ ▪ ▪ ▪ ▪ ▪
b. 1940

Pretext   (*p. 376*)

Points for Discussion and Writing

These two stanzas serve as an introduction to Rodefer's book *Four Lec-tures* (1982). Likewise, "Codex" serves as an afterword to the book. What is the form Rodefer has chosen for his poem? Is it consistent from "Pretext" to "Plane Debris" to "Codex"? What are some of the formal rules?

Do you agree that "It is not the business of POETRY to be anything"?

Rodefer is associated with language poetry. What connection might language poetry poetics have to "the twelve tones of the western scale"? Why would the poet prefer "ninety" tones?

Are you able to make connections among the sentences in these two stanzas? Are connections inevitable, even for readers uninitiated to lan-guage poetry?

FROM *Plane Debris*   (p. 377)

Points for Discussion and Writing

Plane Debris is one of four long poems in *Four Lectures*. Why would Rodefer refer to them as "lectures"? Does this poem attempt to teach or persuade?

"My mind to me mangles iron" refers to the poem "My Mind to Me a Kingdom Is" by Sir Edward Dyer; see also Robert Creeley's poem "Chasing the Bird," which ends, "My mind / to me a mangle is." What other literary references do you find in Rodefer's work?

Is it true that "an error is mirror to the truth"?

Discuss the politics of the lines, "Measurement / means distance, and is political."

Discuss the sentence, "My name will be Money, / but you can call me Change." In a consumer culture such as ours, what connection exists between change (both technological and social) and money?

Rodefer writes, "Just the right hint of everything, / pushed through a sieve." How might these lines refer to a highly selective and therefore overly refined approach to writing? Discuss the issue of selectivity (how much gets "pushed through") in Rodefer's own writing.

Rodefer loves ambiguity. Ambiguity was also favored by the poets of the "New Criticism," such as John Crowe Ransom, Allen Tate, Robert Penn Warren, and others. Like those poets, is Rodefer a formalist and ironist? In what respects does his work radically differ from that of Ransom, Tate, and Warren?

Compare and contrast *Four Lectures* with the writing of Ron Silliman. To what extent to both make use of what Silliman calls the "New Sentence"?

To what extent is the art of poetry "Derivation and other particulars, / affably used"?

To what extent might the ending of stanza 3, "at the tip of the pouring dark" make use of lyric conventions? Discuss the relationship between wit and lyricism in Rodefer's work.

Codex   (p. 378)

Points for Discussion and Writing

Rodefer writes, "Lengthen the line and increasing the leading." Leading is the amount of space between lines in typography, and therefore a reference to the poem at hand. What effect does the reflexiveness of such lines have on the poem as a whole? Why would Rodefer "lay bear the device," to quote the Russian formalist Viktor Shklovsky, rather than create a unified poetic mood?

To what does "so long as you both will breathe" refer?

Is the goal of this poem "sea sounds not yet writ"?

How might language point to its content?

"Codex" contains the final stanza in *Four Lectures*. What impact does this have on the poem's closure?

ROBERT GRENIER ▪ ▪ ▪ ▪ ▪ ▪ ▪ ▪ ▪ ▪ ▪ ▪ ▪
b. 1941

Has Faded in Part but Magnificent Also Late *(p. 380)*

Points for Discussion and Writing

This poem is dedicated to RC (Robert Creeley) and refers to his poetry collection, *Mirrors* (1983). To what extent is the poem a review of Creeley's poetry?

Despite the references to Creeley's life (the "childhood / in Massachusetts" and Buffalo, where Creeley now lives), how does Grenier's poem remain independent of Creeley?

What purpose exists in underlining one word in each line? Is it to stress the word in question or to set those words apart from the rest of the text, as a poem within the poem?

Discuss Grenier's use of the IBM Selectric typewriter in making the typography of the poem an element of its meaning. How significant is the look of a poem on the page? Would the poems here selected have a different meaning if conventionally typeset? To what extent does Grenier's presentation of the poem affect your reading it out loud? Or is the presentation intended exclusively for the reader's eye?

Crow *(p. 381)*

Points for Discussion and Writing

This poem involves the "life" of a sound, a crow's *arr*. How might the poem be considered Imagist in sound?

What connection might this poem have with the writing of Larry Eigner?

Compare and contrast this poem's use of *arr, bark,* and *ark* with "Paradise" by George Herbert (1593–1633), quoted here in part:

> I blesse thee, Lord, because I G R O W
> Among thy trees, which in a R O W
> To thee both fruit and order O W.
>
> What open force, or hidden C H A R M
> Can blast my fruit, or bring me H A R M,
> While the enclosure is thine A R M?

Does Grenier's poem, like Herbert's, acknowledge the pleasure of traditional poetic and metaphysical unity? Or are both interested primarily in literary games and puzzles? Is there any comparison with the work of Harry Mathews, such as his sestina "Histoire"?

Wrath to Sadness   (*p. 382*)

Points for Discussion and Writing

Of how many sentences is the poem constructed? What effect does this delaying of sentence closure have on the poem?

The poem consists of a complex description of a woman's reaction to Grenier's (or "my") "Injury" to her. As narrative, it lacks a beginning and an ending; it is written *in medias res* (in the middle of things). Discuss how the poem moves from the indefiniteness of its beginning to the comparatively grounded certainty of its ending. How might this rhetorical strategy compare to John Ashbery's frequent use of periphrasis, or roundaboutness?

Sunday Morning   (*p. 383*)

Points for Discussion and Writing

In what respect is this poem influenced by Wallace Stevens's poem of the same title?

How does the manner of Grenier's poem change as it proceeds? Compare and contrast the first and fourth stanzas.

What is the effect of underlining words in the poem, especially in the entire last stanza?

In a letter to the editor Thomas Wentworth Higginson, Emily Dickinson wrote, "My Business is Circumference." In this poem, Grenier refers to "that incomparable master Emily Dickinson." He also writes, "each thing born inside vices / beams 'Circumference.'" How might Grenier's own business as a poet be 'Circumference'? Why is 'Circumference' born inside vice? Is Dickinson's poetry quoted in any fashion?

Compare Grenier's final underlined section with William Carlos Williams's poem "Danse Russe," which begins, "If I when my wife is sleeping / and the baby and Kathleen / are sleeping. . . ." Might Grenier's poem include "cut-ups" of Williams's poem?

Does Grenier anticipate the reader's acknowledgement of the Stevens, Dickinson, and Williams sources?

LYN HEJINIAN ▪ ▪ ▪ ▪ ▪ ▪ ▪ ▪ ▪ ▪ ▪ ▪ ▪ ▪ ▪
b. 1941

My Life

A pause, a rose, something on paper   (p. 385)

Points for Discussion and Writing

One of Hejinian's books is entitled *Writing Is an Aid to Memory*. How is writing an aid to memory in this sequence of prose poems? Is memory an aid to writing? How might it serve as a hindrance?

Are the poems in *My Life* autobiographical? Is a consistent chronology of life events followed? Might any part of the work be considered narrative?

Of what significance is the author's use of past tense? Does this lend an elegiac finality to events? Examine Hejinian's use of past and present tenses in the following: "That we sleep plunges our work into the dark. The ball was lost in a bank of myrtle. I was in a room with the particulars of which a later nostalgia might be formed, an indulged childhood."

What is the *form* of this series of poems? Is it a prose poem sequence? Or is each section the chapter of an impressionistic autobiography or memoir? Might it have been intended as "an 'oral history' on paper," as Hejinian writes in this section?

Can you conceive of *My Life* being submitted to a publisher as an experimental work of fiction? What convinces you, finally, that this is poetry rather than fiction?

Of what advantage is the fact that one sentence does not necessarily follow the next in its theme, setting, or kind of reference? Is there an overall consistency of tone despite the poem's discontinuity?

In terms of its form, compare and contrast *My Life* with the excerpt from *Tjanting* by Ron Silliman. Is Hejinian making use of what Silliman calls the "New Sentence"?

As for we who "love to be astonished" *(p. 386)*

Points for Discussion and Writing

Comment on the sentence "There is no solitude."

Is time "more normative" than place?

Is Hejinian referring to the reader when she writes, "Are your fingers in the margin"?

To whom does she refer in writing, "Their random procedures make monuments to fate"? John Cage and Jackson Mac Low? Is the word "monuments" used pejoratively?

The sentence, "There is something still surprising when the green emerges," immediately follows the above reference. Is Hejinian referring to nature as a generative force? What does this mean in the context of the reference to "random procedures"?

Like plump birds along the shore *(p. 387)*

Points for Discussion and Writing

Is Hejinian's poetry personal? What is the position of ego in this series of poems? In this context, examine sentences such as "Now I remember worrying about lockjaw."

Discuss the use of the phrase, "a pause, a rose, something on paper," also the "title" of an earlier work in the sequence. Whom does Hejinian address when she writes the sentence beginning "I want you, too, to have this experience"? Who are the "we" who "love to be astonished"? Is Hejinian herself among them? Are all poets?

The poem refers to "such suchness amid all the bourgeois memorabilia." What is the position of Hejinian's poetry to the bourgeois subject? What is Ron Silliman's? Jayne Cortez's?

Discuss the following in terms of its consciousness of social class: "Did you mean gutter or guitar. Like cabbage or collage."

Yet we insist that life is full of happy chance *(p. 389)*

Points for Discussion and Writing

Comment on the sentence, "Arts, also, are links." Is Hejinian referring to the interdisciplinary nature of the arts? Or to the fact that they link us to other experience? Why "also"? What else serves as "links"?

Comment on the sentence, "I picture an idea at the moment I come to it, our collision." Can ideas be pictured? Are they only pictured briefly, as if at the moment of collision? Hejinian seems to imply that an idea is an entity apart from the self ("I") that is then encountered like an accident on a highway.

Discuss the role of the babysitter who "would gun down everyone in the financial district."

What is meant by "a poetry of certainty"?

Hejinian writes, "Class background is not landscape." Comment on the roles of privacy and collectivity in the poem.

The author writes, "Patterns promote an outward likeness, between little white silences." Is this also true of the kind of poetry Hejinian admires? Can both a narrative and nonnarrative poetry contain "little white silences"?

MIGUEL ALGARÍN ■ ■ ■ ■ ■ ■ ■ ■ ■ ■ ■ ■
b. 1941

Tato—Reading at the Nuyorican Poets' Cafe   (p. 390)

Points for Discussion and Writing

Which language, English or Spanish, dominates in this poem? Is the poem's audience therefore primarily Hispanic?

What are the implications of the "dialogue" of languages?

To what extent does a third language consisting of song appear at the poem's end?

Is it necessary for a listener or reader to understand both languages to appreciate the poem?

How might the poem be more understandable when performed?

A rough translation of the poem's middle section, beginning "no hay que," is: "We don't have to let the little finger pass us by since we have made contact with the eyes of a little girl while I write waiting for the singer to arrive even though his voice is imprisoned, but Tato celebrates it and sweats words in his memory, teasing the rhythm, sucking (or extracting) the universal musical juice, sweating words, casting down his blackness." In this passage, the singer's voice is imprisoned; Tato's voice is liberated and vital, and Algarín's role is that of a recording scribe. Discuss these three elements—singer, poet, and scribe—within the poem.

The Spanish words "esa palabra o coro coroso" means "that word or choirsome choir." The word "coroso" also can refer to a group of acapella singers. How might a poet be considered an acapella singer? Are a poet's words the "choirsomeness" of the choir?

Terms and References

Tato refers to Tato Laviera, a "Nuyorican" poet whose books include *La Carreta Made a U-Turn* (1984) and *Enclave* (1985).

Nudo de claridad   *(p. 391)*

Points for Discussion and Writing

The title means "knots of clarity." Is a poem a "knot of clarity"? Why would Algarín prefer clarity to opacity? Are his own poems "transparent," or do they offer difficulties?

At the poem's end, Algarín calls for an art that is "pure, without lies, a knot of clarity that unties itself." How is such a poetics consistent with a performed, or spoken, poetry?

Discuss the paradox presented by a "knot" of clarity.

Like "Tato," this poem refers to the Nuyorican Poets' Cafe in New York City. Many of Algarín's poems have first been performed in front of an audience at this location. Are the poems specifically designed with this audience in mind? Are the poems necessarily limited to a Nuyorican setting? Or do they speak more universally? Discuss at the larger level what is meant by "universality" in art.

Is Algarín's use of specific time and place—the depicting of present-time events—comparable to that of other poets in the anthology?

Terms and References

El despojo is "spiritual cleansing" in Santeria religious practice.

The phrase *"sacudiendo la cabeza"* means "shaking her head."

"Un nudo que existe / en la confianza del arte, / la confiahza de un poema / que se estalla en el oído, / que inicia la palabra hablada" roughly means "a knot that exists / in the confidence of art, / the confidence of a poem / that explodes in the ear, / that gives birth to the spoken word."

San Francisco   (*p. 392*)

Points for Discussion and Writing

This poem was written on the occasion of visiting San Francisco and being in Diane di Prima's company; Loba refers to the wolf-goddess named in her poetry. What is meant by "I've rambled / through Loba's milk / back or forward to / my shuddering selves"? Why is Loba's breast described as "acid"? Might this poem have been occasioned by an LSD, or "acid," trip?

Discuss the paradox, "or its no thing / becomes a thing / to dissolve into nothing / as soon as it becomes something."

Discuss the poem's paradox of secrecy and revelation. How might complete openness amount to secrecy?

What is meant by the suggestion at the poem's end "that everything / on land goes back to water"? Is water intended as a feminine principle, a going back to beginnings? In general, discuss Algarín's homage to the feminine in this poem. How is the figure of Loba, the white wolf, employed?

TOM CLARK   ▪ ▪ ▪ ▪ ▪ ▪ ▪ ▪ ▪ ▪ ▪ ▪ ▪ ▪ ▪ ▪
b. 1941

You (I)   (*p. 394*)

Points for Discussion and Writing

The poem makes use of the erotic energy and unexpected juxtapositions of surrealist poetry and painting. (See "Terms and References" below.) Discuss Clark's use of surrealist imagery in this poem, paying particular attention to "my André Breton / dream of cutting your breasts off with a trowel." How is such imagery consistent with dreams? Are dreams truer, as the surrealists believed, than waking experience? Discuss the relationship between language and image in surrealist poetry. (See "Terms and References" below.) Is the image dominant?

Compare and contrast language poetry—the discontinuities of what Ron Silliman calls the "New Sentence"—with the montage qualities of surrealism.

How does Clark attempt to bring unity to his disparate images?

Is "You (I)" a love poem?

Terms and References

In *The First Surrealist Manifesto* (1924), André Breton quotes the poet Pierre Reverdy as follows:

> The image is a pure creation of the mind.
>
> It cannot be born from a comparison but from a juxtaposition of two more or less distant realities.
>
> The more the relationship between the two juxtaposed realities is distant and true, the stronger the image will be—the greater its emotional power and poetic reality.[4]

The emphasis for Breton and the surrealists was on the word "distant," with the result that two "realities" might be brought together with surprising effect to create a surrealist image. Breton claimed his first surrealist image to be from a dream of "a man cut in two by the window."[5] He then began applying such images and juxtapositions to language, creating a surrealist poetry essentially based in the visual concept of the collage. An even more essential model of surrealist juxaposition was provided as early as 1868 by Isidore Ducasse, when he published *Les Chants de Maldoror* under the pseudonym of the Comte de Lautréamont. In Canto Six of that novel-length prose poem, Ducasse used the expression, "He is as handsome as . . . the fortuitous encounter upon a dissecting table of a sewing-machine and an umbrella!"[6]

You (III)   (*p. 394*)

Points for Discussion and Writing

Does this poem also have surrealist qualities?

How might "a curtain / of belief" keep the author "away from the tombs / of imagery"? Is Clark making a serious statement about the connection, or lack of connection, between belief and imagery? Or is the sentence written in the spirit of surrealist automatism as a melange of available words?

Compare and contrast the tone and sense of address of this poem with "You (I)." Is Clark in search of beauty in these poems? Is the expression, "the moon / is a gland in the thigh," beautiful?

Clark is sometimes paired with the poets of the New York School. Do you see any evidence of that influence in this poem?

4. *Surrealists on Art*, ed. Lucy Lippard, Englewood Cliffs, N.J., 1970, p. 16. Originally published in *Nord-Sud* [Paris], March 1918.   5. The same, p. 17.   6. Comte de Lautréamont, *Les Chants de Maldoror*, trans. Guy Wernham, New York, 1946, p. 263.

"Like musical instruments . . ." (*p. 395*)

Points for Discussion and Writing

This poem has one image of possible surrealist influence. What is it?

Is the poem as a whole surrealist in manner or intent?

What affect does the poem's stanza form have on its pace and meaning?

Why is the lack of punctuation especially effective?

Baseball and Classicism (*p. 395*)

Points for Discussion and Writing

How might baseball be compared to the Elysian Fields? Are box scores comparable to ancient codes?

How might Clark be influenced by works like Ezra Pound's *The Cantos* in which a simultaneity of ancient and modern experience is achieved?

Terms and References

Eurydice was the wife of Orpheus, a poet whose music could move even inanimate objects. Orpheus was permitted to bring her back from the dead if he would not look at her as she followed him out of Hades. When he couldn't resist looking at her, Eurydice was forced to return to the Underworld.

Elysium, site of the **Elysian Fields**, was a happy land where it never rained or snowed. Heroes would pass to Elysium without dying and live there in perfect happiness.

Suicide with Squirtgun (*p. 396*)

Points for Discussion and Writing

Clark likes to use irony in his poetry. Is this poem ironic, or is it a serious discourse on the nature of an "art experience"? Does Clark really believe that "art is like a soft explosion"?

The poet compares the moment of "illumination" to "trying to keep a firefly's glow in a bottle without the firefly." Is art for Clark the finding of transcendence? Or is the detail of the squirtgun designed to make transcendence seem vaguely silly? Is it possible to create an art that is both silly *and* transcendent? ("Silly" was originally "seely," meaning "happy" or "blessed.")

Is finding "timeless moments" the purpose of art? Or does art speak only to the immediate moment?

How might this poem—and Clark's work in general—be compared with the work of Ron Padgett?

Society   (*p. 396*)

Points for Discussion and Writing

Once again, the seriousness of Clark's purpose is central to understanding the poem. How might the humor of this poem have a serious intent?

Joe Isuzu is an aggressively foolish salesman from a television commercial for Isuzu automobiles. How does the satirically "heroic" figure of Joe Isuzu pretending to be a river god relate to the figures of Sylvia Plath and Edith Sitwell as "ceramic cherubs"? How are all the above "Society"?

Discuss the appearance of Lord Mountbatten, a heroic figure from World War II who was killed by a terrorist bomb aboard his yacht in the late 1980s. How do the falling Mountbatten, Mickey Mouse, Marilyn Monroe, and Madame Pompadour share the same frame?

To what extent does the poem satirize the depredations of popular and consumer culture? Why the repeated references to weightlessness and spinning in midair? Have all the heroes become electronic images tumbling through the cosmic space of television? If so, what meaning does this have for the poets named?

CHARLES NORTH ▪ ▪ ▪ ▪ ▪ ▪ ▪ ▪ ▪ ▪ ▪ ▪ ▪
b. 1941

A Few Facts about Me   (*p. 397*)

Points for Discussion and Writing

The poem's title suggests that it will be factual and personal. Is it either?

What elements serve the joke of the poem, and what elements seem to be written from the heart? In this context, discuss the sentence beginning "As the captain of my fate and steerer of my star."

Is this a love poem, with its central focus the discovery of the "you" in the narrator's life?

Many abstract or poetic words such as "irrevocable," "unfathomable," and "immensities" are used, as well as a periphrastic, or roundabout, rhetoric. Of what effect is the poem's diction?

Is North correct in his evaluation that American textbooks are foreign to American life? What about his distinction between European and American emotional life?

Elizabethan & Nova Scotian Music   (p. 398)

Points for Discussion and Writing

Is it fair to ask what this poem is about?

North uses the word "periphrastic." Is the poem itself periphrastic, or roundabout, in its manner? How might this comparatively smoky style of composition, beautiful but hard to see through, be influenced by the poems of John Ashbery?

Read in sequence W. H. Auden's "In Praise of Limestone," Ashbery's "Flow Chart" excerpt included here, and this poem. How does the poem make use of its literariness and high tone? Does it break with that tone for effect?

The poem consists of two sentences. Trace the logic of the second sentence to its closure in the rhyming couplet (fickleness / gentleness). To what extent does North mock the noble tone of Elizabethan poetry and to what extent does he honor that tradition?

A Note to Tony Towle (After WS)

Points for Discussion and Writing

Read this poem in conjunction with Wallace Stevens's "The Snow Man," which begins, "One must have a mind of winter / To regard the frost and the boughs." Does parody necessarily poke fun at the poem being parodied?

Compare and contrast this poem with Kenneth Koch's "Variations on a Theme by William Carlos Williams."

Discuss North's statement that "deracination is fast qualifying as essence / rather than attribute." "Deracination" means to pull out by the roots or dislocate. Does the rest of the poem comment on deracination?

Is there any particular reason for using the sonnet form besides the compression that its brevity lends? What other formal usages are apparent? How might the fact that the poem employs only one sentence be particularly appropriate for the poem's manner and brevity?

What does this work have in common with the poetry of Tom Clark?

RON PADGETT ■ ■ ■ ■ ■ ■ ■ ■ ■ ■ ■ ■ ■ ■ ■
b. 1942

Wonderful Things   *(p. 399)*

Points for Discussion and Writing

Why does Padgett use the word "are" in "Anne, who are dead"? Is this poem an elegy? If so, how do you explain the humorous tone of "Seriously I have this mental (smuh!) illness"?

Follow the poem's changes in tone. Despite the movement from hilariousness to seriousness, do you feel that "wonderful things" have been communicated?

Discuss the several references to birds, including God's "chirping and chuckling." Is there a thematic purpose to them?

Is the purpose of poetry to "tell you wonderful things"?

The Latin poet Horace wrote that the purpose of poetry is to delight and instruct. Does Padgett's poem have an instructive, or moral, intent?

How do you account for the reference to *"buveur de l'opium chaste et doux"* ("eater of opium chaste and sweet")?

Terms and References

Anne probably refers to Anne Kepler, described in Ted Berrigan's poem "People Who Died" as "my girl . . . killed by smoking-poisoning while playing the flute at the Yonkers Hospital during a fire set by a 16 year old arsonist . . . 1965."

Nothing in That Drawer   *(p. 401)*

Points for Discussion and Writing

The Dada artist Marcel Duchamp once exhibited a store-bought snow-shovel (albeit a Parisian one) as a work of art entitled *In Advance of the Broken Arm*. This is also the title of a poem by Padgett that is included in *Great Balls of Fire* (1969). How might "Nothing in That Drawer" have been inspired by Dada? (See "Terms and References," page 7.)

Wallace Stevens once defined poetry as "that which suffices." In your opinion, does Padgett's poem suffice? In what respect does the poem challenge one's assumptions about poetry?

There are fourteen lines in the poem. Does this make it a sonnet? What kind of rhyme does it employ?

Might this work be staged as performance art?

Ask one of the students to read the poem out loud. Should the reader's inflection change from line to line? Are some lines *more meaningful* than others?

Why is "Nothing in That Drawer" better than "something in that drawer"?

Falling in Love in Spain or Mexico   (*p. 401*)

Points for Discussion and Writing

The poem appears in the form of a very short one-act play. Does it lend itself to performance? Ask two students in the class to perform it.

How might Padgett have arrived at the concept for this poem? By reading a Spanish-English travel guide?

Besides being a "play," what formal characteristics does the poem have? Except for the fact that Padgett has included it in a book of poetry, how can it be considered a poem at all? Does a work take on the status of art simply because the artist *says* it is art?

Is there a narrative development within José's series of statements and comments? If so, what is it?

To what is the Girl saying "Yes!"?

Big Bluejay Composition   (*p. 402*)

Points for Discussion and Writing

What method of composition might have been used in writing this poem?

Compare and contrast this poem with Ted Berrigan's long poem "Bean Spasms" and Paul Blackburn's "Brooklyn Narcissus."

Of what influence are other media—film, television, and cartoon—on the poem?

Other poets in the anthology such as Charles Olson are critical of the role of popular culture and mass media. What is Padgett's attitude toward them? Are they to be feared or a natural part of his field of reference?

What is meant by "to leon the counterpoint"?

Much of the poem is light in manner. Does it become deep or cosmic at any point?

What is Padgett's position on lyricism and other traditional modes?

What do you make of lines like "and I go walkie to nightmare school" and "into which many doggies fell / plunged fiery and screaming / in their machines"?

How is this poem comparable to Padgett's "Wonderful Things"?

Is Padgett's poetry comparable in any way to the work of Kenneth Koch? How?

Who and Each   (*p. 407*)

Points for Discussion and Writing

Look up the word "which" in the *Oxford English Dictionary*. Is Padgett's research correct? Is this, then, primarily a found poem?

The mood is comic throughout much of the work, and the poem's speaker comes off as a somewhat scholarly stand-up comedian. At what point does the mood shift? Does your view of the speaker change, too?

As with the work of Tom Clark and Charles North immediately preceding Padgett's section, discuss the mysterious relationship between high comedy and high seriousness.

ANN LAUTERBACH   ▪ ▪ ▪ ▪ ▪ ▪ ▪ ▪ ▪ ▪ ▪
b. 1942

Mimetic   (*p. 408*)

Points for Discussion and Writing

Compare the last line of the first stanza, "But is the sea a film of the sea, ageless?" with Wallace Stevens's "The Idea of Order at Key West." Is the "you" who is "recumbent against any mirror" also a figure of the singer or maker?

What effect does the reference to painting "your toenails Car Hop Pink" have on the tone of the poem, especially as established by the first stanza?

In her use of Pavese's statement, is Lauterbach suggesting that "sentiment, in art," is inaccurate?

Who is the "she" of the lines "For us, she / Is world, enduring, veracity of was / Being what is"?

If the world fails to reflect itself, is it the fault of language, the poet, or the world? Or is this reflection the forcing of "self" on the world?

Terms and References

Pavese refers to Cesar Pavese, an Italian modernist poet of great importance.

Platonic Subject   (*p. 409*)

Points for Discussion and Writing

What does this poem have in common with "Mimetic"?

Of what importance to the poem is Plato's allegory of the cave?

Discuss the word "here" in the line, "But here is a twig in the form of a wishbone." In what way is the twig "here" in language?

Why is the "I" of the poem aroused by the object of the twig?

Discuss the relationship between the real and the ideal in this poem. Does the final phrase, "and I have a twig," clarify or further complicate the twig's status as a phenomenon?

Here and There   (*p. 409*)

Points for Discussion and Writing

The second section begins with the words, "We almost escape narration." Is narration something Lauterbach's poems usually escape?

How is this poem different from "Mimetic" and "Platonic Subject"?

Is this a personal poem?

Where are "here" and "there"?

In what respects might winter be characterized by "androgyny"? Is the gray of winter an androgyny of color?

Clamor   (*p. 410*)

Points for Discussion and Writing

Does the line "Was this enough to go on, this scrap?" comment on the progress of the poem's own composition? How else is the opening stanza critical of past procedures and positions?

With what are "the old days" associated?

How might it be insufficient to "be magical" as a poet?

How might the charted lists of "the old days" reduce to a single key or unity that will unlock all the codes?

Part 2 focuses on "ruptured attention." The "nerves stray from precision, announcing / Their stunned subject." What does this fraying of attention have to do with affection's being merciless?

The poem invokes the spirits of the dead—he and she, perhaps mother and father. Is the "clamor" that of history, the voices calling out of time? Is the loss of the past a reason not "to count the days"?

Boy Sleeping   (p. 411)

Points for Discussion and Writing

The poem's central figure is a sleeping boy, over whom the forces of memory, the passage of time, and language contend. Of what importance is the terrorist riding a train "at the center of discourse" at the poem's end? Does the train represent the poem?

Lauterbach writes, "I remember when a word / First advanced like a dart at a target, / A star creasing the sky, a lie / Told to save the situation while damning it." Is she critical of a change in cultural or aesthetic decorum? If so, what had the decorum been?

What connection exists in the poem between the abstract and the particular?

When Lauterbach writes, "The precedent of the real mocks us. / Rain spills uncontrollably from above like a test," does she refer to the embattled views of discourse that is postmodern criticism? Or are these lines neoplatonic, questioning the reality of experience, especially in connection with its representation in art?

Who is the person the sleeping boy must escape? Is she "The dead woman" in his face?

Discuss in detail the lines, "Can we follow these new waters / Or are we already too fond, our agility mired / In the scripted river rushing under the bridge." How is the river *scripted*?

WILLIAM CORBETT ■ ■ ■ ■ ■ ■ ■ ■ ■ ■ ■ ■

b. 1942

Vermont Apollinaire   *(p. 413)*

Points for Discussion and Writing

Corbett lives in Boston and spends his summers in Vermont. This poem begins in Vermont ("a crane stands at the stream's mouth") and changes its setting at summer's end to the city. Do the poet's perceptions and language change also?

One of Corbett's books was entitled *City Nature*. How is the paradox of city and nature expressed in this poem?

Is it true, as Corbett writes, that he "cannot carry a tune / Not in a bucket one note"?

Look carefully at the poem's change in music and intensity of expression from stanza 2 to stanza 3. How might the sound of the third stanza be compared with Schuyler's poetry?

Apollinaire refers to Guillaume Apollinaire, the French poet who died in 1918. Does Corbett's manner or interests as a poet resemble those of Apollinaire?

Wickson Plums   *(p. 414)*

Points for Discussion and Writing

Corbett's poems have strong painterly qualities. What painter's work does this poem resemble?

What do this poem and "Cold Lunch" have in common with the work of William Carlos Williams?

What is the effect of not using a comma after "plums" in the first line?

What rhymes does the poet employ?

What means besides precision of observation and short lines does Corbett use to build intensity of expression?

Cold Lunch   *(p. 415)*

Points for Discussion and Writing

As with the previous poem, examine the forms Corbett uses, especially rhyme and assonance: back/clapboard, arrows/brows, beat/feeding, and so on. Does Corbett think in images or in syllables?

Discuss in detail the following passages: "Prudence Dearth / wife of Roderick / stone in Peacham" and "Wind / sets weeds dithering / holds thrush in / piney dark wood / where its song is thin." What is the effect of all the short "i" sounds in the second passage? Where might Corbett have come across the names in the first passage?

After reading the poem out loud and discussing it, ask the class if they can remember its "story." Why might it be difficult to remember? Because its music dominates its narration?

Discuss the relationship between things and language in Corbett's work. How are his poetics, as implied in his poetry, different from those of the language poets? What position does language poetry hold with regard to the subject? What is Corbett's position?

TOM MANDEL ▪ ▪ ▪ ▪ ▪ ▪ ▪ ▪ ▪ ▪ ▪ ▪ ▪ ▪ ▪
b. 1942

Say Ja   (*p. 416*)

Points for Discussion and Writing

What does "Ja" mean in the title? "Yes" in German?

Is it possible to ask what this poem is about? Or is it (as is consistent with language poetry) an ongoing process of composition?

Discuss the degree to which the poem is self-expressive in such lines as "I / wanted the stars overt / and most everything that runs / downhill I wanted to fill / his hand."

How might this poem be compared to Clark Coolidge's "On Induction of the Hand"?

Is this poem written "on location"? How do you explain the proliferation of tropical references? Does the poem consist of the "heat of fantasy"?

Realism   (*p. 418*)

Points for Discussion and Writing

How might this poem argue against the concept of literary realism that language can put its mirror to reality?

Is the "giant" a form of ego, made too large by the presumption that it can practice all it comprehends? Or is Mandel arguing for the burning and incontrovertible realism of "bush, facade, horizon"?

How can recognition dissolve an object?

What is the "transparent monolith" that becomes "opacified"? The window? The language?

Discuss in detail the following: "The limits of the world leak in from its edges, pervade. Thus did he take up the sentence and play it for all he was worth. But what was it worth? The context commands." What value is placed on "the sentence" in the lines quoted? Do sentences have value, or worth? How might "The limits of the world leak in from its edges"?

Jews in Hell   (p. 419)

Points for Discussion and Writing

Why is the poem so titled?

Mandel is Jewish and a student of Jewish thought. Does this poem begin with an assembly of Jews viewed at the gates of Hell? How might such a juxtaposition offer a cultural comment on the status of Jews in a predominantly Christian society?

Are they the "we" of the poem? Who then is the "you" of "You are many, well-organized, and in control of the flow of supplies"?

Is Mandel referring to the marginal position of Jews in history? Is the Holocaust implied by the poem in "we migrate from meeting to meeting in a mutual plan to die"?

Of what importance is the reference to "The spiritual in art," which "finds the door closed tight from the inside and so freezes where it can"? Is this the door to the gas chamber? To history or cultural inclusion?

Is Mandel taking the position, to paraphrase Theodor Adorno, that poetry is impossible after Auschwitz? What is the role of words in such an environment?

MICHAEL PALMER ・・・・・・・・・・・・・
b. 1943

Notes for Echo Lake   3   (*p. 421*)

Points for Discussion and Writing

This poem alternates verse and prose. Do they behave differently, as one might expect?

Comment on the poem's conclusion, "In the poem he learns to turn and turn, and prose seems always a sentence long."

How might the compression of poetry cause it to last longer than prose? Words, however, "come in smoke and go." This suggests the impermanence of language rather than its monumentality. Is this a positive or negative value in the poem?

Who is the "he" of the poem, who, like Palmer, "loved the French poets"? Is it the same as "I," with "a voice that emptied . . . that one with broken back"? Does the "he" fall through the partly open door and the "I" receive the injury? What is the importance of the "he" instructing the "I" on when to talk?

Examine the lyricism of "While April is ours and dark" and the symbolism of "as something always stands for what is."

The prose sections contain different kinds of prose: reminiscence, diary entry, quotation, the dream of four-bearded men, lists of flowers. In this connection, compare John Ashbery's "Variations, Calypso and Fugue on a Theme of Ella Wheeler Wilcox" (in *The Double Dream of Spring*, 1970) despite its great difference in tone.

How do words invent "the letters of the voyage"? What connection exists in the poem between letters, words, and things?

Notes for Echo Lake   5   (*p. 423*)

Points for Discussion and Writing

This poem is entirely in prose. In reading the poem out loud, does it *sound* like poetry?

Scan the first section of the poem for its poetic measure. What is the measure of "a box of marbles in a marble box"?

What roles do figures such as "the interpreter of a cough" and "the inventor of the code" have in the poem? Is the poem which "moves back and forth" connected to "the interpreter of leaves" mentioned in the same section?

Discuss with the class Plato's view of poetry as expressed in *The Republic*. How might this poem embody a Platonic view?

Compare "the empty sleeve waving" in section IV with the sea "waving its empty sleeves" in Wallace Stevens' "The Idea of Order at Key West." Is the poetry of Stevens an influence on Palmer's work in other respects? How?

Who are they who "speak in tongues, correcting the right notes in order to get them wrong"?

How might this poem be considered language poetry? Could you mount an equally convincing argument that it is not?

The Project of Linear Inquiry   (*p. 424*)

Points for Discussion and Writing

From what kind of discourse is the first line taken? How might it compare with Wallace Stevens's opening lines in "Connoisseur of Chaos"?

In the language of syllogisms, statements *a* and *b* usually lead to a conclusion, *c*. Identify in turn *a*, *b*, and *c* in Palmer's poem. Is there a logical or poetic connection among them? Do the first two necessarily lead to the third? How might this "syllogism" relate to a project of "linear inquiry"?

How might the things placed on the table (pomegranates, salt, pepper, books and schedules) share "the same error / and measure of inattention"?

Is the project referred to simply of "seeing things, / so to speak, or things seen"? How does one see things "so to speak"?

How might the woman's speech ("What she says rolls forward.") relate to the project of linear inquiry?

In postmodern poetics, what is the position of the "linear"? How accurate is the word "linear" when it comes to any body of writing? Even the most deliberate of narratives is selective in its use of time. Does most writing consist therefore of a series of broken lines? How much of the "line" of a narrative exists in the transition, or silence, between developments? In discussing this issue, refer back to Lyn Hejinian's "My Life" and related works. To what degree does the occasion of autobiography in Hejinian's work offer an implicit linearity? How "linear," is Frank O'Hara's seemingly narrative poem beginning, "The eager note on my door said 'Call me'"?

Voice and Address   (*p. 426*)

Points for Discussion and Writing

How might one "own" a thought? Moreover, the "you" owns "one complete thought." Might the completeness of this one thought be implicated in ideology? If so, which one?

What is meant by "You are the keeper of one secret thought / the rose and its thorn no longer stand for"? Might Palmer refer here to old-fashioned poetic symbolism of the rose and thorn variety?

Why is "exaggerated music" associated with the experience of "one complete thought"?

How do you explain the poem's metaphors of imprisonment and escape?

What are the "ruins of that place" from which "words as things" arrive?

The poem contains the paradoxes of "studied inattention" and "priapic doubt." What role do they play?

Why is the poem titled "Voice and Address"?

Why are the listeners in the poem "expendable"?

Fifth Prose   (*p. 427*)

Points for Discussion and Writing

What meaning does "I'm writing about the snow not the sentence" have for the poem as a whole? Is Palmer's focus as a poet on the world (snow) or on language (sentence)? Is it the particular interplay of the two that make his work distinctive?

Is it possible to find the poem's center thematically? Might it have to do with the tensions between statue and shadow, razor and fact, and "seeing swimmer and seeing rock"?

What do you make of the poem's circus details beginning with the line "Hassan the Arab and his wife"?

What is "this dialect" to which the poem refers?

RAY DiPALMA ■ ■ ■ ■ ■ ■ ■ ■ ■ ■ ■ ■ ■ ■ ■
b. 1943

[Rumor's rooster]   (*p. 429*)

Points for Discussion and Writing

How might DiPalma's poem be guided by "the strange low / coherences of the ear"?

How is it possible for the thought to walk "when and where there / is no such thing"?

Compare the playful use of analogy and identity ("my A is a vegetable A") with Michael Palmer's "The Project of Linear Inquiry."

[Each moment is surrounded]   (*p. 429*)

Points for Discussion and Writing

Discuss the reference to "the baggy scholar gentry." Is DiPalma questioning his own position in reviling them? What *is* the relationship in general between avant-garde poetry, Bohemianism, and "the baggy scholar gentry"? Might DiPalma be a member of the scholar gentry himself?

Christ fed the multitudes by dividing the loaves and fishes. How can this be compared to the scholar's "sincerities" that "come like the loaves and fishes"?

[A pink maniac]   (*p. 430*)

Points for Discussion and Writing

Unlike the first two poems in DiPalma's section, this one focuses throughout on one subject, the pink maniac and "his bush of violets." Is the pink maniac also "the Orpheus gnome"?

Orpheus is a lyric poet in Greek mythology. The bush of violets may be a figure of imagination. However, it "awakens the pastoral highlands / with a recondite symmetry" and is "a safe and casual elsewhere." Is the pink maniac symbolic of a certain kind of poet? If so, what kind?

[Memory's wedge]   (*p. 431*)

Points for Discussion and Writing

This poem begins with a comment on the effect of memory, how it creates a valley that "tilts the letters" in a certain direction. Does DiPalma desire a poetry free of memory? What are the advantages and disadvantages of a reliance on memory in the writing of poetry? Was the Romantic poet William Wordsworth correct that poetry is "emotion recollected in tranquillity"? Was T. S. Eliot correct in his essay "Tradition and the Individual Talent" when he claimed that poetry "is neither emotion, nor recollection, nor, without distortion of meaning, tranquillity"?[7]

In the second stanza, the "I" turns to a consideration of what "measure" it would make. Does reliance on memory necessarily result in a "selection cut from stone"? Does it inevitably result in "an old measure"?

Is the wedge of memory, which results in clearly defined structures, consistent throughout? What do you make of the last two stanzas?

The lines "the stop for / breath" may also refer to poetry. What meaning might this have for the poem as a whole?

Rebus Tact   (*p. 432*)

Points for Discussion and Writing

A rebus is a riddle composed of words or syllables depicted by symbols that depict the sounds of the words they represent. How might this be seen as a metaphor for poetry?

Does DiPalma give a direction or focus to the rebus reference in the poem itself?

What is "sound grief"?

How might the lines, "Its traditional imagery fills up / With unfamiliar shadows if properly abstract," refer to poetry?

Who are the "farm lads and professors"? Might this be a reference to university creative writing programs, many of which are removed from urban centers?

Of what importance are the lines, "In the cavern you understand how / A shadow works because you've brought your own light"? Might the lines refer to Plato's allegory of the cave in which the human per-

7. T. S. Eliot, "Tradition and the Individual Talent," in *Selected Essays of T. S. Eliot,* New York, 1950, p. 10.

ception of reality is compared to the shadows cast on the wall of a cave by a fire within the cave? In bringing his own light, how does DiPalma challenge Plato's allegory?

MAUREEN OWEN ▪ ▪ ▪ ▪ ▪ ▪ ▪ ▪ ▪ ▪ ▪ ▪ ▪
b. 1943

All That Glitters . . . .   (p. 433)

Points for Discussion and Writing

Kyran is Owen's son. The title refers to the saying, "All that glitters is not gold." Do these facts have any resonance in the poem itself?

Owen writes somewhat out of the daily occasion and is associated with the New York School. Is she completely bound to the present tense occasion?

Discuss the poem's feminism. What affect does the presence of the male baby ("he's a Trolley") have on the statement that she is born "of and through women alone"?

Given the growing importance of her feminist theme, why does Owen turn her attention to other matters, such as Tu Fu and Schubert?

for Emily (Dickinson)   (p. 434)

Points for Discussion and Writing

Discuss Owen's characteristic use of the poetic line. What are the advantages of arranging the poem as she does on the page?

Discuss also her spirited use of capitalization, exclamation, and apostrophe ("O furious Excesses!"). How is the poet's temperament a factor in her poems? Is the author's own temperament necessarily an indication of the mood of her poems?

Owen focuses with great clarity on the actual; we trust the reality of the world she depicts. Does this make her a realist?

Contrast this poem with "Rumor's rooster" by Ray DiPalma. Is Owen's poem easier to understand? Does that make Owen a better poet or simply a different one? DiPalma's poem might be described by a student as more abstract. Does Owen's poem have abstract qualities as well?

African Sunday   (*p. 435*)

Points for Discussion and Writing

Discuss the poem's first lines, "Fuck I want to be bound by devotion! Tortured / by passion!" in terms of the poem's feminist theme. Are these lines necessarily inconsistent with feminism?

Why is D. H. Lawrence an appropriate literary reference in this poem?

Of what importance is the fact that "my deepest Jesuit," a man, authoritatively huffs an opinion about the flight of St. Teresa?

PAUL VIOLI ■ ■ ■ ■ ■ ■ ■ ■ ■ ■ ■ ■ ■ ■ ■ ■ ■
b. 1944

Index   (*p. 436*)

Points for Discussion and Writing

The poem is obviously an index. What is learned about Sutej Hudney in the course of reading the index?

What is the first "narrative" development of importance in the poem?

How might this poem be compared with the fiction of Nabokov, particularly his novel *Pale Fire*?

What kind of artist was Hudney?

How many pages do Hudney's last words occupy?

Violi is associated with the New York School. Which poet of the New York School's so-called first generation (Ashbery, O'Hara, Schuyler, Guest, Koch, Mathews, Elmslie) does Violi's work most resemble?

Rifacimento   (*p. 437*)

Points for Discussion and Writing

"Rifacimento" means a remaking or recasting, especially of literary or musical works. How might that apply to this poem?

The poem offers a series of imagined definitions of individual words. Are these words unusual, or is their meaning generally known?

Each of the definitions works as a joke. Might a poetry consist primarily of jokes? How is this true of some work by Kenneth Koch and Ron Padgett, particularly Padgett's "Nothing in that Drawer"?

Discuss irony as a poetic mode. Does this poem ever break from the ironic mode into meditation or lyric? Is it daring not to?

The creative writing instructor may want to give the class an exercise based on this model; for instance, what do you imagine the meaning of "ousel" or "out sister" to be?

Violi's poem, "Index," can be said to have a beginning, middle, and end of sorts. Does this poem have a beginning, middle, and end?

When to Slap a Woman   (p. 438)

Points for Discussion and Reference

Can this poem be attacked on feminist grounds? As a reader, were you suspicious of it as soon as you read the title? Is the poem, in fact, sexist?

What if the title had been "Loose-strife" instead? Would it have been more beautiful? Or is it more beautiful as it is? In more general terms, is "beauty" a word that applies to the judgment of poetry?

Violi is obviously capable of sustaining a serious poetic mood. Why would he refuse this mood in some of his poetry?

Is there a moral urgency to Violi's poetry, as is often seen in satire? Or is the risk of his project irony for irony's sake?

MICHAEL DAVIDSON   ■ ■ ■ ■ ■ ■ ■ ■ ■ ■ ■
b. 1944

Et in Leucadia Ego   (p. 439)

Points for Discussion and Writing

The title of this poem has a complicated history. It is based on Poussin's painting "The Arcadian Shepherds" in which four shepherds are studying the inscription "Et in Arcadia Ego" ("I too lived in Arcadia") on a gravestone. At the time of writing the poem, Davidson was living in Leucadia, California, a town famous for surfing near San Diego. The overheard speech is of Leucadian surfers. Ask students to discuss the poem before you reveal this information. Then ask them to read and discuss it a second time. To what extent is Davidson's original intention made clear by the text? Are the students' first readings just as legitimate as their second readings?

Davidson has been associated with language poetry. Is this a language poem?

What are the formal constraints under which the poem operates?

Is each of the poem's sections to be read like Allen Ginsberg's "strophes," in one long breath? What pace of reading is suggested by the lack of punctuation?

Does the same person speak throughout the poem or do the speakers change?

What level of diction has Davidson chosen?

Does the poem have a beginning, middle, and end? Or does the poem consist primarily of its development of the author's chosen concept?

The Form of Chiasmus; The Chiasmus of Forms
(*p. 440*)

Points for Discussion and Writing

"Chiasmus" is a literary term indicating a balancing pattern in verse or prose in which the main elements are reversed. *A Dictionary of Literary Terms* by J. A. Cuddon offers the following example from Shakespeare's Sonnet CLIV: "Love's fire heats water, water cools not love." Outside of the title, is chiasmus evident in the poem?

The poet writes, "It is the season of electricity." Is this an attempt to actually set the poem in a season? Is there a consistent point of view or sense of situational development? Why or why not?

Does a narrative or thematic locus develop in the poem? What about the ending of section II, beginning: "They went west seeking not to be at home"?

Discuss the importance of the poem's last sentence: "Welcome to Darkness, you must be tired." With its implications of death and descent into Hell, is this sentence appropriately placed at the poem's end to provide closure?

Thinking the Alps   (*p. 440*)

Points for Discussion and Writing

Why is the name "Bob" in quotes? How does this affect your sense of "his" reality?

How might this poem echo or parody Wordsworth's poetry—for example, "Resolution and Independence"?

Likewise, how might it parody Robert Lowell's "Beyond the Alps," the first poem in his collection *Life Studies* (1959)?

Why is "Bob's" burro named Melancholy?

What is the nature of Davidson's critique of capital and the Industrial Revolution? How does "Bob's" stirring of campfire coals "to become an ad for coffee" mean? Does Davidson intend to implicate the poetry of Wordsworth or Lowell in commodity capitalism and ownership? From what you know of their work, is it possible to do so?

What is the importance of the mirrors in the next-to-last stanza? Is Davidson offering a reaffirmation of Olson's statement in the essay "Projective Verse," "getting rid of the lyrical interference of the individual as ego"? In this connection, look at the next-to-last stanza of Lowell's "Beyond the Alps," which contains the lines, "the blear-eyed ego kicking in my berth."

What do you imagine Davidson's position to be with regard to English Romantic poetry and its legacy?

MARJORIE WELISH ■ ■ ■ ■ ■ ■ ■ ■ ■ ■ ■ ■
b. 1944

Respected, Feared, and Somehow Loved   (p. 443)

Points for Discussion and Writing

A vitrine is a glass case for displaying art objects. Why is it associated with "sins" at the poem's end?

What is respected, loved, and feared in the poem? Art? The gods?

Why must we fix our compass? Have we lost our direction?

There is much reference to the activities of the gods. On two occasions, the gods waver. What is the poem's theology? What does the "instrumentality" of words have to do with the "plea-bargaining" in heaven?

In the context of the poem's cosmic references, what is the role of the line, "Please send for our complete catalogue"? Is this at odds with the poem's elegiac tone? Is the poem, in fact, elegiac?

Veil   (p. 443)

Points for Discussion and Writing

Has someone died? (The first line reads, "An enchanted frame assures the image of a loved one.")

As metaphysics, the poem's last stanza is somewhat more pointed than the rest: "If there is a pattern / of stars beyond the starstruck blue, it spells desire." Discuss these lines in detail, especially regarding the human desire for larger meaning. Are there patterns in the stars? How might they spell desire?

Who is the "you" who is "not even among them [the stars] in question form"? Is "you" the person who has died? Once dead, is a person lost from the pattern of desire?

Within This Book, Called Marguerite   (*p. 444*)

Points for Discussion and Writing

Who are those who are "cunningly blent / to suggest a consensus"? Americans?

Is each sense of history "mutually exclusive"?

Is Welish speaking to herself as a poet when she writes, "I wonder if the mind will ever stop pursuing / rival minds or at least rival murmuring"?

The third section alters the poem's discourse by referring to David Rowland's industrial award. Since Welish is an art critic, she becomes identified as the "I" of the poem. Who then is the "you" of the poem's last two sections?

Skin   (*p. 444*)

Points for Discussion and Writing

Why is the poem so titled? Is its subject really skin?

What is meant by "Our skin, strenuously tutored to appreciate the vernacular / body a feeling might have"? What further references to skin exist in the poem?

What is the importance of the two references to pink? Why is black into pink "devastating"?

What is the "postwar victory" to which Welish refers? Is Welish speaking of the post-Vietnam experience? Why is it a "victory" if the postwar lamplight is "harsher, categorical"?

Ask students to paraphrase Welish's critique of American culture. Why is the spirit "flayed and forbidden / to talk about itself"? In this context, what is meant by "beautiful early work propped against an uphill sea"? Does "beautiful early work" refer to skin or to an aspect of American history and/or landscape?

Welish uses the word *écorché*, meaning "skinned," to suggest that the "American pavilion" has been skinned back or flayed, revealing its internal reality. What is that reality? Discuss further how the word *écorché* relates to the poem's title and themes.

Terms and References

According to *Looking at Prints, Drawings, and Watercolors* by Paul Goldman, the French term *écorché* means "skinned." Goldman writes, "From the Renaissance onwards artists frequently drew studies from clay or plaster figurines representing the human body with the skin removed to show the muscles. The term '*écorché*' is applied both to the figurine and to the drawing made from it."[8]

Crossing Disappearing Behind Them   (*p. 445*)

Points for Discussion and Writing

How are this poem and "Skin" different from the other poems in Welish's section?

The poem describes and meditates on a street scene where strangers pass circumstantially. This creates "their pretty accident." To what extent does this poem treat the theme of circumstantiality?

Does this poem contain more than one reality? What do you make of the different kinds of shadows and rain in the poem?

The first six stanzas comprise one movement of the poem. The seventh stanza, beginning "And on the fortieth day" comprises a commentary on having written the earlier stanzas: "and I saw myself / stepping onto a movie set of rain imitating rain, / a central fiction." Likewise, "the ruin has memorized the ruin." How might this mirroring and theme of replication relate to the line, "This application is lengthy / and comes with two interleaved carbons"?

What is the condition of being "minor" in this poem?

Who is "he who is truly original"? God?

What effect does the rain have on the poem's "many heads" early and late? Does the rain become more original? Do the people?

8. London, 1988, p. 26.

LORENZO THOMAS ▪ ▪ ▪ ▪ ▪ ▪ ▪ ▪ ▪ ▪ ▪ ▪

b. 1944

The Marvelous Land of Indefinitions   *(p. 447)*

Points for Discussion and Writing

Is poetry "FULL OF LIES" or is Thomas being ironic?

Is poetry everyone's business or is it an activity primarily of the white middle class? Is poetry any different in this respect from any of the other arts?

Is the avant-garde implicated in Thomas's lines, "Everyone else is a part of the problem / And we're in the 'in' crowd"?

What is "the 51st State" to which the poem refers? Does it consist of the people at the poetry reading where Thomas now speaks?

Is this a scathingly honest poem, or is it just another bourgeois art product in its own right?

A language poet might argue that the language and form of Thomas's poem bear the stain of ruling class hegemony. How might Thomas respond to such a charge?

Is there a necessary connection between a poet's social group and his or her *kind* of poetry? Do poets of privileged circumstances tend to be committed to the oral tradition in letters? Or are they on the whole more devoted to the written word? Do working-class poets, or those from the culture of poverty, tend to be committed to deconstructive theories of language? Can you tell a poet's social class, religion, and ethnicity by reading his or her poems? Is this a poem of the oral tradition?

Instructions for Your New Osiris   *(p. 450)*

Points for Discussion and Writing

In what respect is Thomas himself "your new Osiris"? To whom does "your" refer: the reader or the woman who left him?

To what does "the full name on the door" refer?

What is the importance of the line, "The day my best friend laughed dead in my face"?

Terms and References

A **Canopic vase or jar** is one with a top in the form of a human head. It was used in ancient Egypt to hold the viscera of embalmed bodies.

In Egyptian mythology, **Osiris** was the god of the Underworld.

ANNE WALDMAN ▪ ▪ ▪ ▪ ▪ ▪ ▪ ▪ ▪ ▪ ▪ ▪ ▪ ▪
b. 1945

Makeup on Empty Space   (*p. 452*)

Points for Discussion and Writing

What formal constraints does Waldman use in this poem? How might her work compare in this respect with that of Allen Ginsberg and Jerome Rothenberg?

How does Waldman advance and retard the poem through the use of repetition?

The poem has often been performed in front of an audience. What elements in the poem lend themselves to being spoken out loud?

Why are the offerings made to empty space? Is it to be worshipped?

Why would the "I" of the poem "wish to venture into a not chiseled place"? Is poetry generally a "chiseled place"? Is this poem?

Discuss the poem's feminist details. Why is the feminine deity bound with briar and other things? Must she be restrained?

How does the information provided below about Vajrayogini, the quintessential female deity principle of Buddhism, affect your reading of the poem? Is putting makeup on empty space comparable to summoning the spirit of Vajrayogini? To what extent might Waldman herself, and by analogy, any female poet, compare to the figure of Vajrayogini?

Terms and References

In Hindu mythology, *amrita* is the ambrosia of immortality.

The female figure to which this poem refers is **Vajrayogini**, the quintessential Buddhist female deity principle visualized to "bring up energies." Vajrayogini is often depicted wearing a necklace of skull bones and holding one leg in the air in the act of stomping on the corpse of ego. Thus she adorns the phenomenal world at the same time as she dissolves this adornment.

Berthe Morisot (*p. 455*)

Points for Discussion and Writing

How does this poem differ from Waldman's other work in this selection?

In what respect might Waldman identify with Morisot? Has she too worked for most of her career in a male-dominated art form?

What claims does the poem make for the feminine? For the woman artist as lunatic?

Terms and References

Berthe Morisot (1841–1895) and her sister Edma were the first women to be involved in the Impressionist movement. A student of Corot, she frequently modeled for the paintings of other Impressionist painters.

skin Meat BONES (chant) (*p. 456*)

Points for Discussion and Writing

Directions for the reading of this poem are appended to it. Why are these necessary?

How does the poem's typography lend meaning?

When Waldman writes that she is boning up on her "Dante, William Carlos Williams, / Campion and Gertrude Stein," is she listing a pantheon of her poetic heroes? Is their influence felt in her writing?

The poet refers to this work as a "chant." Is "Makeup on Empty Space" also a chant?

ALICE NOTLEY ▪ ▪ ▪ ▪ ▪ ▪ ▪ ▪ ▪ ▪ ▪ ▪ ▪ ▪ ▪
b. 1945

Poem ("You hear that heroic big land music?")
(*p. 459*)

Points for Discussion and Writing

This poem is an elegy for Notley's father, who lived in Needles, California. Is it the father who "starred, had lives, looks down"?

What is the meaning of the lines, referring to one's own land, "We / were all born on it to die on / with no writin' on it"? Why "no writin' "?

Examine the same lines carefully for their sound, especially the skillful use of syntax and repetition of the words "on" and "it." The same thing might be done with "windmill still now they buy only / snow cows."

How might Notley have been influenced by the poetry of William Carlos Williams?

Jack Would Speak through the Imperfect Medium of Alice (p. 460)

Points for Discussion and Writing

Jack is Jack Kerouac, the Beat fiction writer and poet. Kerouac speaks, therefore, through Alice Notley. From what you know of his poems from this anthology's selection, is the manner of this poem Kerouac's or Notley's? Are the "facts" consistent with Kerouac's life? Did Kerouac begin as a drunkard and end as a child? Why has Notley reversed the chronology of his life in this way?

Look closely at section III, beginning "But I began in a word & I ended in a word." What is the word to which he (she) refers? How can "My body my alcohol my pain my death" be "the perfect word"?

A California Girlhood (p. 461)

Points for Discussion and Writing

This is a list poem but one unlike most such poems in the anthology. Compare and contrast it with Anne Waldman's "Makeup on Empty Space."

To what extent is the poem autobiographical? Like Wordsworth's *The Preludes*, might it depict the growth of the poet's mind?

What event might have occasioned the poem? Discovering a shelf of Notley's childhood books during a visit home? Discuss in general the tendency of some New York School poets to base a poem in occasion. Are some occasions more important than others? Why might so much occasional poetry have elegiac qualities?

How Spring Comes (p. 462)

Points for Discussion and Writing

The last word of this poem is "Joy." How might Notley's work exhibit W. H. Auden's definition of poetry as "happiness of language"? In what way does her exuberance of language relate to the title of the poem?

Discuss the meaning of the lines, "a semi-colon / is blue window / to me." How is a semi-colon also "a semi-precious garnet cluster / telegram"?

The poem is diaristic and casual. What poets might have influenced Notley in such an approach? What are the risks and advantages of the diaristic mode?

Where is the poem set and to whom is it addressed in such lines as "I offer you my heart over Tucson"?

How would Notley define a "true woman"?

What is the position of Notley as a woman with regard to the "you" addressed in the poem?

Look at the change in point of view that occurs with the line, "She didn't kill nothing," as well as the almost immediate return to first person. Is "she" Notley herself? Is the "I" Notley?

How might Notley's ending, "Not saints but always pupils / pupils dilated fully black in full achievement of / gut-feeling. Joy." serve as a statement of her poetics?

FROM *Beginning with a Stain*   (*p. 465*)

Points for Discussion and Writing

Compare and contrast this poem with the others in Notley's section.

Discuss the imagery of the stain in the poem. How might the figure of the stain serve as a metaphor for memory?

In some detail, dwell on the lines, "This is the stain that / invents the world, holds it together in the color of / color of, color. Color of love." What is the effect of the staggered repetition of the last words?

How does the metaphor of the stain change at the poem's end?

What is "the song of one breath"?

Who is the "you" addressed in the poem? Might it be Notley's deceased husband, the poet Ted Berrigan? How might this be her declaration "to begin again, with & from" Berrigan's ghost? Discuss the use of "with & from" in this context.

BERNADETTE MAYER ● ● ● ● ● ● ● ● ● ● ●
b. 1945

Gay Full Story   (*p. 467*)

Points for Discussion and Writing

In what ways is the title an accurate or inaccurate description of the poem? Is it a story? Is it full? Is it gay?

The poem contains the words "vim," "verve," "vivacity," "veracious," and "veritable." Is there a compositional scheme—such as those used by Harry Mathews, Ron Silliman, and others—that would bring such words into play? Are these words descriptive of the writing at hand?

Mayer writes, "Winners are nothing at all," but continues, "You get a yam, a rail, a tag, a charm, a set, a bet, a man, a bed, a rub, a run, and growing Sally the sterling bereft of life heart doll that grows...." Is any or all of this list expressive of Mayer's own winnings in life? Does the poem have a personal element?

Compare and contrast this poem with the work of Kenward Elmslie, also known for a lively vocabulary.

Mayer is associated with the New York School, yet her work also appears in some anthologies of language poetry. In what ways might "Gay Full Story" be considered language poetry?

In her essay, "The Obfuscated Poem" (see "Poetics" section in *Postmodern American Poetry*), Mayer writes, "The best obfuscation bewilders old meanings while reflecting or imitating or creating a structure of a beauty that we know." Is this poem an example of successful obfuscation?

Read Mayer's essay and discuss the issues of transparency and opacity in the writing of a poem, especially as they relate to her work. Might a poem be confusing and also wonderful? Must every element of a poem be fully understandable in order to give the reader pleasure?

Sonnet ("Beauty of songs your absence
I should not show")   (*p. 468*)

Points for Discussion and Writing

To what or whom is the poem addressed: the "beauty of songs" or someone who comes knocking for a "tylenol"? If it is the "beauty of songs," how is being precise to be equated with abdicating decorum?

What does Mayer mean by the lines, "You've come and gone—to write the perfect poem / And not ten like men or blossoms, but I am profligate / I strike the ground for ruin while you sensibly sleep"? What is suggested if men and blossoms write ten perfect poems while the author only writes one? Profligate means lost to vice or recklessly extravagant. In what sense does Mayer use the word?

"Lysistrata" is the title of a poem by John Milton. What meaning does it have here?

Compare and contrast Mayer's style as a sonnet writer with that of Thomas Wyatt (1503–1542), who introduced the form to England, and William Shakespeare, its best-known practitioner. Has Mayer actually taken any lines from Shakespeare, as Ted Berrigan did in "Sonnet LXXXVIII"? What about the line "And so in this at least a poem can have an end"?

Compare and contrast Mayer's sonnets with Ted Berrigan's.

Sonnet ("A thousand apples you might put in your theories") (*p. 468*)

Points for Discussion and Writing

Compare this poem with "They Flee from Me" by Thomas Wyatt, included in *The Norton Anthology of Poetry*.

To whom is the poem addressed?

In what way is the theme of this poem consistent with that of many Elizabethan sonnets? How do Mayer's diction and manner of phrasing compare and contrast with those of the Elizabethans?

Birthday Sonnet for Grace (*p. 469*)

Points for Discussion and Writing

The word "hypnopompic" refers to the state between sleeping and waking in which fantasies and dreams occur; "hypnagogic" means inducing sleep or the mental condition just before sleep. How are the two distinguished in this poem?

Is the "Grace" addressed in the poem a person, the sonnet form, or the state of Grace?

How is the self-reflexiveness of Mayer's sonnets—her references to the act of writing, authorship, and so on—consistent with Elizabethan sonnet conventions?

First turn to me. . . .   (*p. 469*)

Points for Discussion and Writing

Discuss the directness and clarity of Mayer's sexual language. What are the advantages of *not* being discreet? Can profanity be beautiful? What about the lines, "you suck my cunt for a thousand years" or "at last I remember my father's anger and I come"?

Why is it appropriate to refer to the tired lovers as "exhausted couplets"?

Is this poem feminist?

JOHN GODFREY ▪ ▪ ▪ ▪ ▪ ▪ ▪ ▪ ▪ ▪ ▪ ▪ ▪ ▪ ▪
b. 1945

Our Lady   (*p. 471*)

Points for Discussion and Writing

One thing doesn't necessarily follow another in this poem. Does it nevertheless communicate?

Why is the poem titled "Our Lady"?

Might a key to interpretation lie in the final lines, "when a momentary greatness of description / rewards our straining nerves with / Her atomized refreshments: / a fleeting reverence that bares us / to no one else, her seductive plea / to which, sometimes, we add our names"?

How might this poem be concerned with the poetic muse?

Wings   (*p. 472*)

Points for Discussion and Writing

Discuss the lines, "you must realize the material world / is constantly crumbling under my eyes."

The poetry of sixteenth-century British poets John Donne, George Herbert, and Andrew Marvell was described by Samuel Johnson as metaphysical. Johnson charged that within their poetry, characterized by the use of poetic conceits (concepts) and a packed, often twisted syntax, "the most hetogeneous ideas are yoked by violence together." The poet Ron Padgett has referred to Godfrey as a metaphysical poet; with Johnson's words in mind, how might this poem provide proof of Padgett's assertion that Godfrey is metaphysical?

What is "the most furious little / chunk of history" to which Godfrey refers?

What is to be made of the transmutation of the poem's "we" into "champ pigeon teams" and finally, "American birds"?

So Let's Look at It Another Way   (*p. 473*)

Points for Discussion and Writing

Discuss the poem's references to monkeys, such as, "killer monkey doing all this too close to prayer," "the marks your monkeys made," and "Invisible monkeys blow into the naked eye." Is there consistency within these references, or does Godfrey simply use the word "monkey" as a compositional "trigger"?

Like Godfrey's other poems, this one begins with great linguistic exuberance. Does that tone change as the poem develops?

To what extent might this poem depict Godfrey's actual experience? In this respect, focus on the figure of "a thin girl with long wavy hair."

Whom does the poet address in the line, "In some crazy way I am running for your pleasure"?

Where the Weather Suits My Clothes   (*p. 473*)

Points for Discussion and Writing

Discuss the connection in Godfrey's work between invention and expression. To what extent does Godfrey create figures and scenes that are expressive of his real feelings and personal situation? In this context, consider the sentence, "So there's a hole tonight in daddy's heart where the vinegar goes, and the salt of my eyes meets the soft-shelled crab."

What *is* Godfrey's situation in this poem? Has the reader just been in a bar fight, taking "the guy on the left"?

WANDA COLEMAN ■ ■ ■ ■ ■ ■ ■ ■ ■ ■ ■ ■

b. 1946

the ISM (*p. 474*)

Points for Discussion and Writing

Which of the isms does the poem mean? Capitalism? Racism?

How might the presence of the "ism" be located in "stares of neighbors" or "overhead flashing lights"?

If Coleman is referring to racism, why isn't she more declaratory in approach?

Brute Strength (*p. 475*)

Points for Discussion and Writing

Coleman is interested in questions of power. Does the poet announce an interest in the connection between personal power (or powerlessness) and political power at the larger level? Does she argue for one power interest over another—for example, women over men or vice versa?

What is the role of "aunt ora" in the poem as an authority figure? Is her use of power justified? Is Coleman's use of force with her "geechie lover" justified?

Of Lee Marvin, Coleman's laughing brother, her "geechie lover," and her first husband, who does the author most respect? Are any of these figures to be disdained for his use or misuse of power?

What is the position of women in this poem?

Coleman acknowledges that she was attracted as a young poet to the work of Charles Bukowski. Do you see any connection between this poem and those of Bukowski?

Essay on Language (*p. 475*)

Points for Discussion and Writing

Can a poem work as an essay and still be effective? To what extent might all poems be considered essays?

Discuss the assertion by "she" that "blacks think in circles." Is "she" black? Is it racist to make such distinctions? Do whites think in a linear way? What ideologies might be buried in the distinction between circularity and linearity?

Much postmodern poetry attempts to escape from the linear for sometimes a feminist purpose. Is Coleman's own language linear or circular? Is sentence structure in English, normally subject-verb-object, linear in its own right?

What meaning do the italicized snippets from the children's clap game "Who Stole the Cookie?" have for this poem?

Discuss Coleman's use of the metaphors of mirror and glass. How do they relate to one's sense of identity? What meaning do they have in the context of language, especially poetry?

What connection does the "he" who "hates me" have with the rest of the poem?

African Sleeping Sickness (*p. 477*)

Points for Discussion and Writing

Coleman connects her own physical and emotional disorders with those of slavery. What is "the curse of ever-dreaming"?

What connection does section 2, concerning "my father," have to the rest of the poem? Is his song, which represents strength and family continuity, a curative for the ills of the "sleeping sickness"? Likewise, what is the importance of the line, "sing to me of rivers" at the poem's conclusion?

Why is morphine necessary "for the pain of becoming"?

ANDREI CODRESCU ▪ ▪ ▪ ▪ ▪ ▪ ▪ ▪ ▪ ▪ ▪ ▪ ▪
b. 1946

Work (*p. 481*)

Points for Discussion and Writing

This poem mixes the elements of the surrealist catalogue (though its surrealism is mild) and a Whitmanesque sense of communal ego ("i sleep all the sleep that is given me plus / the sleep of those who can't sleep and the sleep / of great animals who lie wounded / and unable to sleep"). Compare and contrast this poem with Walt Whitman's poem "The Sleepers."

Where is the "elsewhere" to which Codrescu wishes to move?

Against Meaning   *(p. 481)*

Points for Discussion and Writing

What is the connection between "the obvious" and meaning in the poem?

Why would Codrescu want to oppose meaning? How does this relate to the police?

Does the importance of meaning (and the police) change from one political climate to another?

In 1978, the year the poem was published, might "the obvious" differ in Romania under the dictator Nicolae Ceausescu from that in the United States?

Is Codrescu writing as a Dada prankster at the ending of this poem? Or is he making a serious observation about the ability of humans to construct meaning?

Paper on Humor   *(p. 482)*

Points for Discussion and Writing

Discuss the relationship between humor and seriousness in poetry. Can a funny poem become sad because the reader (or anthologist) projects his desire for sadness on it? Can the opposite happen? Of what significance are the prizes ("the cross, the guillotine / and the hot pepper") that Codrescu wins for his sad poems?

Circle Jerk   *(p. 482)*

Points for Discussion and Writing

A circle jerk is an activity in which a group of men compete to see which one can first "jerk off," or masturbate, successfully. How is this activity related to the concerns of the poem?

Who is "that hombre" whose activities are the focus of much of the poem? Is he related to "ideology and addiction"? Is he the ultimate consumer or "the class enemy" within the (middle) class?

How might Don Juan, described as a narcissist, "upset order / and the authority spent / establishing it"? In this poem, is the narcissist an heroic figure or part of an economic and social "circle jerk"?

What are the conditions under which "a man loses his taste for himself"?

In the political view of the poem, "Two careless lovers are worth one thousand bankers." How?

What are the politics of the references to Betamax and sobriety?

Telyric *(p. 484)*

Points for Discussion and Writing

Codrescu has appeared with some frequency on National Public Radio and "Nightline," the television show. How does this poem relate to his experience with mass communications? Discuss also how the poet's "TV-less childhood" is connected to the situation.

What does the word "telyric" suggest? What is the "telyric self" that "bends in the sun- / solitude of its large puppethood"? Why "puppethood"?

Is the poem a dream or a fantasy of appearing on television as a bizarre sacred ritual?

Why does Codrescu "throw the first pitch into the sun"? Does "pitch" have a double meaning in the context of television?

PAUL HOOVER ▪ ▪ ▪ ▪ ▪ ▪ ▪ ▪ ▪ ▪ ▪ ▪ ▪ ▪
b. 1946

Poems We Can Understand *(p. 485)*

Points for Discussion and Writing

Is Hoover genuinely calling for poems "we can understand"? Or is his argument for a "complex nothingness / amounting to a song"?

Is it the poet's role to rename "the flowers and trees, / color-coding the scene, / doing bird calls for guests," or is Hoover being ironic?

Of what importance is "no sea that moves / with all deliberate speed, beside itself / and blue as water, inside itself and still"? Is the sea a positive or negative value in the poem? How might it be seen as a figure of imagination?

Are "the fingerprints on mother's dress, / pain of martyrs, scientists" of positive or negative value for the author?

What relationship of poetry to audience is posited by the poem? Is the "we" the audience that is incapable of understanding? Does this "we" understand the demands it is making with regard to poetry?

Heart's Ease (p. 486)

Points for Discussion and Writing

"Heartsease" is another name for pansy or violet; it also means freedom from sorrow. How does this information affect your reading of the poem?

How might pine trees "father"? How does this image of procreation relate to "creating calm attention / from nothing like a mother"?

What is "this plenitude" in the sentence, "This plenitude exists."?

The poet announces his consciousness of the reader and himself as author. How might authorship figure in the lines, "revealing a new heroism where the system says / I AM, a scattered Adonis gathered"?

What is the importance of the poem's rural setting? What might this rural setting have to do with the comfort inherent in the name "heartsease"? In the same context, who is the "dismayingly quiet child in that now crumbling town"? Is it the author?

Desire (p. 487)

Points for Discussion and Writing

According to critic John Sturrock, "There are two distinct modes of response to a Text. There is *plaisir*, or 'pleasure,' and there is *jouissance*, or 'enjoyment'. The connotations of *jouissance* in French are sexual, and those connotations are crucial to Barthes's distinction. *Plaisir* is a homely feeling . . . appropriate to the fireside and to writing that is *lisible* [readerly]; *jouissance* on the other hand is extreme and disconcerting, and appropriate to writing that is *scriptible* [writerly]."[9] How does the author's title, "Desire," relate to these concepts?

How does the epigraph by French critic Roland Barthes affect your understanding of the poem? It describes a situation of imprisonment in language in which satisfactory communication seems impossible. Is this the condition of language as the poem "Desire" sees it? Is there any escape from this condition?

Many references in the poem are from the realm of literary criticism— for example, "makes metaphor / aesthetic crime / in realism's mind." How might realism take offense at metaphor? Why would the eye want "to coincide / with incidental / things, making / distance rare"?

To what extent is this poem also an argument or essay?

How might it be that "Rupture [see "Terms and References" below]

9. John Sturrock, *Structuralism and Since*, Oxford, 1979, p. 72.

loves the difference"? What kind of poetry is based on loving the difference? Does this poem therefore offer an argument against such writing?

How does this theme compare with the lines, "Synthesis is / its merit, / the unity in / scatter / coming on / like trucks"? Does Hoover favor unity over scatter, or are both of value?

To what extent does "intimate conviction" offer the antidote to both an excessive unity and disunity?

"the body's packed / in lime / beneath the author's / house" refers to the ghoulish acts of Chicago mass murderer John Wayne Gacy. How does this relate to "the unity in / scatter"?

Discuss how the poem's final movement, beginning "I can touch / you now," with its reference to Beijing's Tiananmen Square, relates to the literary jargon of the first part. What might be the politics and related literary concerns of the author?

Terms and References

Rupture is a term from deconstruction theory denoting the *aporia,* or impasses of meaning, in which, according to critic Terry Eagleton, "texts get into trouble, come unstuck, offer to contradict themselves."[1]

RON SILLIMAN ▪ ▪ ▪ ▪ ▪ ▪ ▪ ▪ ▪ ▪ ▪ ▪ ▪ ▪
b. 1946

FROM *Tjanting*   (p. 490)

Points for Discussion and Writing

What is the relationship between Silliman's use of the Fibonacci number sequence, an arithmetic progression frequently found in nature (such as the geometrically increasing number of whorls on a mollusc shell), and Denise Levertov's concept of "organic form"? Might Silliman's form in this instance also be considered "organic"?

Because the Fibonacci number sequence may expand toward infinity, does it provide Silliman with a form that frustrates closure? What are the political implications of closure in poetry?

How might this poem express Silliman's desire for "maximum productivity"? (See Silliman's essay, "Of Theory, To Practice" in the "Poetics" section of *Postmodern American Poetry.*)

1. Terry Eagleton, *Literary Theory: An Introduction,* Minneapolis, 1983, pp. 133–134.

Discuss the "sentence-centered poem" to which Silliman refers in "Of Theory, To Practice." Is it different from free verse?

In what respects does this prose poem differ from the prose poems of Maxine Chernoff and Russell Edson?

Discuss the poem's self-reflexiveness (references to its own activity as *writing*). In what respects is the poem *not* self-reflexive?

What are the implications of beginning with the phrase, "Not this"? How does the phrase "Not not this" relate to "Not this"?

When Silliman writes, "I cld have done it some other way," is he referring to the writing of this poem or to some other activity?

The poet also writes, "Each sentence accounts for all the rest." Is each sentence in the poem's progression *necessary* to the other sentences?

Discuss the *form* of the following: "Cat on the bear rug naps. Grease sizzles & spits on the stove top."

Certain elements of the poem, such as, "mute pleonasm" and "planarians, trematodes," are repeated. What effect does this have on the poem as a whole? Is it a poetic refrain? How might it be compared with Ted Berrigan's use of repetition in *The Sonnets*?

Is any aspect of the poem personal? Is the reference to "Dear Bruce, dear Charles" (probably Bruce Andrews and Charles Bernstein) an example of personal poetry?

On the other hand, how might the poem be considered impersonal?

The long poems of Walt Whitman and John Ashbery are agglomerative, or touch on a large number of things. How is Silliman's work comparable in this respect?

FROM *Paradise*   (*p. 493*)

Points for Discussion and Writing

According to Anne Mack and J. J. Rome, *Paradise* "is a sequence of paragraphs each of which was written in one sitting, with these paragraphs arranged in 'monthly' groupings, and with the whole comprising 'a year's diary.' "[2] What diaristic tendencies do you find in the two sections of the poem here represented?

Compare and contrast this work with Frank O'Hara's "I do this I do that" poems.

How might the sentence, "As for we who live to be astonied, basil makes the pesto," relate to Lyn Hejinian's *My Life*?

2. "*The Alphabet*, Spelt from Silliman's Leaves (A Conversation on the 'American Long-poem')," *South Atlantic Quarterly*, Fall 1990, p. 755.

Comment also on the following sentence, "Yet as *USA Today* makes clear, condensare [poetic compression] is not itself sufficient for dichtung [poetry]."

In the section beginning "DEEP IN GENITAL SOUP," comment on the sentence, "The burns on my father's body." Silliman's father was a fireman. Does this make his poem personal?

Comment on the sentence, "To try and tell a story is to make a purgatory of the real." How is it possible to take a moral position by opposing storytelling in poetry?

Comment also on the sentence, "Masturbating, I think of you." Is "you" the reader? Is it possible for an author to be voyeuristic with regard to his reader?

Discuss the poem's other uses of sexual references, including the final sentence, "The tip of his penis against the back of her throat." Of what effect are such references on the reader? Are they more or less shocking for having been removed from a narrative context?

Silliman writes, "The bottom of the page is only a dotted line across the screen. A flock of starlings high over the valley. These are not facts." Does the sentence, "These are not facts," refer to the sentences that precede it? If so, in what respect are they "not facts"?

BOB PERELMAN ▪ ▪ ▪ ▪ ▪ ▪ ▪ ▪ ▪ ▪ ▪ ▪ ▪ ▪
b. 1947

Cliff Notes   *(p. 498)*

Points for Discussion and Writing

What is the significance of the poem's title?

The poem focuses on television and language in relation to the image. What is the "word window" to which the poem refers in the first stanza? Is each language private to itself but nevertheless a "way of undressing"? How so?

What is the importance of the reference to Plato and Socrates in the fourth stanza? Is Perelman implying that knowledge and consequently opinion are received hierarchically?

Of what significance is class difference to the politics of the poem? What is meant by "scarcity of meaning / spread out over the proletariat as a visible economic ether. / You can look, but it costs"?

What is Perelman's critique of contemporary culture in the last four lines? Does the "postcard of ageless windwashed marble / posing for recorded history" refer to Western civilization as framed by Plato and Aristotle?

To what extent does a depiction of culture, whether by Plato or TV, *become* the culture?

Let's Say   (*p. 499*)

Points for Discussion and Writing

This poem is concerned with the politics of reading. What is the relationship between the page and the "face of 'things' "?

How do both the page and "things" relate to the "scrapbook of desire" located "inside" the narrator? How is language related to desire? In what respect is the floor "sexualized"?

How might the inner life of the "I" be read like a book?

Are the "you" and the "I" of the poem the reader and author?

What are the implications of "reading water" at the poem's end?

In general, what is the nature of Perelman's comment on language and society? Why are the farms described as "strafed"?

Things   (*p. 500*)

Points for Discussion and Writing

To reify is to make real or concrete, especially abstract concepts. What is meant by "Reification won't get you out of the parking lot"?

In what respects is this poem an essay on matters of concern to the language poets? What is meant by "Glamor of the thing"? To what extent is transparency a value in Western culture? Why might opacity, on the other hand, be of moral and artistic value?

What roles do *The New Yorker* and the *New York Times* play to give an empty glass "poetry water" and "germ-free water"? Why is this "germ free water" described as "rational" and "apolitical"? Would an improved poetry be irrational and political?

In the same context, discuss the line, "whole histories pounded into simple binaries for lunch."

Is language by its nature reductive in relation to the "truth," or is it equal to the task of communicating the experience of our "psychodramas"?

Is a poem less capable or more capable than a novel of capturing lived experience? The Russian critic Mikhail Bahktin was of the opinion that novels capture better than poetry the heteroglossia (or complex blending of diverse voices) of modern life. How might language poetry be an attempt to compete with novels in capturing the diversity and fullness of experience?

How might reification ("the frozen reified narrative") be considered "a past you can count on / safest investment"? Parking lots are known as the safest investment for an entrepreneur. What kind of poetry is equivalent to a parking lot?

What is "the simple law of outward push"? How might "outward push" serve as a metaphor for the expansion of empires?

Chronic Meanings   (*p. 501*)

Points for Discussion and Writing

In a statement written for a poetry anthology, Perelman wrote, " 'Chronic Meanings' was written on hearing that a friend had AIDS; it is an attempt on my part to see what happened to meaning as it was interrupted. If one expects a poem to be more or less narrative, focusing sharply or softly on spots of time, 'Chronic Meanings' might feel evasive. But in fact I was trying to be direct; the sentences came as matter-of-factly from my experience and imagination as I could manage."[3] How does this information affect your reading of the poem? Is the poem an elegy? Is it elegiac?

Discuss the inconclusiveness of many of the poem's lines—for example, "On our wedding night I." Does this curtailment of meaning parallel the curtailment of Perelman's friend's life?

Discuss other aspects of the poem's form. How many words does each sentence contain? Does Perelman ever abandon the use of sentence fragments in favor of complete sentences? What is the resulting effect?

A frequent complaint among the avant-garde is the dominance of the elegiac mood in mainstream poetics. Discuss Perelman's use of the elegiac occasion in the context of this antipathy.

3. *The Best American Poetry, 1991*, eds. Mark Strand and David Lehman, New York, 1991, pp. 302–3.

NATHANIEL MACKEY ▪ ▪ ▪ ▪ ▪ ▪ ▪ ▪ ▪ ▪ ▪

b. 1947

Ghede Poem   (p. 505)

Points for Discussion and Writing

Read and discuss the excerpt from Mackey's essay, "Sound and Senti-ment, Sound and Symbol," located in the "Poetics" section of *Postmodern American Poetry*. How does Mackey's poem exhibit his theory of "polyrhythmicity and heterogeneity"? Does it contain the "limp" of the social outcast or orphan?

The figure of Ghede is phallic. Does this mean that Mackey is a phallocentric poet? Discuss the politics of sexual representation in general among experimental poets. Are different constraints in place for men than for women in the depiction of sex?

How might Ghede's priestly taunt ("You love, I love. . . ."), designed to mock worshipper's pretensions, serve as a metaphor for the corrective role of poetry?

The Shower of Secret Things   (p. 508)

Points for Discussion and Writing

Who are the "they" of this poem? Who is "she"?

Discuss the male and female figures of the poem in relation to the references to drought and rain. Is the dousing of the "witch" a means of bringing rain?

Discuss the form of the poem, especially its consistent use of enjamb-ment, or line breaks. How might Mackey's line breaks be compared with those of Robert Creeley, Gustaf Sobin, and Art Lange?

Compare and contrast this poem with Mackey's other work, "Ghede Poem." To paraphrase a statement of Wallace Stevens, how might Mackey's change of form be considered a change of subject?

DAVID SHAPIRO ■ ■ ■ ■ ■ ■ ■ ■ ■ ■ ■ ■ ■ ■
b. 1947

The Counter-Example   (p. 511)

Points for Discussion and Writing

The sentence, "The morning star is not the evening star," is the kind of
identity statement that Frege would have considered in his first philosophical work, *Begriffsschrift* (Idea Writing), 1879. With regard to
Frege's philosophical interests, how does the information below affect
your reading of "The Counter-Example"? Does the poem offer counter-
examples to its own propositions? In this respect, give special attention
to the poem's last two lines.

Terms and References

Gottlog Frege was a German mathematician whose achievements included the definition of "number" in 1884. According to Bertrand Russell, "It is remarkable that, before Frege, every definition of number
that had been suggested contained elementary logical blunders. . . .
From Frege's work it followed that arithmetic, and pure mathematics
generally, is nothing but a prolongation of deductive logic. This dis-
proved Kant's theory that arithmetical propositions are 'synthetic' and
involve a reference to time."[4] Frege's work in mathematics led to the
understanding that "a great part of philosophy can be reduced to something that may be called 'syntax.' "[5] Frege belatedly became a central
figure in the philosophy of language; his thought led to an important
break with Aristotelian logic.

A **counter-example** is commonly used by philosophers to test their
propositions.

Commentary Text Commentary Text Commentary Text   (p. 511)

Points for Discussion and Writing

What part of Shapiro's poem is commentary and what part is text? Or is
commentary indistinguishable from text? In this context, examine
closely the lines: "Nonobservance, nonappearance, noncompletion. /
Like the bright male cardinal on the red maple." Is the first line commentary and the second line text? Why would the male cardinal serve

4. Bertrand Russell, *A History of Western Philosophy*, New York, 1945, p. 830.
5. The same.

as a simile for "nonobservance, nonappearance, noncompletion" rather than observance, appearance, completion?

Examine the paradox of *"Present I flee you | Absent I have you."*

Whose name is written "like landscape" across the middle of the page? To what "page" does Shapiro refer?

A Realistic Bar and Grill (*p. 512*)

Points for Discussion and Writing

The poem is concerned with a number of issues, among them the speed of change in modern culture ("Everything that is me would rush up and meet you / Like the front of a subway / Rushing into a cave painting"). Shapiro also alludes to issues of representation in art—the play versus its performance and the "real" John Clare versus his image as lionized author. How does the title of the poem relate to these issues?

Can one bar and grill be more realistic than another? To what extent does the word "realistic" presuppose the bar and grill's depiction as art?

How might one step on "a nonreferential ladder"? Do things, including ladders, refer to anything other than themselves?

What do the references to John Clare and Percy Shelley, British poets of the Romantic period, have to do with the rest of the poem? Is the unjust celebration and abuse of the "naive" poet John Clare comparable to the drowning of Percy Shelley "in a dull historic terrain"?

How might a fire balloon launched among mountains compare to "the front of a subway / Rushing into a cave painting"? Are these Shapiro's way of expressing an historical paradox? How do these paradoxes compare to the play and its performance?

To what extent is Shapiro concerned with the nature of poetic celebrity ("pomp") and the uncertainties of fame?

Tracing of an Evening (*p. 513*)

Points for Discussion and Writing

The poem has a dreamlike setting in which "Snow falls on the phonograph." How might Shapiro have been influenced by surrealist painting such as Rene Magritte's *The Menaced Assassin* (1926) which depicts a man listening to a phonograph in the same room with a naked corpse?

The second stanza continues a mood of menace and dislocation. In this context, discuss the lines "The old man was watching from a book" and "The floor is so far from the earth."

What is the relation of the transparent ocean to the opaque one? Can the same ocean be both transparent and opaque? How might these references to the transparent and opaque relate to the concerns of language poetry?

A Book of Glass (*p. 513*)

Points for Discussion and Writing

Shapiro is a professor of art history. Is the book of glass his own invention, or does he refer to a preexisting work of art? In this respect, compare "A Book of Glass" with Marjorie Welish's poem, "Within This Book, Called Marguerite."

In the first line of Shapiro's work, the book of glass exists; in the last line, however, he states that he will make it. Discuss this presentation of the book of glass.

How might this poem be based on a dream ("I should / Wake and render them!") in which his mother figures?

Is naming the book of glass in a poem the same as making it?

Discuss the book of glass as a metaphor for authorship. Is it legible? Are the words on its pages to be considered transparent or opaque?

RAE ARMANTROUT ▪ ▪ ▪ ▪ ▪ ▪ ▪ ▪ ▪ ▪ ▪
b. 1947

Necromance (*p. 514*)

Points for Discussion and Writing

Necromancy is divination by means of communication with the dead. Is necromancy in evidence in the poem? Or is the title a pun meaning "dead romance"?

Who is the "she" of the poem? Is she the Siren who "always sings / like this"?

Armantrout writes, "Hard to say where / this occurs." What evidence exists of the poem's setting? What "story" or situation does it depict?

How does the "roar / of a freeway" relate to "The mermaid's / privacy"? Might this contemporary mermaid have appeared in a story by Raymond Carver?

Armantrout is associated with language poetry. How might the lines, "Morbid / glamor of the singular," relate to language poetry theory? In the context of such poetics, why would "separate / dust motes / afloat in abeyance" be described as an "Ideal / republic" in the poem?

Language of Love   *(p. 515)*

Points for Discussion and Writing

Identify the narrative elements of this poem. What "story" is being related?

Is "the boss" the same person who "stroked her carapace / with his claw"?

Of what importance is the distinction between Petite Impressions and Town Square?

Is this poem an allegory about sexual relations in the workplace? Is the "boss" guilty of sexual harrassment?

"Micturation" means the act of urination. Is this word spoken mincingly by "the boss," or does the male character ("he") change from section to section?

Attention   *(p. 516)*

Points for Discussion and Writing

Robert Creeley once defined poetry as "an act of attention." Is this poem about poetry? How is ventriloquy "the mother tongue"? Is poetry a form of ventriloquy?

What is meant by "colonize rejection"? What overture is being rejected?

The poem contains several references to absence; "the holes / in dead leaves" correspond with "that flutter / of indifference," "lapses," and "the 'you' / in the heart of / molecule and ridicule." Discuss the relationship between absence and presence in the work.

MEI-MEI BERSSENBRUGGE ▪▪▪▪▪▪▪▪▪

b. 1947

Alakanak Break-Up   (p. 518)

Points for Discussion and Writing

The poem repeats the line, "This is where they have concentrated you." Who are the "they" to whom Berssenbrugge refers?

Is the "you" of the same sentence the author, the reader, or a second-person character in the poem's fictive setting? How does this "you" relate to the poem's "she" ("She prefers to lie down like a river")? In whose perspective is the poem written: that of she or you?

Discuss the words "plane" and "plain" in the following: "This is the breakthrough in plane. The plane itself is silent. / Above and behind the plain lies the frozen delta."

In part 3 of the poem, the first-person point of view is introduced. How does this point of view relate to the earlier use of "you" and "she"?

Berssenbrugge writes, "The summer / is an interruption of intervals that disappear, like his little dance / before the main dances, a veridical drug." To what extent might this poem be descriptive of a landscape undergoing the change of seasons? What is the nature of the human perception of this change?

Discuss the sentence, "When her attention is discontinuous, this no longer means that she / is inattentive." To what extent might the discontinuity of attention be a theme of "Alakanak Break-Up"?

Is Berssenbrugge's manner as a poet discontinuous yet not inattentive?

Is the poem realistic? If so, how might one "balance three horizons" or "take the window and place it in your mouth"?

Comment on the reference to dashes in "The dashes you had applied so carefully, in order to record rotation / in the sky have been washed away, leaving milky traces of themselves / and of their trails." Does Berssenbrugge mean the punctuation mark or dashes on a map?

To what extent might Berssenbrugge write as a literary Cubist, selecting her references according to their shape ("A square of the board lights up") and movement ("You are a blur of speed concentrating on heading in one direction")?

Discuss the role of "the human" in this poem, especially in the following: "The human shines through from behind / and below seams and holes in the ice. The human hovers like a mood. / On a molecular level, the human remains, as a delicate glittering accent / on the dateline...."

Texas   (p. 522)

Points for Discussion and Writing

As with "Alakanak Break-Up," discuss the changing point of view in this poem. The poem begins in the first person ("I used the table as a reference"), but in the second stanza the third person is dominant. Are the first and third persons interchangeable in the poem?

What are the implications of this shifting point of view for the poem as lyric?

Focus on the narrative elements of the poem. Who are the characters in this narrative? Where is the "story" set?

What is the significance of the references to visual art in the lines, "Now, / she turns her camera on them to change her thinking about them into a thought / in Mexico, as the horizon when you are moving can oppose the horizon inside / the elevator via a blue Cadillac into a long tracking shot"? What other evidence do you see in Berssenbrugge's work of a cinematic approach to poetry?

Discuss the lines, "First the table is the table. In blue light / or in electric light, it has no pathos." As a poet, what is Berssenbrugge's relation to pathos?

Jealousy   (p. 523)

Points for Discussion and Writing

Discuss Berssenbrugge's statement that "nature never provides a border for us." How might it relate to her practice as a poet?

Given the comparatively novelistic references to a love triangle and to the exploding of fireworks, how do you account for the meditative rather than passionate quality of the poem's concluding lines, "A starry night, like a fully reflecting surface, / claims no particular status in space, or being of its own"?

LESLIE SCALAPINO ▪ ▪ ▪ ▪ ▪ ▪ ▪ ▪ ▪ ▪ ▪ ▪ ▪

b. 1947

Crowd and not evening or light

The series - 3   (*p. 524*)

Points for Discussion and Writing

This poem and "Flush, a play" are part of a book-length work, *Crowd and not evening or light*. Students who are interested in the interconnectedness of the poem's parts will want to obtain this 1992 volume. What similarity do you observe between "The Series - 3" and "Flush, a play"?

Discuss critic Tyrus Miller's assertion that Scalapino's poetry is influenced by "the grammaticalism of Gertrude Stein, and the typographical quirkiness of Emily Dickinson."[6]

To what extent might *both* poems be considered plays? What emphasis is placed on what would be called "stage directions" in a play?

In "The Series - 3," who does Scalapino mean by "my / people"?

"Weatherman" refers to the radical leftist group of the 1960s which took its name from Bob Dylan's song lyric, "You don't need a weatherman to know which way the wind blows" (in "Subterranean Homesick Blues"). Of what importance is Weatherman to the poem's themes of rebellion and gender?

How might the repeated word "flaccid" act to unify the poem's political views?

How are "a version" and "the real event" related in this poem and in Scalapino's work in general?

Flush   a play   (*p. 527*)

Points for Discussion and Writing

Note the similarity in this poem's ending ("- and only in that") to the ending of "Series - 3" ("which it does - or has / - and is that"). Is the treatment of male sexuality similar to or different from that of "Series - 3"?

6. Review of *that they were at the beach—aeolotropic series, Conjunctions*, No. 9, 1986, p. 224.

What are the advantages of having written this poem for alternating male and female voices?

Is this a play to be acted or simply spoken? Can such a differentiation be made?

Of what importance is the poem's central "act" of a man masturbating on the street? How does the dramatic intensity of a such an act relate to the rest of the poem? Of what importance is the distance of the man's act of masturbation from the woman who sees it?

Is the figure of the "stowaway" metaphysical (in the manner of Emily Dickinson) or actual?

To what extent is "movement," including that of the author's mental associations, the central focus of the poem rather than the actions of the exhibitionist?

BRUCE ANDREWS ▪ ▪ ▪ ▪ ▪ ▪ ▪ ▪ ▪ ▪ ▪ ▪
b. 1948

Stalin's Genius   (p. 531)

Points for Discussion and Writing

Examine this poem as discourse. What is the role in each paragraph of the topic sentence? How do the prose sections of the poem relate to the use of line breaks? Is information necessary to a given paragraph because of its subject? What other forms of organization do you observe?

What is meant by "Woman's place = sexual deviance, doesn't it have pockets?"

Compare and contrast the poem's political nature with the genre of political satire. Andrews is clearly political. Is he satirical as well, or simply observant? As political comment, discuss the sentence, "CIA Julie Andrews push-ups."

Why is thinking "a nice guy not a growth industry"?

Is totalitarianism linked to the literacy rate?

What are the politics of the line, "I think of documentation as domination"?

Biko is the murdered South African black leader, Steven Biko. Of what importance is the reference to the poem?

To what uniqueness does Andrews refer in the line, "this uniqueness old hat"?

Species Means Guilt   (*p. 532*)

Points for Discussion and Writing

Discuss the line, "are 'make it new' & 'make it even' compatible?" Does Andrews wish to "make it new"? Does he desire to "make it even"? How might the two be in conflict? To what extent are the two interdependent?

Discuss the line, "classical means what, fake sense of order?" What is the sense of order in Andrews' poem? Does his poetry reject the classical? What connection does Andrews's poetry have to the Romantic? The metaphysical?

Discuss the truth of the epigrams: "to get to the top, step on yourself," "no human has a history," and "men are capital, women are the baby labor factory?"

Discuss the phallic references of the third and fourth sections: "Suds down the dick in the outfield" and "I was castrated for seducing the local tax collector's wife." How might these be compared to sexual references in Ron Silliman's *Paradise* poems.

Bomb Then, Bomb Now   (*p. 534*)

Points for Discussion and Writing

Discuss the line *"fantasy causes stress:* the universe is perfect." Might it be taken as a statement of poetics? Is the universe, in fact, perfect? Does fantasy cause stress?

Is realism a category more acceptable to Andrews than fantasy? If so, what is the character of that realism?

In an essay, "Total Equals What: Poetics & Praxis," Andrews writes, "Laying bare the device remains as a task but it becomes a more social act, of social unbalancing, of a social reflexivity of content, rather than some kind of (what I have called in the past) preppie formalism. . . . if something's going to be disruptive, or disrupted, it's going to have to be *method,* seen in a more social sense—as the social organization of signs, as ideology, as discourse; those are the more broadly social things that need to be shaken up: historicized, politicized, contextualized, totalized—by laying bare the social devices, or the social rules which are at work."[7] Does Andrews' poetry use method? What is it?

What are the social rules Andrews is intent on disrupting? Is he a formalist? How is his poetry to be distinguished from the "preppie formalism" to which he refers?

7. Bruce Andrews, "Total Equals What: Poetics & Praxis," *Poetics Journal*, No. 6, 1986, p. 57.

BARRETT WATTEN ▪ ▪ ▪ ▪ ▪ ▪ ▪ ▪ ▪ ▪ ▪ ▪ ▪

b. 1948

Statistics   (*p. 536*)

Points for Discussion and Writing

How might this poem be read as a manifesto for language poetry? What is the poem's stance toward dramatic monologue? Toward difficulty? Toward speech? Toward persona? Toward self?

Why is the poem titled "Statistics"?

Discuss the frequent use of quotation marks. What effect do they have on the poem's meaning? As an interruptive gesture, how do they serve to constantly remind the reader that the text is *written*?

Read the poem out loud in class. How do the quotation marks affect the spoken word? What is the position of this poem with regard to the oral tradition?

Radio   (*p. 537*)

Points for Discussion and Writing

How does this poem differ from "Statistics"? Is it more lyrical? If so, in what sense? How do the forms of the two poems affect their manners?

Does the subject of radio continue throughout the poem? To what extent might radio serve as a metaphor for all communication, including poetry?

How might the line, "edges of stations start to come in," describe the purposely oblique and multivalent approach of language poetry in which "peripheries meet"?

FROM *Progress*   (*p. 538*)

Points for Discussion and Writing

This is an excerpt from the beginning of a book-length work. Given the aims of language poetry, why is the title *Progress* appropriate to the work?

What formal methodology do you observe in this poem?

Watten writes, "The idea / *Is* the thing." Discuss the connection between Watten's statement and William Carlos Williams's "No ideas but in things."

What are the politics behind the line, "Stalin as a linguist. . . ."?

Why would Watten write, "I trust replication"? Isn't such a statement contrary to the Romantic concept of originality? Is Watten therefore anti-Romantic or neoclassical in orientation?

How is "I trust replication" consistent with the later phrases, "I trust wheat" and "I trust the thing itself"?

Discuss the statement, "Only I trust the materials." What if Watten had written "I only trust the materials"?

Is the "I" of the poem always the same person?

Is it true that "I write, as in a mirror, / This present"? What connection exists between the present as moment of composition and the present as moment of reading? Does the present exist, or must it be imagined? What about the past and the future?

Watten writes, "Then I erupt my articulation." Is such eruption in fact a part of his project?

Discuss the form of the poem. When *Progress* was published in 1985, each page of the book consisted of five stanzas of five lines. Is each group of five stanzas independent in theme or style?

DAVID LEHMAN ▪ ▪ ▪ ▪ ▪ ▪ ▪ ▪ ▪ ▪ ▪ ▪ ▪ ▪ ▪
b. 1948

The Difference Between Pepsi and Coke (*p. 542*)

Points for Discussion and Writing

Is this poem really about the difference between the two soft drinks?

Of what social class is Pop a member? How is this evident?

Is the poem a satire on Pop's beliefs or does it confirm his wisdom in opposing the war and forgiving the maid?

How might the manner and topic of this poem be associated with the practices of the New York School poets?

Toward the Vanishing Point   (*p. 543*)

Points for Discussion and Writing

Compare and contrast this poem with John Ashbery's sestina, "Farm Implements and Rutabagas in a Landscape." Is Lehman's poem a sestina, a double sestina, a *faux* sestina, or none of the above?

The poem consists of 5 twelve-line stanzas followed by a five-line *envoi*. Is Lehman's use of his chosen form consistent from stanza to stanza?

Despite its high degree of artifice, is the poem beautiful? Discuss the popular belief that beauty is related more to sincerity and truth-telling than with the shapeliness of the poem as a made thing. Are poems that strive to be natural therefore more "true" than poems that place their craftsmanship in the foreground?

Compare and contrast Lehman's use of poetic form—and the New York School's generally—with that of the language poets.

Following a discussion of traditional poetic forms, instructors of creative writing might invite students to invent their own poetic forms. It is often useful to require that each student employ at least two (but not more than two) formal constraints such as stanza size, line length, and use of rhyme and other word patterning. In doing so, the poem is designed formally before it is written. What effect does this placing artifice in the foreground have on the composition of the poem? What is the role of the arbitrary in writing poems? Is it different from writing a work of fiction or a play? Might a poem that began as an exercise in form later seem necessary as expression?

First Offense   (*p. 545*)

Points for Discussion and Writing

The poem is a villanelle, a form requiring the repetition of the poem's first and third lines, as well as five tercets followed by a quatrain. Before informing students of the poem's form, ask them to study its formal elements on their own.

Is it true, in general, that poets in this anthology of experimental poetry are more interested in the formal concerns of poetry? Why might this be true? Why would a formal approach to poetry be distrusted by more mainstream poets? Has this always been the case?

How does the poem's form relate to its content? Is the content less important because it is trivial? How might its triviality be *more* useful to Lehman's project than the material of elegy?

GEORGE EVANS ■ ■ ■ ■ ■ ■ ■ ■ ■ ■ ■ ■ ■ ■ ■ ■
b. 1948

A Renaissance Drunk (*p. 546*)

Points for Discussion and Writing

The lines, *"The leaves drop (horohoro) / weaving down drunk / from their trees,"* are Evans's translation of a Santōka haiku. The lines, *"The shape of the traveler / in the puddle is the traveler,"* are Evans's own, written in imitation of Santōka. How might the figure of Santōka, whose life is described below, serve as a Bohemian poetic ideal for Evans?

Who are "they" who have never read their Hedylos or Santōka?

Terms and References

Hedylos was an ancient Greek poet whose work appears in *The Greek Anthology*. Active until 270 B.C., Hedylos refers in his poems to his contemporary, Sokles, who was a superior poet when drunk. Hedylos' poem is therefore an exhortation to keep drinking.

Santōka (1882–1940) was the last great haiku poet of Japan. Writing during the Meiji Era, a period of modernization and openness to outside influence that has been considered a "renaissance" period, Santōka gave up his family and professorial position at Waseda University for the life of a wandering Zen Buddhist monk who owned only the bowl in which he ate his rice. He was also given to drunkenness.

The Japanese word *horohoro* is an onomatopoeia for the sound of falling leaves. It is very similar to the Japanese word for "wanderer."

Revelation in the Mother Lode (*p. 546*)

Points for Discussion and Writing

This poem is set near Sutter's Mill, California, where Evans's father-in-law owns a vineyard. How soon in your reading of the poem does its subject become apparent?

What is Evans's political position in the poem? In this regard, discuss the third stanza:

> And is this guilt, or the product of being swept up
> in a time on human earth when few do more than raise
> the cause of their own names—and am I one, or is all this
> death just sloth which one pretends
> to work against the belly of
> but which in fact
> controls?

What is Evans's position with regard to ego? Compare and contrast it with Charles Olson's statement about "getting rid of the lyrical interference of the individual as ego."[8]

Discuss the penultimate stanza, which contains the lines, "I don't want to heal, and am sick of those who do. / Such things end in license." How might forgetting the war end in license?

How are newspapers and monuments to be equated with taxidermy?

Who is the soldier Evans comes upon at the poem's end? His own ghost?

Horse on a Fence   (p. 547)

Points for Discussion and Writing

Each New Year's Day, Evans writes a poem involving the animal that figures in Chinese astrology for that year. The year this poem was written was the Chinese Year of the Horse. Is this also a poem about the Vietnam War? How might the detail of "standing now on a fence / between two worlds" combine the occasion of New Year's Day and Evans's memory of the Vietnam War? Do these worlds also include the living and the dead?

Who are the "we" who "might have died by now"?

Discuss the form of this poem. How is it different from that of "Revelation in the Mother Lode"? Is the form of each poem consistent with its content? What similarities exist between the two poems?

AUGUST KLEINZAHLER ▪ ▪ ▪ ▪ ▪ ▪ ▪ ▪ ▪ ▪
b. 1949

An Autumnal Sketch   (p. 549)

Points for Discussion and Writing

The poem satirizes the poetry of "the professors." How might this poetry be described?

Of what importance is the site the professors chose for their revelations ("where the field begins and the suburb ends")? Do the professors arrive from the direction of the fields or the suburbs?

The professors are described as making the mallard in the reeds "their own." Does all poetry possess its subject in this way? How can these

---

8. Charles Olson, "Projective Verse," in *Selected Writings*, p. 24.

professorial poets make the mallard "both more than a duck / and less"?

Is there such a thing as an academic poem? If so, how does it behave? Is the academic poem the same today as it was in 1950? Or has the term "academic" become meaningless? Is it fair to say that all poets who teach in a university are academic? Is a Bohemian poet someone who resists formal education? Might a Bohemian poetry, on the other hand, display a good deal of learning? Was William Carlos Williams academic, Bohemian, or neither?

Hamburger   (*p. 549*)

Points for Discussion and Writing

In the tradition of William Carlos Williams, Kleinzahler makes good use of everyday American speech. In this poem, idiomatic voices appear in italics. Are both italicized sections in the same voice?

Kleinzahler gives minimal external clues as to how the voices in the speeches sound. Is the accent of speech nevertheless clear when the poem is read out loud in class?

What formal devices does the poet use? Is the poem entirely free verse? What gives it organization?

How does Kleinzahler's position on speech differ from that of the language poets? Is his work comparable in any way to that of William Corbett?

Poetics   (*p. 550*)

Points for Discussion and Writing

In what respect is this poem a statement of poetics? Statements of poetics usually deal in literary matters, and privilege one element of the literature over another. What does Kleinzahler privilege? How might the value placed on the liquor store and "pizza crust" place Kleinzahler in the tradition of William Carlos Williams?

Is the poet sincere, or tongue-in-cheek, when he writes, "I have loved the air outside Shop-Rite Liquor / on summer evenings"? Is it possible to be somewhat tongue-in-cheek and still express a love for such things?

What is Kleinzahler's position with regard to American culture? Is he critical of its consumerism, like Charles Olson and some of the language poets? Or does he appreciate its actuality?

What is the effect of using the past perfect tense ("I have loved") in the poem's first line?

Spleen   (p. 550)

Points for Discussion and Writing

Is the poem, in fact, splenetic?

The poem is concerned with Canadian politics. Can it be described as a political poem? Is it of significance that "Bankers were generally pleased" with the budget? Or does the poem's "spleen" concern itself more with issues of mortality?

Of what importance to Kleinzahler's style are such elegant asides as: "et voilà: / catkins dripping from ash"?

One of William Carlos Williams's poems was entitled "Proletarian Portrait"; it described a woman eating plums from a paper bag. To what extent is Kleinzahler committed to making portraits of everyday experience?

Kleinzahler is masterful in his ability to control the mood of a poem. Discuss his use of tone and diction in this work, especially in the first stanza. What is the effect of having the phrase "shit-faced in the bar" in close proximity to "brilliantly scarved"?

The Lunatic of Lindley Meadow   (p. 551)

Points for Discussion and Writing

Is this poem written in a traditional poetic measure? Are its concerns formal as well as social? What is the nature of Kleinzahler's social commentary? How might his social critique resemble that of fellow New Jerseyan William Carlos Williams?

A screed is a prolonged tirade or harangue. Discuss Kleinzahler's word choice in the expression "chummy screed."

For its formal characteristics, discuss the line, "the snaps of the beak your hand becomes cease."

Who is the poem's "you"?

Ebenezer Californicus   (p. 551)

Points for Discussion and Writing

At what season of the year is this poem set? To whom does the title refer?

Is Ebenezer the speaker at the poem's beginning?

What social observation does the poem contain? Who is described by the line, "the Bob Hope Holiday Leer of Delight"?

Discuss Kleinzahler's use of the American idiom and characteristic mixing of demotic and hieratic language.

Who speaks at the poem's end, starting with "O Christ"? Who is Baby Teapot?

A Case in Point   (*p.* 552)

Points for Discussion and Writing

The "he" of the poem "takes refuge in a text / of a text"; this love of textuality is set at opposition to "the authentic." Of what kind of poet— and reader—is this poem critical? Is Kleinzahler referring to a specific individual or the representative of a group?

In Kleinzahler's view, of what does the authentic consist? What is characteristic of the inauthentic?

Discuss the lines, "Because he honors not the made thing / nor can he recognize it when coming upon it." How might these lines have been influenced by Ezra Pound's poem, "Hugh Selwyn Mauberley"?

Do you recognize other Pound influences in Kleinzahler's approach?

EILEEN MYLES   ▪ ▪ ▪ ▪ ▪ ▪ ▪ ▪ ▪ ▪ ▪ ▪ ▪ ▪
b. 1949

December 9th   (*p.* 553)

Points for Discussion and Writing

How does Myles's poem reflect the life of poet John Milton?

Does Myles speak as herself in her poems? Why might the use of a persona be philosophically offensive to the poet?

Discuss Myles's use of both everyday and heightened poetic tones. Is her work different from or similar to August Kleinzahler's in this respect?

Is Myles a personal or a confessional poet? What aspects of her poem suggest an interest in New York School poetics?

New England Wind (p. 554)

Points for Discussion and Writing

One aspect of New York School poetry is its casualness. Is this poem casual? What formal elements in the poem work against a casual, diaristic mode?

Discuss the formal qualities, including rhyme and rime riche, of the first two stanzas.

Who is addressed in the poem? The New England Wind? Who is the "who" referred to at the poem's end?

The Sadness of Leaving (p. 555)

Points for Discussion and Writing

Myles writes, "I won't / kill myself today. It's / too beautiful." What occasion inspires these feelings?

Who is the "you" of the poem? Do you need to know her or his specific identity?

What are the advantages in Myles's use of extremely short lines of one to four words? Does the effect of enjambment change from short poems like "December 9th" to long ones like this?

Some of Myles's passages are casual, the observations of a pedestrian, and some are emotionally intense. How does the poet manage both tones in the same poem? Does one tone lend credibility to the other?

Would the poem be as effective if it used a longer poetic line? Robert Creeley uses a very short line. Is Myles as conscious of her use of the line as Creeley? Does the content of each line seem formally necessary to that line? Or are the lines broken arbitrarily? In what respect does the short line lend tension to the poem's "narrative"?

VICTOR HERNÁNDEZ CRUZ   ▪ ▪ ▪ ▪ ▪ ▪ ▪ ▪ ▪
b. 1949

Areyto   (p. 558)

Points for Discussion and Writing

What is the "old calendar" to which Hernández Cruz refers?

Discuss the relationship between the poem's traditional figures such as Yukiyu and Queztalcóatl and its reference to "Plush media inventions" and "cars and consumer junk/" Why does the author stress that "Yukiyu has not abandoned you"?

What is meant by the advice to "go horizontal into the circle"? The "circle" apparently refers to the *batey* where the *Areyto*, or tribal meeting, would take place. What security does it offer?

What kind of America does Hernández Cruz see today? What America does he envision for the future?

Compare and contrast his America with that of Allen Ginsberg in his poem "America." Is Hernández Cruz influenced by Ginsberg when he writes, "Linda America just rise and take / off your clothes"?

Does Hernández Cruz speak as an insider or outsider to Linda America? What is Ginsberg's position?

How might the "Old fire of agricultural guitar / spreading North" serve as a cultural corrective? Is the guitar a metaphor for the migration of Latin Americans north to the United States? Why "agricultural"?

How might Hernández Cruz's emphasis on the inherent morality of agricultural society compare and contrast with that of the agrarian traditionalism of the so-called Fugitive poets John Crowe Ransom and Allen Tate?

Discuss the importance of the poet's distinction between *unidos* (united) and *único* (singular). How might this distinction relate to the "conquistadors' wishes"?

Terms and References

Areyto refers to a tribal meeting of the Taino tribe in Puerto Rico. These meetings would take place in a *batey*, or circle.

A **flamboyans** is a tree with bright red flowers that grows in Puerto Rico.

Yukiyu is the god of the rain forest.

The national symbol of Guatamala, a **quetzal** is a bird of brilliant plumage regarded as a deity by the ancient Mayas, whose chiefs alone were permitted to wear its plumes.

Quetzalcóatl is a traditional god and heroic figure of the Aztecs.

José **Betances** and Eugenio María de **Hostos** were Puerto Rican intellectuals who struggled for national independence.

José **Marti** was the legendary Cuban hero who fought for independence from the Spaniards.

Raza cósmica means "universal race."

Guaguanco is a dance music that originated in Cuba of African, Spanish, and French influence.

Trio **Los Diamantes** and Trio **San Juan** are musical groups renowned for their performances of boleros.

Johnny Albino is a singer for Trio San Juan.

La'uds refers to a Latin American lute.

Unidos means "united."

Único means "singular" or "unique."

The *maraca güiro* is a long gourd impressed with ridges; it is played by rubbing the ridges with a stick.

The *tambor* is a drum.

An Essay on William Carlos Williams   (*p. 561*)

Points for Discussion and Writing

Compare and contrast this poem with "Williams: An Essay" by Denise Levertov. What poetics do Williams and Hernández Cruz share?

What are the political implications of a speech-based poetry? Of directness? What might Hernández Cruz's position be with regard to language poetry? The theory behind language poetry holds that a speech-based poetics is inevitably implicated in ruling class ideology; in other words, that language is a means of social control. Do you believe this is true?

Discuss the relationship between public and private discourse in poetry. Is "An Essay on William Carlos Williams" an example of public or private discourse? Is a completely private poetry possible? Is a completely public poetry possible? What kind of poetry does Hernández Cruz argue against?

Would "the desert and Mecca" be undesirable because they don't represent local conditions?

Problems with Hurricanes   (*p. 561*)

Points for Discussion and Writing

A *campesino* is central to this poem and also figures strongly in "An Essay on William Carlos Williams." Of what importance is the *campesino* in Latin American culture?

The word *campo* means country or field. How would you translate the word *campesino* to English? Is there a North American equivalent to the *campesino*?

On the surface, this poem is not overtly political, yet Marxist criticism holds that all texts are political. Do you believe this to be true? Is "Problems with Hurricanes" secretly political? What would the politics be in Ron Padgett's sonnet "Nothing in That Drawer"?

JESSICA HAGEDORN   ▪ ▪ ▪ ▪ ▪ ▪ ▪ ▪ ▪ ▪ ▪ ▪
b. 1949

Latin Music in New York   (*p. 563*)

Points for Discussion and Writing

What is the relationship in the poem between "the white girl" (heroin) and revolution? How might the white girl be equated with "the trace of vampires"?

What does "miss harlow's house" represent in the lines, "i danced with you / in a roomful of mirrors / in miss harlow's house"? Is the poet referring to the screen actress Jean Harlow, who died at a young age?

Who is "you" in the sentence, "i danced the tasty freeze shuffle with you"?

"the reds   the blues" may be a drug reference. How many other drug references can you locate in the poem? What is the position of this poem with regard to drugs? In the context of the drug theme, what is meant by "i saw the white girl smiling / la cucaracha was up all night / hiding her spoons   her mirrors   her revolutions"? What connection does the word "revolutions" have to drugs? Why must "her revolutions" be hidden along with other drug paraphrenalia?

Terms and References

Tito and **Eddie** refer to the Latin jazz musicians Tito Puente and Eddie Palmieri.

Ray is probably Ray Barretto.

Lady Day refers to the singer Billie Holiday.

"The white girl" refers to heroin.

The word *cucaracha* means cockroach.

Something About You   (*p. 564*)

Points for Discussion and Writing

The poem is written as a charm and homage to poets and artists of Hagedorn's acquaintance. What is the chief force of healing and magic in the poem? Of what connection to this theme are the lines "and the beautiful blueness / of the water of my voices"?

Hagedorn writes, "the music will save you / from madness." How?

Why "shredded" blossoms in the water at the poem's end? Is this consistent with the poem's themes of sadness and death?

In what respects are this poem and "Latin Music in New York" designed for performance?

Terms and References

Ntozake is the poet, Ntozake Shange.

Pedro is most likely the deceased New York poet Pedro Pietri.

Thulani is poet and playwright Thulani Davis.

Lena Horne is the noted African-American singer and film actress.

Dorothy Dandridge was also an African-American film actress of note.

CHARLES BERNSTEIN ■ ■ ■ ■ ■ ■ ■ ■ ■ ■ ■
b. 1950

The Klupzy Girl   (*p. 566*)

Points for Discussion and Writing

The poem's first line suggests that the work may proceed, at least in part, as an essay on the art of poetry. Does this prove to be the case?

How might a "Sense of variety" be equated with "panic"?

Discuss the meaning of the lines, "The / Protest-ant's voice within, calling for / this to be shepherded, for moment's / expression's enthroning." Is "this" the language? If so, who acts as its shepherd? Why would it be undesirable to enthrone expression?

What is meant by the lines, "I fumbled clumsily / with the others—the evocations, explanations, / glossings of 'reality' seemed like stretching / it to cover ground rather than make / or name or push something through." Is the passage a commentary on the failures of realism as a literary mode?

Discuss the issue of realism in poetry. How could it be that poetry "brings you to your senses," to quote Bernstein's first sentence? That is, if traditional realism causes one to "swoon," how might a more accurate realism be achieved through language poetry?

Is Bernstein's use of the word "swoon" positive or negative in connotation? How might "absorptive" writing ("By *absorption* I mean engrossing, engulfing . . . hypnotic, / riveting, enthralling"[9]) mean putting the reader under an undesireable spell such as a swoon? In this respect, discuss Bernstein's statement, in his essay "Artifice of Absorption," that "the project is to wake / us from the hypnosis of absorption."[1]

Compare and contrast "The Klupzy Girl" with John Ashbery's "How Much Longer Shall I Be Able to Inhabit the Divine Sepulcher . . ." and "Leaving the Atocha Station." To what extent do both poets make use of found material? How much reliance does each place on the parody of other literary genres?

What is the position of self in Bernstein's work? Does Bernstein himself speak in the lines, "I shall ever / remember you in my prayers, and I / wish you the best for the future."?

Who speaks in the lines, "Or I originate out of this / occurrence, stoop down, bend on"?

Whose Language   (*p. 570*)

Points for Discussion and Writing

Why is the poem so titled? Is the poem centered on the ownership or possession of language?

Why would the poet begin with a reference to the famous baseball skit by the comedy team Abbott and Costello? Might Bernstein be interested in the skit's humorous confusion of identities and directives?

Discuss the lines, "The door / closes on a dream of default and / denunciation (go get those piazzas), / hankering after frozen (prose) ambiance / (ambivalance)." What is a "frozen (prose) ambiance"? Is such an ambiance to be equated with ambivalence? Or is Bernstein simply composing the above sentence by ear, allowing alliteration and assonance to

9. Charles Bernstein, "Artifice of Absorption," in *A Poetics*, Cambridge, 1992, p. 29.
1. The same, p. 54.

194

guide his word choices? Is "a skewed and derelict parade" of language
(and authorship) to be preferred? Of what importance, then, is the final
line, "My face turns to glass, at last."? Is the subject of the line the
rhyme between "glass" and "last"? Or is the poet concerned with the
issue of transparency (versus opacity) of language?

Of Time and the Line   (p. 570)

Points for Discussion and Writing

In the lines, "if it's in prose, there's a good chance / it's a poem," how
might Bernstein parody Frank O'Hara's "Personism: A Manifesto"?

Bernstein writes, "When / making a line, better be double sure / what
you're lining in & what you're lining / out." Is all language a delineation
that results in lining people in or out? How might language poetry be
seen as an attempt to line people in? How might its complexities serve
to line some people out?

Which comedic style would Bernstein himself prefer, that of George
Burns or Henny Youngman?

Does the poet sincerely advocate writing with a chisel? Why might
Bernstein desire to avoid "chiseled" lines of poetry?

To what purpose does Bernstein employ elision in the word "fact'ry"?

What is meant by "The lines of an / imaginary are inscribed on the /
social flesh by the knifepoint of history." Why "an imaginary"?

George Burns and Henny Youngman are associated with burlesque (the
Italian word *burla* means ridicule or joke). Burlesque is also a literary
mode. Is this poem an example of burlesque? What other poets in the
anthology use jokes or one-liners in their poetry? Might Bernstein's
poem compare to some of the poetry of Kenneth Koch and Paul Violi in
this respect?

Wait   (p. 571)

Points for Discussion and Writing

Discuss the reflexiveness of the poem's first sentence: "This is the way
to start a sentence about startling a sentence." Language poets frequently put the mirror up to their own literary devices. Is there a moral
purpose to doing so? What might it be?

Discuss Bernstein's use of antique diction—for example, "What am I to
do sayeth the elderly man." Is he making use of found material, perhaps
a Shakespeare text? Or is he parodying an outworn poetic manner?

Discuss in detail the sentence, "I will goes into these houses that you have made for me and will tell you all I slate." Is "I will" a singular entity in the grammar of this poem? How might it compare with Ron Padgett's line, "Anne, who are dead" in the poem "Wonderful Things"? Or does Bernstein have in mind the statement by the French poet Arthur Rimbaud, "I is another"? What is meant by "I . . . will tell you all I slate"? Does this sentence refer to the author as a kind of recording instrument who writes first and "tells" (makes public) later?

JOHN YAU ▪
b. 1950

Chinese Villanelle   (*p. 572*)

Points for Discussion and Writing

Compare and contrast this poem with David Lehman's villanelle, "First Offense." Is the tone of Yau's poem more serious than Lehman's? Which poem is more beautiful?

Does Yau ever signal a break in the lyrical tone he adopts in the opening line?

How might a mountain be "worthy of its insolence"?

What is the importance of the statement, "the song does not melt"? Is a song supposed to melt?

What is the role of the word "description" in the poem? Is this poem descriptive? Why is it described as a "wandering description"?

Yau has said that "to write about one's life in terms of a subjective 'I' . . . is to fulfill the terms of the oppressor."[2] What is the role of the poem's "I"? Is it subjective or objective?

Of what significance is the repeated phrase, "I am a lute"? What connection exists between the poet as singer or lute and the word "description"?

Cenotaph   (*p. 573*)

Points for Discussion and Writing

A cenotaph is an empty tomb or a monument to the dead that does not contain the remains. How might the family photograph album relate to the title?

2. Edward Foster, "An Interview with John Yau," *Talisman*, No. 5, Fall 1990, p. 49.

In part III of the poem, one section of the album has missing photographs; only the captions remain. How might this detail relate to the title?

Referring to the album, Yau writes, "I understood someone had tried to erase this history of excerpts." How is his poem itself a "history of excerpts"?

Of what is the importance of Yau's imagined caption, *"Mound of Heads, Shanghai, 1946"*?

What is the role of the word "white" in this poem?

Much experimental poetry rejects lyrical representations of the bourgeois subject. Does this poem?

Engines of Gloom and Affection (*p. 575*)

Points for Discussion and Writing

How does this poem differ from "Cenotaph"?

How might this be an example of a poem composed by means of word substitution games?

How might the poem reflect Yau's interest in movies: the *"speed* of seeing, the seamless jumps, the echoes, and the way something dissolves something else"?[3] Is this poem seamless, or does it make sudden and distant jumps? Is the previous poem, "Cenotaph," even more cinematic in terms of sustaining and connecting its scenes?

What evidence do you see of a surrealist influence in this poem?

Given the strangeness of some of the poem's details, what do you make of its comparatively austere ending sentence, "Someone claims to be your friend."?

How might this poem be compared to what has been called the metaphysical style of early De Chirico paintings?

---

3. The same, p. 48.

JIM CARROLL ■ ■ ■ ■ ■ ■ ■ ■ ■ ■ ■ ■ ■ ■ ■ ■

b. 1951

Withdrawal Letter (*p. 575*)

Points for Discussion and Writing

Discuss the lines, "so many gulls / seen and jammed into poems / this one just glided onto the reef / it was easy to include, and I trust it." Does the acknowledgment of having written the gull into the poem heighten or diminish its reality? Compare the gull on the reef to the gull that "glows in my sweat."

Of what significance are the lines, "and one loves again / in this marvelous hollow decoration / each moves slowly within"? What is meant by "this marvelous hollow decoration"?

How might words "shoot up" other scenes? Are words comparable to heroin?

The phrase, "treating someone I love badly," refers to Guillaume Apollinaire's "Chanson du Mal Aimé," translated as "Song of the Poorly Loved." How might Apollinaire's street-wise lyricism attract Carroll? Does the poem contain any other literary acknowledgments?

Maybe I'm Amazed (*p. 577*)

Points for Discussion and Writing

What is "the most false of revolutions" to which Carroll refers? What is the music that is piped into it?

Is Carroll's work influenced by a specific poetics? What might these influences be?

Of what significance are the references to the fictional character Sherlock Holmes and the (now deceased) Hippie writer Richard Brautigan?

The poem contains references to drug use—for example, Marty's death at the Cloisters and blue pills. To what extent is the lyricism of the poem dependent on your knowledge as a reader of Carroll's drug habit?

What is the poem's source of amazement?

Paregoric Babies (p. 578)

Points for Discussion and Writing

The title of this poem is taken from William Burroughs's introduction to his novel *Naked Lunch:* "Paregoric Babies of the World Unite. We have nothing to lose but Our Pushers. And THEY are NOT NECESSARY." What other connection do you see between Carroll's poem and the Burroughs's novel?

This poem describes the experience of using the drug paregoric, a camphorated tincture of opium. Discuss the poem's "vision." How might Carroll be seen as a poet? Like the opium eaters Coleridge and DeQuincey of the Romantic tradition?

Does Carroll's poetry emphasize content over technique, or are the two inseparable in his work?

Discuss the relationship of Carroll's often lyrical use of language to his transgressive subject matter. Can his poetry be said to have a moral function?

CARLA HARRYMAN ▪ ▪ ▪ ▪ ▪ ▪ ▪ ▪ ▪ ▪ ▪ ▪
b. 1952

My Story (p. 579)

Points for Discussion and Writing

To what extent is "My Story" a story? Who are the "incognito striplings" that occupy much of paragraph 4? What is the relationship between the striplings and the "I" who narrates the poem? Why are the striplings unable to "show me my face," and why can't they be consoled?

What do you make of the specific naming of the town of Nemole, given that no other such details are provided in the poem's "fiction"?

Why is the poem called "*My* Story" (my emphasis)? Since the narrator refuses to disguise herself "in the habit of that body, the one that isn't mine," is the story really "my" story at all?

What cautions does Harryman offer with regard to "fidelity to the subject"?

Why is this "a braggart's tale"?

Who is the author who describes a woman climbing a hill?

Realism   *(p. 580)*

Points for Discussion and Writing

Is the poem an example of realism? Of what kind?

What is the relationship between the expanding "I" of the poem and the giants that "expound around us"?

What is the nature of information in a poem? Why does it consist of "the bald-faced bold bleak wall of descriptive intonations"?

Does Harryman oppose the "unconditional exactitude" that "wants us to believe in this darkness and partialness"? Of what importance is the poem's last paragraph in terms of its argument?

Is the "I" of this poem the true realist? What are the conditions of this realism?

Harryman writes, "The world is going to seed." Is going to seed a useful metaphor for the poetic imagination?

The Male   *(p. 580)*

Points for Discussion and Writing

Describe the Male as Harryman presents him. Do the actions of the Male represent stereotypical male behavior? Are all males "prosaic" or just the Male? Do all males exhibit, for instance, "a deep, ponderous blank"?

Is the poem that the Male sings a good poem? Is it meant to be bad? Are men more pretentious (and sententious) than women? Does their constant bluster leave the female in a state of inarticulateness? Does this poet depict male and female behavior as you recognize it in your own experience?

Is the critique of sexual identity primarily aimed at men? If so, is the poem at risk of being sexist? Or is it rescued from such an accusation by its sense of humor?

Do you imagine that this poem was written out of some personal experience that Harryman had in Wales? Or is its setting fictional?

Of what significance is the epilogue?

Are words the realm of the Male ("Words come to the Male") and not the Female?

Are "endless spontaneity and lack of preference" beneficial characteristics?

A bolus is a large pill or mass that is difficult to swallow. The poem presents a bolus in the pregnant female narrator's throat. Of what significance is the fact that the Male must name everything, including this obstruction to female speech?

Harryman writes, "The desire to be touched is overwhelming. But whose desire is it?" What is the role of desire in the experience of the narrator and the Male?

What do you make of the narrator's alternating use of "I" and "she"? Is the use of the third person a means for the "I" to see herself objectively?

MAXINE CHERNOFF ■ ■ ■ ■ ■ ■ ■ ■ ■ ■ ■
b. 1952

The Man Struck Twenty Times by Lightning *(p. 583)*

Points for Discussion and Writing

Chernoff's prose poems often begin with a conceit or *donnée* of fantastic proportions. How might this relate to the fabulistic fiction of Robert Coover's *Pricksongs & Descants* and Donald Barthelme's *Unspeakable Practices, Unnatural Acts*?

Is the poem realistic? Is it unrealistic? Does the realism of a work have anything to do with its literary value?

The poem has comedic elements and might be compared to Kenneth Koch's "Permanently" or "Alive for an Instant" as conceptual or metaphysical art. Does this mean that the work has no serious intent? What elements of the poem are lyrical and deep?

What connection might exist between this poem and poetry of the deep image?

Lost and Found *(p. 583)*

Points for Discussion and Writing

To what extent is the poem written in a persona? To what extent might the "I" be Chernoff herself?

Compare and contrast the poem with John Yau's "Cenotaph."

Is the photo for which the "I" is searching of deep personal significance? What does it depict?

Breasts   (*p. 584*)

Points for Discussion and Writing

This poem is written in verse lines rather than in prose. What does it have in common with Chernoff's prose poems? To what extent does it represent a *break* in style with her prose poems?

The poem also makes use of the catalogue, or list, form. To what extent do "The Man Struck Twenty Times by Lightning" and "Lost and Found" also make use of lists?

How might the tendency toward self-sufficient images be consistent with the metaphysical tradition in poetry? (See a description of metaphysical poetry in the John Godfrey section of this guide.)

Compare and contrast this poem with surrealist poet André Breton's blazon "L'union libre," which begins:

> My wife with the hair of a wood fire
> With the thoughts of heat lightning
> With the waist of an hourglass
> With the waist of an otter in the teeth of a tiger.[4]

FROM *Japan*

Amble *and* Black   (*p. 585*)

Points for Discussion and Writing

An abededarium is a poetic sequence guided by alphabetic progression. "Amble" and "Black" are the first two poems in Chernoff's collection, *Japan,* an abecedarium of poems of twenty-seven lines; each title consists of a five-letter word. What else do the poems have in common formally?

Read the works out loud at a relatively fast pace; allow connections to develop between consecutive lines. Is a "story" developed in the process? What is the narrative effect of the lines, "recant / panic / bodily / orbit" (from "Black")?

To what extent is the composition of the works dictated by the sound of neighboring syllables? In this respect, discuss the prosody of the lines, "mental / trappings / hair and / tangents / fruited / fingered / lily / alley / alabaster" (in "Amble").

---

4. André Breton, "Freedom of Love," in *Young Cherry Trees Secured Against Hares,* trans. Edouard Roditi, Ann Arbor, 1969, n.p.

How Lies Grow (*p. 586*)

Points for Discussion and Writing

This prose poem was written somewhat later in Chernoff's career than the first two in this section. How does it differ from the others? In what respect is it similar?

Is there a psychological reality to the poem's conceit or concept?

How might this poem reflect Chernoff's growing interest in prose fiction, which resulted in the publication of two short story collections and a novel?

ART LANGE ▪ ▪ ▪ ▪ ▪ ▪ ▪ ▪ ▪ ▪ ▪ ▪ ▪ ▪ ▪ ▪ ▪ ▪

b. 1952

Sonnet for the Season (*p. 587*)

Points for Discussion and Writing

Compare and contrast this sonnet with those of Bernadette Mayer and Ted Berrigan.

How does the poem reflect Lange's work as a jazz and classical music critic?

Of how many sentences does the poem consist? What effect does this extension of syntax have on the poem?

The poem has lyric elements, especially in the musical sense. Is it possible to say what the poem is about?

To what season does Lange refer in the title?

Perugia (*p. 587*)

Points for Discussion and Writing

Perugia is a city in central Italy where Lange attended a jazz festival. As you read the poem, is your focus primarily on Lange's description of things seen there or on the beauty of his word choices and rhythm?

How is the form of the poem appropriate to Lange's halting and advancing pace of language?

Working a sentence at a time, examine the relationship of Lange's syllables—the "in" sound in the lines, "cadences / like / warm creme in / cappucino, curdling— / who / drinks it?" and the "u" and "i" sounds in the passage, "The summer / sky so / high, so / blue, the few / clouds / seem / an intrusion. Lewd / landscape / lousy / with figures, none / of them / ghosts, none of them / you." What use does the poet make of parallelisms? Of alliteration?

If Lange were a jazz musician, which one would he be? Both Lange's magazine, *Brilliant Corners,* and one of his poetry collections, *Evidence,* are also titles of Thelonious Monk compositions. Is Lange's cadence that of Monk?

Is the music of Lange's poetry tuneful or dissonant?

In what respects might Lange's poetry be compared to that of Robert Creeley and Gustaf Sobin? How does his work differ from theirs?

JIMMY SANTIAGO BACA ▪ ▪ ▪ ▪ ▪ ▪ ▪ ▪ ▪ ▪
b. 1952

Voz de la Gente   (*p. 590*)

Points for Discussion and Writing

The title means "voice of the people." How is the "voice of the people" expressed in the poem?

Late in the poem, the description of drumming on the sandbar is revealed to be a dream. What purpose does the drumming serve? Why is it significant that the drumming ceremony occurs at the Rio Grande?

How might Baca's dream of drumming equate with his role as poet?

What is meant by the line, "wild weed doctor covering night with my cure"?

What responsibility does Baca feel as a result of the dream?

Terms and References

A *llano* is an open field or plain.

Bosque means woods or forest; figuratively, it may imply confusion.

Matachines refers to a grotesque clowning dance, in this case, of the drummer's hands.

Mi Tío Baca el Poeta de Socorro   (p. 591)

Points for Discussion and Writing

The poet describes the death of his uncle, Antonio Ce De Baca, at the hands of masked men in *"Rinche* uniforms." Does this imply that the men were "turncoat" Mexicans working at the behest of powerful interests?

How might this poem be compared to "Voz de la Gente"? Both poems, for instance, contain visions that serve as a normal reminder to the poet. How are they different?

Terms and References

Socorro means rescue, aid, or salvation.

Rinche means turncoat.

Viga refers to a wooden beam, in this case of cane.

La Virgen De Guadalupe is the patron saint of Mexico.

Matanza to Welcome Spring   (p. 593)

Points for Discussion and Writing

After vividly describing the sacrifice of the sheep, Baca writes, "and tomorrow I will go / to church." Discuss the relationship between the matanza and Christian ritual.

Baca later repeats the words, "I commit myself!" How might his poetry be seen as one of ceremony and commitment?

Is the "ba-ba ba-ba" sound of the poem's ending chorus intended to have a double meaning in relation to the sheep's death? What might those meanings be?

Baca could be described as a public rather than a private poet. To what extent does his interest in sacred occasions and ritual lend his poetry a shamanistic quality?

What elements of this poem lend themselves to public performance?

Terms and References

Matanza means, literally, slaughter. Thus the title means "Slaughter to Welcome Spring." Baca himself describes a *matanza* as a "barrio social event where people gather to talk and eat, involving butchering and dressing an animal."[5]

Duende means spirit or goblin.

5. *Black Mesa Poems*, New York, 1989, p. 126.

DAVID TRINIDAD ▪ ▪ ▪ ▪ ▪ ▪ ▪ ▪ ▪ ▪ ▪ ▪ ▪ ▪

b. 1953

Movin' with Nancy   (*p. 596*)

Points for Discussion and Writing

This poem is a pantoum (also pantun), a Malaysian form in which the second and fourth lines of each stanza become the first and third lines of the next. A pantoum can be of indefinite length. What is the advantage to Trinidad, given his love of the materials of popular culture, in using the pantoum form?

Are you concerned as a reader about the poet's lack of depth? Is Trinidad's insistence on a poetry of surface the transgressive nature of his work?

Wallace Stevens once defined poetry as "that which suffices." Does Trinidad's work suffice? Discuss the minimal requirements (in the opinion of the class) for a poem. Might a poem consist, for instance, of a single word? Are there conditions in which two words might prove too much?

Given that he uses popular culture and sometimes writes in eccentric traditional forms, might Trinidad be described as a poet of the New York School?

Double Trouble   (*p. 597*)

Points for Discussion and Writing

Patty and Cathy were the identical cousins on television's *The Patty Duke Show* of the 1960s. Are the two monologues intended to be read simultaneously or one after the other? If one after the other, what is the purpose of positioning the "twin" columns side by side?

How might Trinidad's insistent focus on popular culture be considered *more* realistic than that of poets of depth?

Is watching television a form of lived experience? Is it by definition less important than other forms of experience?

Do you feel that Trinidad is too accepting of consumerism and celebrity culture? Or does "Double Trouble" reflect the experience of living in the United States as you know it?

Is Trindidad's work antiheroic or does it simply honor new heroes?

As a poet, how might Trinidad be considered a mythmaker?

ELAINE EQUI
b. 1953

A Bouquet of Objects (*p. 599*)

Points for Discussion and Writing

Equi has been described as a minimalist, yet she might also be described as an insouciant urban Deep Imagist. Discuss these strains in her poem. How might Ron Silliman, who often writes lengthy poems, also be described as minimalist?

In what respect might Equi's work be compared with that of Charles Simic? For example, both Simic and Equi make use of fully shaped images in strongly visual poetry. Both are ironists, and both were raised in Chicago and now live on the East Coast. Is there such a thing as a regional temperament in poetry?

With regard to the question of regional perspective, to what extent does art exist in proportion to large bourgeois populations?

The figure of the muse in "A Bouquet of Objects" is male. Is the poem therefore feminist?

Of what significance is the poem's form?

Puritans (*p. 600*)

Points for Discussion and Writing

This poem is more sharply satirical than some of Equi's other work. Who are the puritans to whom she refers? White Anglo-Saxon Protestants? What are their characteristics? From what perspective are her barbs aimed?

Is satire a form of moral literature? Or does it act to divide one group from another? Is Equi's use of satire kind or mean-spirited? To what extent does your judgment of the "correctness" of a work of satire depend on your own allegiances? Is it acceptable, for instance, to satirize the powerful but not those excluded from power?

In a Monotonous Dream (*p. 601*)

Points for Discussion and Writing

Like the prose poems of Maxine Chernoff, this poem develops from a given conceit or concept. It also makes use of the catalogue or list form. Is their work similar in any other way?

How might it be true that the language "created the landscape"? Is the poet announcing a position on language? In this respect, compare and contrast this poem with Kenneth Koch's poem "Permanently."

A Date with Robbe-Grillet (*p. 601*)

Points for Discussion and Writing

Alain Robbe-Grillet is the French author of *Jealousy* and other novels noted for their purposeful lack of character, development, plot, and other traditional characteristics of fiction. "A Date with Robbe-Grillet" is a pantoum. How might the circularity of the pantoum form be appropriate for a "date" with Robbe-Grillet?

What happens to the figure of Robbe-Grillet ("you") at the end of the poem? Is he lost in the forest?

Discuss the use of doubles and mirror-imaging in this poem. For instance, there are two forests, one within the other, that are identical to each other. Equi writes, "You, for example, made a lovely girl." Is the "lovely girl" Robbe-Grillet? If Equi's narrator, perhaps herself, survives alone to tell the story, has she triumphed over Robbe-Grillet as an author? With respect to the use of doubles, consider the fact that half the poem's lines are repeated word for word.

DENNIS COOPER ▪ ▪ ▪ ▪ ▪ ▪ ▪ ▪ ▪ ▪ ▪ ▪ ▪
b. 1953

Being Aware (*p. 603*)

Points for Discussion and Writing

Is this poem personal or is Cooper writing a "fiction"? The poem has narrative qualities, yet it is also carefully structured in six-line stanzas. Of what importance is form to the poem?

How does the poem's address to "Dad" add to its transgressiveness?

Is Cooper making a moral or political point about the hypocrisy of the father figure, and thereby the "straight" world?

No God   (*p. 604*)

Points for Discussion and Writing

Cooper has been associated with the so-called blank generation of the 1980s. What is the relationship between the poem's title and the numbness experienced through sex?

Of what significance is the fact that the "I" drives a Mercedes? Why is the car comparable to a "wishing well" to the "young / man who looked like a shadow"?

Drugs   (*p. 605*)

Points for Discussion and Writing

Who is the "you" in the poem? Why is "a friend" not more clearly identified? Is the blankness of their identities a part of Cooper's point in the work?

The poet prefers transgressive content. Is his language also transgressive?

To what extent might Cooper be considered a poet of moral longing?

AMY GERSTLER   ▪ ▪ ▪ ▪ ▪ ▪ ▪ ▪ ▪ ▪ ▪ ▪ ▪ ▪
b. 1956

The True Bride   (*p. 606*)

Points for Discussion and Writing

What distinguishes this prose poem from a short story?

Of what importance is the fact that Elaine is "crippled"? Is she intended to represent the condition of all women? Must true brides be crippled in order to become "ideal" to men?

What is the significance of Gerstler using a male persona?

Is the poem's narrator a man? Why would the desires of crippled women searching for husbands in a desert represent the narrator's "ideal pornography"?

BZZZZZZZ   (*p. 607*)

Points for Discussion and Writing

Like "The True Bride," this poem presents a bizarre love match. In this case, the speaker is female and declares her love for a beekeeper. How is the language of the poem different from that of "The True Bride"?

How might Gerstler's metaphysical compression and subject matter compare with Sylvia Plath's beekeeper poems in *Ariel*, including "The Bee Meeting," "The Arrival of the Bee Box," "Stings," "The Swarm," and "Wintering"?

Bitter Angel   (*p. 607*)

Points for Discussion and Writing

Gerstler writes, "A terrible succession of images buffets you." How might this describe the manner of her own writing?

What does the bitter angel represent? Is it a figure of the muse? If so, is its appearance triumphant or anticlimactic?

Gerstler writes, "There's no nightlife or lion's share, none of the black-and-red roulette wheels of methedrine that would-be seers like me dream of." Does the angel arrive in a gray light only to find the poet-seer unwilling or unready to cooperate? How might the "smudged, undone paperwork" represent Gerstler's own anxieties about creative work?

Compare and contrast this poem with James Merrill's poem, "Angel," with its "evidently angelic visitor."

Marriage   (*p. 608*)

Points for Discussion and Writing

The majority of Gerstler's poems, and all of our selections, are in prose. How is this form well-suited for her use?

Many of her poems deal, albeit strangely, with themes of love and marriage. There is also the frequent appearance of a failed savior or guide. In this poem Gerstler writes, "O bride, fed and bedded down on a sea of Dexatrim, tea, rice, and quinine, can you guide me? Is the current swift?" How might her poems be seen as fables of postmodern psychology? Likewise, despite its numerous anxieties and doubts about marriage (romance is "perilous as a clean sheet of paper"), how might this poem be seen as an affirmation of marriage? Of what significance is the repetition of "I kiss" and "I do"?

DIANE WARD ■ ■ ■ ■ ■ ■ ■ ■ ■ ■ ■ ■ ■ ■ ■ ■

b. 1956

Immediate Content Recognition   (*p. 609*)

Points for Discussion and Writing

"Immediate content recognition" is a term from the worlds of marketing and packaging that refers to the ability of the consumer to immediately recognize what a package contains. How might this relate to the line, "well-marketed cigarette packs" and "well-lighted glossy magazine ads"? Like Charles Olson, is Ward concerned with the triumph of consumerism and billboards?

How does "immediate content recognition" work with regard to a poem? Even before it is "opened," does a poem announce what it is about and to whom it is addressed?

What does Ward mean by "the post love world"? Is this poem concerned, at least in part, with the breakup of a love affair or some other disappointing relationship?

Who are the chief "actors" of the poem? The narrator and who else? Who is the "you" in the line, "the times I used you without mentioning you to decline invitations"?

Ward writes, "these thoughts that occur simultaneously are without any immediate content recognition." Is it possible for several thoughts to occur in the mind at the same time? Or does the mind work consecutively, albeit very quickly? How might such simulaneity be the purpose of the poem's several references to light—for example, "light that's blinding the river"?

Discuss the poem's ending passage, especially with regard to its image of speech. How might they be "composed for the moment"? What relation do these images of speech ("words in comic strips / or even thought bubbles") have with "a sort of on-call improvised emotional flow"? To what degree is language influenced by the emotion under which it is written? Is this less true of writing than of speech?

Glass House   (*p. 611*)

Points for Discussion and Writing

Why is this poem so laden with specialist jargon (see "Terms and References" below), especially that of a scientific nature?

Describe the social setting Ward presents. What social class is portrayed at the party in the glass house? What is the relationship of "she" to "Daddy"? Of what importance are the references to the "over-controlleds" and "his control / tower over-manned by chronoscope controllers"? Is this poem a satire on upper-middle-class behavior?

How might the words "subreception" and "monogenesis" be important to the poem's political comment?

Terms and References

A **positron** is a positively charged particle of an atom, with a weight equal to that of an electron.

The initials **"crt"** stand for cathode ray tube and so refer to television or computer display screens.

A **halation** is an appearance somewhat like a halo; it may also refer to a ghost.

"Subreception" means an inference resulting from concealment or a misrepresentation of essential elements or facts.

A **chronoscope** is an instrument that graphically measures a minute interval of time.

Lactescent means having or secreting a milky juice.

Monogenesis is the doctrine of the descent of all living organisms from a single cell.

Arrack is a strong Oriental liquor distilled from rice or, in this case, coconuts.

Infanta refers to the daughter of a Spanish or Portuguese king.

Lovely Stuff   (*p. 611*)

Points for Discussion and Writing

What is the "lovely stuff" to which Ward refers?

Is this poem about poetry and authorship? Do "this" and "here" refer to the poem itself?

How might the lines, "The didactic food that feeds / it is controllable," refer to the moral or didactic impulse of authorship?

How might the poem's ending be a statement of the (lovely) impermanence and conditionality of poetry? Should poetry consist of "perfect peeks / beneath frantic erasures"? Are erasures "lovely stuff," too?